T0320035

Ageing Labour Forces

Ageing Labour Forces

Promises and Prospects

Edited by

Philip Taylor

Faculty of Business and Enterprise, Swinburne University of Technology, Australia

Edward Elgar
Cheltenham, UK • Northampton, MA, USA

Published by
Edward Elgar Publishing Limited
Glensanda House
Montpellier Parade
Cheltenham
Glos GL50 1UA
UK

Edward Elgar Publishing, Inc.
William Pratt House
9 Dewey Court
Northampton
Massachusetts 01060
USA

A catalogue record for this book
is available from the British Library

ISBN 978 1 84542 425 1

Printed and bound in Great Britain by MPG Books Limited, Bodmin, Cornwall

Contents

Figures

Tables

Contributors

Martin Cooke, Assistant Professor, Faculty of Applied Health Sciences, University of Waterloo, Canada.

Sol Encel, Professor Emeritus of Sociology, Social Policy Research Centre, University of New South Wales, Australia.

Frerich Frerichs, Professor of Ageing and Work, Institut für Gerontologie, University of Vechta, Germany.

Anne-Marie Guillemard, Professor of Sociology, Centre d'étude des Mouvements Sociaux, University of Paris V Sorbonne, France.

Kène Henkens, Head of Social Demography Department, Netherlands Interdisciplinary Demographic Institute (NIDI), Den Haag, the Netherlands.

Annie Jolivet, Economist and Researcher, Institut de Recherches Economiques et Sociales, Noisy le Grand, France.

Julie McMullin, Associate Professor, Department of Sociology, University of Western Ontario, Canada.

Gerhard Naegele, Professor of Social Gerontology, Director Institute of Gerontology, University of Dortmund, Germany.

Masato Oka, Professor, International College of Arts and Sciences, Yokohama City University, Japan.

Sara Rix, Senior Policy Advisor, Public Policy Institute, AARP, Washington, DC, USA.

Joop Schippers, Professor of Labour Economics and the Economics of Equal Opportunity, Institute of Economics, Utrecht University, the Netherlands.

Philip Taylor, Professor of Employment Policy, Faculty of Business and Enterprise, Swinburne University of Technology, Melbourne, Australia.

Terri Tomchick, Advisor in Equity and Human Rights Services, University of Western Ontario, Canada.

Introduction: the promise of ageing labour forces

Philip Taylor

INTRODUCTION

From debates about the restructuring of economies, to the adjustment of social welfare systems, to redefining the concept of old age, older workers have been at the vanguard of developed economies' efforts to respond first, to industrial decline and reorganization in the last three decades, and latterly, the so-called looming crisis facing social welfare systems, associated with population ageing. This volume examines the notion of retiring later, considering the evolution of national policymaking and the behaviour of employers, addressing the question of whether older workers can look forward to the prospect of longer working lives with choice and security and make successful transitions to non-work.

Listening to policy makers and some commentators might make one optimistic that older workers are on the threshold of a new era of opportunity, a 'golden age' of job openings and flexible retirement. This volume tests the validity of this claim, focusing on developments in a small number of industrialized nations: Australia, Canada, France, Germany, Japan, the Netherlands, the United Kingdom and the USA. Nowadays, the necessity for economies, and the value for both industry and older people of extending working lives seems to be taken for granted and dissenting voices are seldom heard. Quickly it seems that a remarkable consensus among policy makers, employers, trade unions and social commentators has emerged. This volume takes a close look at the relatively recent shift away from rhetoric and action of early retirement towards that of 'active ageing', seeking to understand the motives and behaviour of key actors, examining recent trends in older workers' labour force participation and offering an assessment of their likely position into the future.

This chapter begins with a brief overview of the recent history of older workers before moving on to discuss the changing policy landscape.

DECADES OF EARLY EXIT

The final quarter of the twentieth century saw the growth of early retirement as a phenomenon. Most industrialized nations, and some European ones in particular, have seen a decline, sometimes marked, in labour force participation rates (defined as the proportion in employment and those seeking work) among older workers. Table I.1 shows the scale of the decline, substantial in much of Europe, rather less in Japan and the USA. The range within Europe is also striking. This downward trend continued until recently, but noticeable is a recent slowing and in some countries, a modest reversal. Perhaps older workers are on the verge of a new era of employment opportunity, the subject of this volume.

As a backdrop to current debates, it is important to consider their changing status in some detail. Their declining participation is explained, to a large extent, by massive restructuring of industry, which has been a feature of most major economies, and has frequently involved the removal of those considered no longer able to do the job or unwilling to change, as industries such as manufacturing and finance sought to reorganize. For others, their jobs disappeared along with whole parts of the industries in which they worked. Relatively generous pension or redundancy settlements have sometimes been used to lever such workers out of jobs. In some countries, early retirement pathways emerged with generous state support. 'Redundant' older workers often made the transition to retirement while aged in their 50s, sometimes without the need to look for alternative employment, with state support that frequently undermined normal ages at which pensions could be claimed.

The result has been the breakdown of the three phase model of the life course: education, work and rest. 'Socially assigned' economic inactivity has, for some, made the last stage 'unforeseeable and uncertain' (Guillemard and Argoud, 2004: 168). Guillemard argues that the passage from work to retirement has undergone a profound shift, with 'an increasing number of in-between, usually unstable, statuses between work and retirement' (1997: 451). While early retirement has often been portrayed as an opportunity to enter a life of leisure, free from the stresses of working life and while in good health, in fact, the reality, as some older people have found out too late, is often very different. Research studies have shown that while, for some, it is welcomed and can come as a relief, many others would have preferred to stay on or at least have chosen their time of retirement. Most thought they might easily move into new, often part-time, jobs but the reality is that a lifetime's experience has often counted for little. What should be a period of winding down and relaxation can turn into an anxious wait and an inevitable scaling back of ambitions.

Table I.1   *Trends in labour force participation rates among people aged 55–64 among the OECD countries (%)*

	Men					Women				
	1983	1990	1995	2000	2004	1983	1990	1995	2000	2004
Australia	62.0	63.2	60.8	61.2	64.4	20.5	24.9	28.6	36.1	43.1
Austria	–	–	42.6	44.5	38.6	–	–	18.8	18.9	19.3
Belgium	50.6	35.4	35.9	36.3	41.0	12.3	9.9	13.3	15.8	21.8
Canada	72.4	64.0	58.9	61.0	66.0	33.5	34.8	36.3	41.6	49.0
Czech Republic	–	–	52.0	54.5	60.1	–		21.3	23.7	31.3
Denmark	67.2	69.1	67.9	64.5	73.3	41.7	45.9	40.1	48.2	57.6
Finland	54.1	47.1	44.6	48.1	55.7	47.4	40.8	41.9	45.2	54.3
France	53.6	39.3	41.5	41.7	44.3	32.7	26.9	30.9	33.0	35.0
Germany	63.1	55.9	54.5	52.4	54.8	26.3	24.7	31.3	33.5	33.8
Greece	70.8	59.5	61.1	57.3	58.7	25.7	24.3	24.5	25.5	25.3
Hungary	–	35.3	28.6	34.1	39.7	–	15.1	9.7	13.3	25.8
Iceland	–	93.5	92.7	94.7	89.7	–	81.1	84.8	76.8	78.8
Ireland	78.0	65.0	63.9	64.7	66.6	20.2	19.9	21.2	27.8	34.5
Italy	56.2	53.0	44.1	42.7	44.0	15.0	15.5	13.8	16.1	20.4
Japan	97.1	83.3	84.8	84.1	82.5	46.1	47.2	48.5	49.7	50.1
Korea	–	77.2	79.7	71.0	73.5	–	49.6	50.4	48.6	46.5
Luxembourg	37.8	43.2	35.1	38.6	39.1	14.7	13.8	13.3	16.8	23.3
Mexico	–	85.9	80.7	80.8	81.5	–	24.4	26.9	28.6	32.0
Netherlands	54.1	45.8	42.3	50.8	58.7	13.4	16.8	18.6	26.4	33.6
New Zealand	–	56.8	65.3	72.2	78.2	–	30.7	39.0	48.0	59.6
Norway	80.3	72.8	72.3	74.4	74.3	53.1	53.9	57.4	61.6	63.1
Poland	–	48.1	45.5	40.4	41.3	–	29.6	27.6	23.7	23.3
Portugal	70.7	66.5	61.9	64.5	62.8	32.6	32.3	34.5	41.9	44.8
Slovak Republic	–	–	–	41.0	51.9	–	–	–	10.7	14.8
Spain	71.5	62.5	54.9	60.5	62.7	20.3	19.4	19.9	22.6	27.2
Sweden	77.0	75.5	70.7	72.8	76.0	59.7	65.8	63.7	65.9	70.2
Switzerland	–	86.4	82.3	79.3	79.1	–	43.8	58.7	51.3	55.7
Turkey	–	61.3	60.9	53.4	49.0	–	26.6	26.1	21.6	19.8
UK	70.0	68.1	62.4	63.3	68.0	36.1	38.7	40.8	42.6	48.3
EU-15	62.8	55.4	51.9	52.3	55.2	26.6	25.7	28.0	30.9	34.5
EU-19	–	54.3	–	51.1	54.0	–	25.8	–	29.5	33.1
EU (OECD Europe)	62.9	55.5	52.4	51.9	54.2	27.6	26.4	27.8	29.5	32.7
USA	69.4	67.8	66.0	67.3	68.7	41.5	45.2	49.2	51.9	56.3
All OECD	80.6	65.0	62.7	62.8	64.7	34.5	34.7	36.4	38.8	42.2

Source: OECD Employment Outlook (various).

However some older workers are denied even this minimal level of security. These workers have been caught on the tide of massive shifts in industry which have taken place over the last 25 years. Gone are many of the industries in which they predominated. When they disappeared, some older workers were left high and dry without even a modest financial settlement. Once out in the job market many found their skills ill-suited to the demands of the new economy or that their age counted against them. Many never worked again. This has often meant years of unemployment, or something akin to this, before reaching the relative safety of retirement. Of course, any savings are usually long since exhausted, eliminating any prospect of a relatively comfortable old age.

What accounts for the problems faced by many older workers? First is society's preference for youth. The young are seen by many as our future while older people are seen as having nothing new to offer. A large body of evidence demonstrates that older workers face considerable discrimination in the labour market. Not only are they overrepresented among those targeted first for redundancy; once in the labour market they find themselves facing considerable age barriers. An OECD study found that, among nine European Union countries, the share of older workers among recent job hires was almost 13 percentage points lower than so called 'prime-age' workers (OECD, 1998a). For example, managers sometimes express concerns about the pay-back period on investments in training, that older workers are marking time until retirement, and that their work performance in key regards is lower than younger workers (for instance, see AARP, 2000; Taylor and Walker, 1994). As a result, non-working older workers may find it difficult to find re-employment, except on the low-pay/low security periphery of the labour market. Older workers in employment sometimes find themselves denied access to training opportunities or are passed over for promotion, simply because they have crossed a particular age threshold. This makes them vulnerable if a reduction in the workforce headcount is required.

Second, and importantly, until recently, many European governments gave tacit, and some overt support to employers wishing to dispense with older labour. For some individuals, the ability to make use of early retirement pathways alleviated much of the distress of unrealistic job-search. This particular part of the recent history of older workers has been considered thoroughly by others, particularly Kohli *et al.* in the seminal *Time for Retirement* (1991) and more recently by Casey (1998) and there is no need to cover old ground, but it should be noted that this backdrop to present-day policy efforts explains their origins, scope and some of the challenges they are facing. This particularly applies to countries with well-developed early exit pathways such as France and Germany. As Guillemard and Argoud (2004) note, while popular, early retirement in France has created other problems, contributing to a general devaluation of older labour at earlier and earlier ages. Companies, trade unions and employees have colluded in the perpetuation of a system where 55 has become 'the normal age for definitively leaving the labour market' (p. 177). Such a situation has not only had a profoundly negative effect on how such workers are viewed by managers and supervisors, but moreover, workers aged in their 40s are now viewed as 'nearly old' and find their career prospects severely curtailed (p. 178).

Third, evidence shows that older workers sometimes help perpetuate ageist myths. Some wrongly believe that retraining is unnecessary or that they are too old to retrain. Others believe that, at their age, no employer would take them on anyway. On the other hand, some believe that the barrier is their age when it is not. Thus, 'ageism' is often internalized by older people and making way for younger workers has even been presented as a reason for taking early retirement (Taylor and Walker, 1996a, b).

Of course, and this often appears to have been overlooked recently by public policymakers keen to emphasize a clear shift in favour of older workers' employment as, they argue, industry increasingly recognizes the business case for employing older workers, early retirement and what appear to be overtly ageist employment practices continue into the twenty-first century. A couple of examples will serve to illustrate this point. One is the German firm KSB (Taylor, 2006), a world-leading manufacturer of pumps and valves for private and industrial applications. This company implemented a 'programme for older employees' in 2003, which included a range of measures aimed at the integration and retention of its older workers. However any positive vision of workforce ageing this attempted to engender was subsequently threatened as management responded to changing business conditions. One year after launching this measure, a rationalization and reorganization programme was implemented by the company, which led to a wave of compulsory early retirements. This approach was regarded by management as the most socially acceptable solution to the company's problems.

Another recent example again demonstrates that competitive pressures can lead companies into actions that could be viewed as being overtly ageist. The company is Ericsson, which announced in the spring of 2006 that it was offering voluntary severance to up to 1000 employees aged 35 to 50 in order to make way for younger workers. The telecommunications equipment maker stated that its workforce had become unbalanced after major job losses at the beginning of the decade and it needed to recruit younger staff in order to ensure competitiveness. It was stated that the measure would include a generous financial package and retraining (*Financial Times*, 2006).

These are not unusual occurrences as corporations seek to maintain competitive advantage. It is possible to counter that the literature is littered with examples of good employment practice and guidance aimed at supporting the integration of older workers (for instance, Buck and Dworschak, 2003; Buck *et al.*, 2002; Dennis, 1988; Health Education Authority, 1994; Ilmarinen, 1999; Kuhn, 1997; McNair and Flynn, 2005; Naegele and Walker, 2006; Pack *et al.*, 1999; Taylor, 2006; The Commonwealth Fund, 1991; Walker and Taylor, 1998; Worsley, 1996). In the drive for competitiveness and greater efficiency businesses have often being unwittingly drained of vast reservoirs of skills and experience which are then lost forever, but recently, a few employers have begun to recognize that older workers have things to offer and that a blend of youth and experience has business benefits. Some have recognized that the tacit knowledge amassed by older workers can be an important source of competitive advantage and have thus abandoned early retirement schemes in favour of compulsory, performance-based, schemes, thus retaining the best team on the pitch, not necessarily the youngest. Organizations that have not, have often subsequently regretted the loss of corporate memory caused by the removal of older workers. Additionally, some employers are beginning to look at other ways in which they can remove age barriers. For example, some have included statements such as 'older people welcome to apply' in recruitment advertisements, some provide age awareness training for staff while others provide career planning workshops for workers aged in their 50s. Others offer special leave for those caring for elderly relatives and a few encourage older people to come back in a consultancy capacity after they have officially retired or run mentoring schemes whereby older workers can pass on the benefits of their experience to younger workers. Some leading companies and government departments are implementing policies aimed at making retirement more flexible. Employers have reported business benefits in terms of employee job satisfaction, increased sales and better customer relations.

Yet against the background of a scarcity of labour and relatively buoyant economies, it is hardly a surprise that some organizations have demonstrated an interest in older workers. What is not generally acknowledged is the continuing pressure that older workers are under as they confront what Sennett (2006) describes as the 'spectre of uselessness' as the forces of globalization undermine their position in labour markets, with jobs they could do moving elsewhere and employers being unwilling to invest in the level of skills training that might give them a solid foothold in the labour market. Sennett's is a rare cautionary voice nowadays.

MEETING THE CHALLENGES OF AN AGEING SOCIETY. TOWARDS ACTIVE AGEING

Paradoxically, as the age at which we have retired has been lowered, our societies have been ageing. Global ageing is a fact and the populations of the developed economies are the oldest. It is projected that Europe will be most affected by population ageing, with the proportion of people aged 60 or over increasing from 20 per cent to 35 per cent by 2050. Southern Europe is the world's region with the oldest population – 22 per cent in 1998 – and predicted to increase to 39 per cent by 2050. In 1998, Italy had the world's oldest population, followed by Greece, Japan, Spain and Germany. By 2050 Spain will have the world's oldest population, followed by Italy. After Europe and Japan, the other areas particularly affected by ageing are, in decreasing order, North America, Oceania, Asia and Latin America and the Caribbean (Auer and Fortuny, 2000).

Europe and Japan, in particular, with the most rapidly ageing societies, are increasingly viewing this as a strategic issue, though it is also on the agenda elsewhere. Our economic futures, it is argued, depend on meeting the challenges of an ageing society. The OECD summed up much of the tone of the current debate in its publication: *Maintaining Prosperity in an Ageing Society* (OECD, 1998b). Shrinking populations and labour shortfalls, which most observers think will only be partially offset by immigration, are predicted. In a relatively short space of time, discussion of the attainment of a leisure society has been replaced by a work-centred perspective.

Consideration of the needs of older workers is far from new. For instance, in 1980 the General Conference of the International Labour Organization made a number of recommendations which stand scrutiny today. But in recent times, a huge number of official reports, conferences and programmes of research in the industrialized nations have considered issues of workforce ageing. An exhaustive review would be virtually impossible and anyway, almost immediately out of date, but the theme is always a similar one: working lives need to be extended if social welfare systems are to be sustainable and there is to be an adequate supply of labour going forward. Many observers have pointed to the failure of early retirement to create jobs for younger people, a key objective (for instance, World Bank, 1994), and there is a burgeoning literature concerning economic and social aspects of population ageing which serves to provide an evidence base for the argument that working later is a necessity (for instance, Access Economics Pty Limited, 2001; Bertelsmann Foundation, 2006; Bundesministerium fur Bildung und Forschung, 1999; Committee for Economic Development, 1999; Confederation of German Employers' Associations, 2003; Employment

Observatory, 1999; Eurolinkage, 1997; European Foundation for the Improvement of Living and Working Conditions, 1992; Johnson and Zimmerman, 1993; Pearson, 1996; Performance And Innovation Unit, 2000; Productivity Commission and Melbourne Institute of Applied Economic and Social Research, 1999; The Geneva Association and GINA, 2002; The Victorian, South Australian and Western Australian Equal Opportunity Commissions and the Australian Employers' Convention, 2001).

Principal among recent reviews is a major thematic study undertaken by the OECD of older workers and employment policy among member states (OECD, 2005) which shows that, at national level a range of reforms are now stepping up efforts aimed at stopping early exit and extending working lives, while noting barriers to progress (for other recent reviews, see also ETUI, 2002, 2003; Frerichs and Taylor, 2005; Reday-Mulvey, 2003; Taylor, 2002). This builds on earlier national reviews conducted by the International Labour Organization and the European Foundation for the Improvement of Living and Working Conditions into the labour market situation of older workers, age and training and the behaviour of the social actors (for instance, Frerichs, 1996; Guillemard, 1996; Oka, 1992; Sutter, 1989; Taylor and Walker, 1996a, b; Thomas *et al.*, 1992; de Vroom, 1996; Yocum, 1992).

Meanwhile, many media reports of the issue have adopted an almost hysterical tone, characterizing older people as a burden on the young and for the latter's sake, needing to work on, if the 'crisis' that is global population ageing is to be averted. To be fair, much of both the policy and academic literatures on the ageing of populations has been similarly strident, using the language of crisis and threat rather than challenge and opportunity. Again, there have been a modest number of attempts to provide qualifications and critical commentary (for an example, see Working Group on the Implications of Demographic Change, 2002). It should also be noted, because it helps put present discussions in context, that only recently older workers were being pressured to make way for the young. Either way, it seems, they are quite often viewed as a 'problem'.

According to Burniaux *et al.*, (2004), in many OECD countries demographic changes will result in significant declines in the growth (and sometimes the levels) of the labour force and aggregate participation rates over the coming decades. They calculate that the overall participation rate could fall by 4–5 percentage points for the OECD on average between 2000 and 2025. At the same time, there will be an increasing share of older workers in the labour force and a significant increase in old-age dependency ratios.

They and many others have argued that by utilizing measures involving additional work incentives for older workers and women and raising the propensity of youth to combine work and education, it will be possible to mitigate, offset or, even reverse these adverse demographic effects, at least for the time-being. Reforms with the largest potential effects on participation concern pension systems, particularly those achieving actuarial neutrality of old-age pensions. Additional work incentives for women are also influential and may be politically easier to implement.

Concern about the escalating costs of supporting a growing inactive older population with fewer younger people means that the issues of age discrimination in employment and the extension of working life are now high on the agendas of national governments and increasingly business. It is argued that companies, chasing a shrinking pool of young skilled labour, will face an increasing wage bill if they are to compete in the labour market. They will also risk having a workforce which, in its composition, does not reflect that of the population as a whole, with the possibility that they will lose touch with the needs of their, increasingly older, customer base, who will also be demanding a different type of service and product. For both government and business therefore, population ageing potentially presents serious challenges.

The responses of national governments are addressed in each chapter, but to begin, a brief discussion of European policy will illustrate how far some countries have gone and the distance they will need to travel in order to reach the end of early retirement. The remarkable scale of early exit and the perceived challenges confronting Europe as its population ages explains why European policy makers have devoted so much recent effort to redefining retirement. An 'active' employment policy is central to the vision of Europe set out at the Lisbon Council of the year 2000 where a strategic goal for the decade of becoming 'the most competitive and dynamic knowledge-based economy in the world capable of sustainable economic growth with more and better jobs and greater social cohesion' was established (http://www.europarl.europa.eu/summits/lis 1_en.htm).

Developing this vision, three European level agreements affecting older workers have aimed at influencing public policy at national levels. These are the European Equal Treatment Directive, and the Barcelona and Stockholm targets. In the year 2000 the European Union Council Directive 2000/78/EC established a general framework for equal treatment in employment and occupation. The Directive required all EU countries to introduce legislation proscribing direct and indirect discrimination in terms of labour market activities and vocational training on the grounds of age. The directive allowed Member States until the end of 2006 to implement the provisions on age and allowed considerable latitude as to how the directive was to be implemented. A recent review concluded that transposition of the directive had been uneven, progress being slow in some countries, while others had complied technically, though more could be done. Also, while the Directive called for consultation with a range of stakeholders, this had been lacking (Baker, 2004).

Additionally, the EU's taskforce on employment led by Wim Kok (European Union Task force on Employment, 2003), submitted a report to the European Council calling for Member States to take three key measures to meet European targets:

1. Provide incentives for workers to retire later and for employers to hire and keep older workers.
2. Promote access to training for all regardless of age and to develop life-long learning strategies.
3. To improve the quality of work to provide attractive, safe and adaptable work environments throughout the working life, including the provision of part-time work and career breaks.

Given their status in the European labour market, the European Council of Stockholm in 2001 agreed a remarkably ambitious target for the employment rate of older workers of 50 per cent by the year 2010. This stood at 38.8 per cent in 2001 (European Council, 2001). At the Barcelona European Council it was stated that the burden represented by an ageing population will need to be shared between the generations: 'A progressive increase of about 5 years in the effective average age at which people stop working in the European Union should be sought by 2010' (European Council, 2002). The average exit age from the labour force, regardless of whether they are receiving a pension or not, for the EU was 59.9 years in 2001.

There are a few positive signs, though progress remains modest overall. Only a handful of European Member States have achieved the Stockholm target so far and the European Commission (2003) concludes that the employment of older workers remains a major challenge. In a recent report to the Stockholm European Council it stated that:

> For older workers, despite various policy initiatives by the MS [Member States] (as reported in NAPs [National Action Plans]) there is little evidence that these have resulted in significant increases in labour market participation among older workers. To a large extent this reflects a deep-rooted early retirement culture and the persistence of early retirement schemes (often coexisting with schemes aiming at extending older workers' working life) and negative attitudes which remain not only among employers but also trade unions and policy makers. (European Commission, 2001: 23)

In fact, Burniaux *et al.* (2004) suggest that the kinds of reforms they suggest for the European Union would suffice to meet targets, though they think it unlikely that the effects could materialize by 2010, as is hoped.

Table I.2   Changes in employment activity rate for the age group 55–64 years old between 1979 and 2004

	Men								
	1979	1983	1990	1995	2000	2001	2002	2003	2004
Australia	67.4	59.6	59.2	55.3	58.5	56.6	58.1	60.7	61.7
Canada	72.9	66.4	60.0	54.0	57.7	57.3	58.9	60.8	62.0
EU-15	–	–	52.3	47.2	48.5	48.6	49.8	51.3	50.4
France	67.0	50.4	37.0	38.4	38.5	34.9	38.1	39.7	41.9
Germany*	63.2	57.4	52.0	48.8	46.4	46.4	47.2	47.1	48.8
Japan	81.5	80.5	80.4	80.8	78.4	77.5	76.8	77.4	78.1
The Netherlands	63.2	44.2	44.5	31.5	50.0	50.5	54.9	57.4	56.4
United Kingdom	–	62.4	62.4	56.1	59.8	61.6	62.1	65.0	65.4
United States	70.8	65.2	65.2	63.6	65.7	66.0	66.3	65.6	66.0
	Women								
Australia	19.8	19.9	24.2	27.4	35.4	35.7	38.0	39.4	41.7
Canada	32.3	30.9	32.8	33.4	39.4	39.4	41.4	45.3	46.2
EU	–	–	24.3	25.6	28.5	29.0	30.3	32.0	30.9
France	37.0	30.4	25.0	28.9	30.3	26.7	29.6	32.7	32.5
Germany*	26.8	24.0	22.4	27.0	29.0	29.4	30.0	30.9	29.8
Japan	44.8	45.1	46.5	47.5	47.9	47.3	47.1	47.5	48.6
The Netherlands	14.0	13.2	15.8	14.0	25.8	28.0	29.0	32.2	32.5
United Kingdom	–	–	36.7	39.3	41.4	43.2	44.7	46.4	47.3
United States	54.8	40.4	44.0	47.5	50.6	51.7	53.2	54.5	54.3

Note: * Reunified from 1989.

Source: OECD Employment Outlook (various).

Table I.2 places current the present European debate in sharp relief. This shows employment rates among the 55–64 age group for the countries which formed the case studies for this volume. Europe, overall, clearly lags far behind Japan and the USA, and other industrialized nations such as Australia and Canada. Despite this, as will be demonstrated, reform is also under way in these countries. Japan, like parts of Europe, faces looming problems due to the rapid ageing of its population. Although early exit has never been a major feature of its labour market, immigration, which could offset the effects to some extent, has not found wide acceptance as a policy approach. Pension and labour market reforms are under way in order to maintain the viability of its economy (Kano, 2002). For the USA the problem is somewhat less urgent, due to the relative youthfulness of its society, and as with Japan, though to a lesser extent, the participation of older workers in the labour market did not deteriorate as much as it did in Europe. The National Strategy for an Ageing Australia (Department of Health and Ageing, 2002) identified the 'need for and value of better utilising skilled mature age workers [which] will increase as the supply of younger workers declines. Ongoing engagement of mature age workers will be important to achieve sustained economic growth as the population ages' (p. x).

Added to the obvious benefits for economies of people working later, there is a body of evidence which shows that the option of paid work for an older individual can improve their prospects of experiencing a healthier, a wealthier and a happier old age, offering, according to Robert Butler, continuing social engagement, a sense of purpose and meaning, control over one's life and, on top of this, a wage (www.cenekreport.com/storage/npr% 20interview_dr%20robert%20butler_health%20benefits%20of%20workin g% 20.pdf).

However the real situation is clearly rather more complex. To return briefly to the discussion of international comparisons of early retirement, Gruber and Wise (1999a) show that social security provisions in many countries have sometimes offered enormous incentives to retire early, which may account for a significant part of the long-term decline in economic activity rates among older males. In continental Europe disability and unemployment programmes have provided generous early retirement benefits well before the official retirement age. Research places the USA alongside Japan in having low levels of non-work among those aged 55–59 and a low implicit tax on work at older ages. This research also places the UK and France together as countries with high levels of non-work among those aged 55–59 and a high implicit tax on work at older ages. Canada and Germany fall between these high and low groups (Gruber and Wise, 1999b). On the other hand, it is also the case that it is Japan and the USA where joblessness among older workers is more likely to be associated with poorer mental health (Taylor, 2003). Moreover, while employment rates among older workers have increased recently, some observers have argued that they have been overrepresented in the expansion of precarious work, and risk ill-health and injury associated with poor work organization, inadequate training and poorer knowledge of hazards and managing them (Quinlan *et al.*, 2001; Quinlan and Bohle, 2003; McGovern *et al.*, 2004). Their job security is also threatened by work intensification and the loss of soft and bridge jobs caused by the introduction of lean production processes (Tros, 2004), while research also points to declining levels of job satisfaction (Green, 2002), associated with the propensity to retire. Importantly, for many of the young and those with high skill levels, temporary jobs provide a stepping stone to jobs of higher quality. Among older and low skilled people, however, less than a third and less than

40 per cent, respectively, move from a temporary to a permanent job within three years. For these same groups, the risk of becoming unemployed is more than twice as high compared to young people and those with high-level skills (Taylor, 2006).

It seems, therefore, that early retirement's detractors have overlooked some potential benefits, while 'activation' appears to have its problems. While working later may be better, this is probably not all work, and in what sense is unemployment a better scenario than early retirement, other than perhaps in a narrow economic one?

Nevertheless in recent times, the term 'active ageing' has largely replaced 'early retirement' in the policy vernacular (Prager and Schoof, 2006) and bodies such as the World Health Organization (2002) and the European Commission (1999) have been busy promoting the concept. A policy framework for active ageing has been set out by the World Health Organization. Here the concept is defined as: 'the process of optimizing opportunities for health, participation and security in order to enhance quality of life as people age' (WHO, 2002: 12).

Active refers to:

> continuing participation in social, economic, cultural, spiritual and civic affairs, not just the ability to be physically active or to participate in the labour force. Active ageing aims to extend healthy life expectancy and quality of life for all people as they age, including those who are frail, disabled and in need of care.

However while a broader term than 'productive ageing', which has been coined to refer to 'any activity by an older individual that produces goods or services, or develops the capacity to produce them, whether they are to be paid or not' (Bass *et al.*, 1993: 6), in reality much of what has emerged from the 'active' ageing recipe book has had a strongly economic flavour. European commentators and policy makers, in particular, have begun to flesh out an active or activating approach to tackling specific issues associated with the extension of working lives. According to Naegele (1999) such an approach concerns both measures aimed at the prevention of unemployment and the reintegration of unemployed workers. It includes tackling age discrimination in the labour market, adapting learning approaches to the circumstances of older people and the adaptation and improvement of working conditions. The primary objective should be to prevent involuntary early retirement.

The European Commission has set out its vision for realizing the greater integration of older workers with the following list of requirements:

- improving their skills, motivation and mobility;
- good practice in lifelong learning is promoted and disseminated;

- adapting workplaces to workforce ageing to reduce the erosion of work-ability and to extend working lives;
- facilitating access to more suitable and flexible forms of working; and
- removing age-discriminatory attitudes and practices (p. 5).

Elsewhere, it has referred to the need for action in the following domains.

1. A joint government and social partner initiative to extend working lives:
   - access to company training;
   - improving quality in working conditions and work organization; and
   - changing views about the value of early retirement.
2. A targeted review of tax/benefit systems towards enhancing work incentives:
   - removing incentives encouraging early retirement both for individuals and for enterprises;
   - promoting a partial/gradual transition to retirement;
   - reviewing the effects of current policy combinations affecting participation.
3. Reforms aimed at making the care system more responsive to the needs of an ageing population (European Commission, 2002: 12–13).

The European Commission (1999) states that 'Successful active ageing policies involve all generations. All actors (government, firms and workers) need to adopt lifecycle strategies enabling workers of all ages to stay longer in employment' (p. 5). In his keynote introductory report to the European Commission Conference on Active Ageing in 1999, Alan Walker (1999) identified these key themes among others:

- Active ageing has the potential for major social and economic impact via the development of new, more active and employment/activity-friendly approaches with regard to pensions, employment, health and social care and citizenship.
- Bringing together the different elements of policy is essential if active ageing is to become more than a slogan. A multidimensional strategy will integrate individual and collective action and concentrate attention on the whole of the life course, not only older people.
- Achieving active ageing across the life course requires policy makers to adopt holistic and 'joined-up' approaches.

Similarly, the OECD (1998b) has set out the following list of reforms in order for active ageing to be achieved:

- Greater emphasis on prevention: making inexpensive interventions such as providing public information at an early stage of life and thereby reducing the need for later remedial action.
- Use of remedial interventions that are less fragmented and that are concentrated at critical transition points in life – early identification of problems, use of case management techniques, coordination among various agencies and measurement of outcomes.
- Better balance in the lifetime costs and benefits of programming to provide less constrained choices and greater responsibility at the level of individuals – such as greater linkage of lifetime pension contributions and benefits.
- Without a common strategic framework for reform, changes in one area can offset reforms in another; reforms necessarily cut across traditional programme boundaries.
- A common framework would also improve the quality of ground service delivery by facilitating cooperation among many agencies. There would be opportunity for sharing of lessons learned across disciplines and exchange of data and research results.

The Australian Council on the Ageing (Sheen, 2001; see also Sheen, 2000) goes further, arguing for a five-point strategic plan for older workers which includes issues of labour demand and an adequate social safety net. To summarize:

- maintaining economic growth which will generate sufficient jobs, combined with effective labour force management;
- tackling age discrimination;
- providing adequate opportunities for learning and training;
- flexible jobs and social security provision; and
- an adequate safety net for those unable to work.

The 'active' approach, thus offers a radically different vision of the ageing worker from that of the past. According to Walker (2002: 137) 'it is a strategy that makes sound economic sense, by responding to the economic challenges of ageing and extending employment, and, at the same time, it improves quality of life'. A recent report concluded that 'the most effective and plausible social, and policy, response to an ageing population is to increase the employment rate of the over 50s' (Working Group on the Implications of Demographic Change, 2002). Therefore, in considering such issues, this volume is timely. However although early exit pathways would seem to be anathema to the activating approach, Naegele recommends a cautious examination and weighting of social security features for an ageing workforce in order for the activating approach not to be under-mined. In his view, an approach which substitutes one kind of exclusion: early retirement, for another: long-term unemployment would be a failure. It is notable that for the WHO also, activation is not just a one way street:

> It allows people to realize their potential for physical, social, and mental well being throughout the life course and to participate in society according to their needs, desires and capacities, while providing them with adequate protection, security and care when they require assistance (p. 12).

Although it added that:

> The current trend toward early retirement in industrialized countries is largely the result of public policies that have encouraged early withdrawal from the labour force (p. 17).

While in one sense this statement is true, it confuses cause and effect, over-looking a critical factor which lay behind the rise of early retirement, namely declining demand for older workers and the loss of industries in which they predominated. Thus, any consideration of active ageing from a labour market perspective must consider both labour supply and demand. Activating older workers is one thing, but if ageing is to be 'successful' then it would seem that considerations such as opportunity and choice should be applied.

The cautious approach advised by Naegele and others underpinned the construction of this volume. Although proponents of active ageing seem to have a strong case, this needs to be tested. While early retirement now has few defenders, it may still have an important role to play in protecting older workers from the vagaries of labour markets. Chapters are provided by leading experts in the field of age and work in Europe, North America, Japan and Australia. These consist of country reviews where the authors seek to compare the promise of active ageing with the reality of older workers' experiences in the labour market. They examine the ageing of workforces and the changing status of older workers, consider the reform of retirement income systems, the emergence of active labour market policies and the rationale for current actions. They ask whether real progress is being made towards active ageing and set out the critical barriers to extending working lives.

REFERENCES

AARP (2000), *American Business and Older Employees*, Washington, DC: AARP.
Access Economics Pty Limited (2001), *Population and the Economy*, Canberra: Commonwealth Department of Health and Aged Care.

Auer, Peter and Mariangels Fortuny (2000), *Ageing of the Labour Force in OECD Countries: Economic and Social Consequences*, Geneva: International Labour Organization.

Baker, Richard (2004), 'Age discrimination: implementing the directive in the EU', accessed at http://lawzone.thelawyer.com/cgi-bin/item.cgi?id=110183&d=pndpr&h=pnhpr&f=pn.

Bass, Scott, Frank Caro and Yung-Ping Chen (eds) (1993), *Achieving a Productive Ageing Society*, London: Auburn House.

Bertelsmann Foundation (2006), *Active Aging in Economy and Society*, Gütersloh, Germany: Bertelsmann Stiftung.

Bohle, Philip and Michael Quinlan (2000), *Managing Occupational Health and Safety*, Melbourne: Macmillan.

Buck, Hartmut and Bernd Dworschak (eds) (2003), *Ageing and Work in Europe. Strategies at Company Level and Public Policies in Selected European Countries*, in the booklet series Demography and Employment, Stuttgart: IRB Verlag.

Buck, Hartmut, Ernst Kistler and Hans G. Mendius (2002), *Demographic Change in the World of Work. Opportunities for an Innovative Approach to Work – A German Point of View*, Stuttgart: Bundesministerium für Bildung und Forschung.

Bundesministerium für Bildung und Forschung (1999), *Congress Ageing and Work*, Berlin, November.

Burniaux, Jean-Marc, Romain Duval and Florence Jaumotte (2004), 'Coping with ageing: a dynamic approach to quantify the impact of alternative policy options on future supply in OECD countries', OECD Economics Department working paper 371, OECD, Paris.

Casey, Bernard (1998), 'Incentives and disincentives to early and late retirement', OECD working paper Awp 3.3, Paris.

Committee for Economic Development (CED) (1999), *New Opportunities for Older Workers*, New York and Washington: CED.

The Commonwealth Fund (1991), *New Findings Show Why Employing Workers Over 50 Makes Good Financial Sense for Companies*, New York: The Commonwealth Fund.

Confederation of German Employers' Associations (2003), *Proage – Facing the Challenge of Demographic Change*, Berlin: Confederation of German Employers' Associations.

Dennis, Helen (1988), *Fourteen Steps in Managing an Aging Workforce*, Lanham, MD: Lexington Books.

Department of Health and Ageing (2002), *National Strategy for an Ageing Australia. An Older Australia, Challenges and Opportunities for All*, Canberra, accessed at www.health.gov.au/internet/wcms/publishing.nsf/Content/ageing-ofoa-agepolicy-nsaa-nsaa.htm-copy2.

Employment and Social Affairs European Commission European Employment Observatory (1999), 'Older workers and the labour market', *Trends*, **33** (Winter), SYSDEM network, Berlin.

Employment and Social Affairs, European Commission (1999), *Active Ageing. Promoting a European Society for All Ages*, Brussels: European Commission.

European Union Task Force on Employment (led by Wim Kok) (2003), *Jobs Jobs Jobs: Creating More Employment in Europe*, Report to the European Council, November, Brussels: European Commission.

European Trade Union Institute (ETUI) (ed.) (2002), *Active Strategies for Older Workers*, Brussels: ETUI.

European Trade Union Institute (ETUI) (ed.) (2003), *A Lifelong Strategy for Active Ageing*, Brussels: ETUI.

Eurolinkage (1997), *Policy Options to Assist Older Workers*, London: Eurolinkage.

European Commission (1999), *Active Ageing. Promoting a European Society for All Ages*, Brussels: European Commission.

European Commission (2001), *Increasing Labour Force Participation and Promoting Active Ageing*, Brussels: European Commission.

European Commission (2002), 'Increasing labour force participation and promoting active ageing', COM(2002) 9 final, Brussels.

European Commission (2003), 'The Stockholm and Barcelona targets: increasing employment of older workers and delaying the exit from the labour market', accessed at http://europa.eu.int/comm/employment_social/employment_analysis/work/exit_en.pdf.

European Council (2001), *Presidency Conclusions, Stockholm, 23 and 24 March*, Brussels: European Council.

European Council (2002), *Presidency Conclusions, Barcelona 15 and 16 March*, Brussels: European Council.

European Foundation for the Improvement of Living and Working Conditions (1992), *Ageing at Work*, Luxembourg: Office for Official Publications of the European Communities.

Financial Times (2006), 'Pushed aside for younger model', 27 April.

Frerichs, Frerich (1996), 'Combating age barriers in job recruitment and training: Federal Republic of Germany', European Foundation for the Improvement of Living and Working Conditions, working paper no. wp/96/40/EN, Dublin.

Frerichs, Frerich and Philip Taylor (2005), *The Greying of the Labour Market: What Can Britain and Germany Learn from Each Other?*, London: Anglo-German Foundation for the Study of Industrial Society.

The Geneva Association (2002), 'The future of pensions and retirement', *Geneva Association Information Newsletter*.

Green, Francis (2002), 'Work intensification, discretion and the decline in well-being at work', paper prepared for the Conference on Work Intensification, Paris, 20–21 November.

Gruber, Jonathan and David A. Wise (eds) (1999a), *Social Security Systems Around the World*, Chicago, IL: University of Chicago Press.

Gruber, Jonathan and David A. Wise (1999b), 'Social security, retirement incentives and retirement behaviour: an international perspective', Employee Benefit Research Institute issue brief 209, Washington, DC.

Guillemard, Anne-Marie (1996), 'Combating age barriers in job recruitment and training: France', European Foundation for the Improvement of Living and Working Conditions, working paper no. wp/96/41/EN, Dublin.

Guillemard, A-M. (1997), 'Re-writing social policy and changes within the life course organisation: A European perspective', *Canadian Journal on Aging*, **16** (3), 441–64.

Guillemard, Anne-Marie (2001), 'Reforming employment and retirement in an ageing society: difficulties in finding a way out of the end-of-career inactivity trap in France', presentation to the Japan Institute of Labour Workshop/Symposium 2001 – Towards Active Ageing in the 21st Century – Japan/US/EU Joint Program, Tokyo.

Guillemard, Anne-Marie and Dominique Argoud (2004), 'France: A country with a deep early exit culture', in Tony Maltby, Bert de Vroom, Maria-Luisa Mirabile and Einer Øverbye (eds), *Ageing and the Transition to Retirement. A Comparative Analysis of European Welfare States*, Aldershot, UK: Ashgate, pp. 165–85.

Health Education Authority (1994), *Investing in Older People at Work. Contributions, Case Studies and Recommendations*, London: Health Education Authority.

Ilmarinen, Juhani (1999), *Ageing Workers in the European Union*, Helsinki: Finnish Institute of Occupational Health.

Ilmarinen, Juhani (2005), *Towards a Longer Worklife! Ageing and the Quality of Worklife in the European Union*, Helsinki: Finnish Institute of Occupational Health.

Johnson, Paul and Klaus F. Zimmerman (eds) (1993), *Labour Markets in an Ageing Europe*, Cambridge: Cambridge University Press.

Kano, Yasu (2002), *Improving Employment Opportunities for Older Workers*, final report, European Commission, Japanese Ministry of Health, Labour and Welfare, and The Japan Institute of Labour, p. 10.

Kohli, Martin, Martin Rein, Anne-Marie Guillemard and Herman van Gunsteren (eds) (1991), *Time for Retirement – Comparative Studies of Early Exit from the Labour Force*, Cambridge: Cambridge University Press.

Kuhn, Karl (1997), *Design for Integration. Five Case Studies from Germany*, Dortmund: Federal Institute for Occupational Safety.

McGovern, P., D. Smeaton and S. Hill (2004), 'Bad jobs in Britain', *Work and Occupations*, **31** (2), 225–49.

McNair, Stephen and Matt Flynn (2005), 'The age dimension of employment practices: employer case studies', Department of Trade and Industry, Employment Relations, research series no. 42, London.

Naegele, Gerhard (1999), *Active Strategies for an Ageing Workforce*, Luxembourg: Office for Official Publications of the European Communities.

Naegele, Gerhard and Alan Walker (2006), *A Guide to Good Practice in Age Management*, Luxembourg: Office for Official Publications of the European Communities, accessed 12 April, 2007 at http://www.eurofound.eu.int/pubdocs/2005/137/en/1/ef05137en.pdf.

Organisation for Economic Co-operation and Development (OECD) (1998a), *Employment Outlook*, Paris: OECD.

OECD (1998b), *Maintaining Prosperity in an Ageing Society*, Paris: OECD.

OECD (2005), *Ageing and Employment Policies*, synthesis report, Paris: OECD.

Oka, Shinichi (1992), *Older Workers: Conditions of Work and Transition to Retirement*, Tokyo and Geneva: International Labour Office.

Pack, Jochen, Hartmut Buck, Ernst Kistler, Hans G. Mendius, Martina Morschhäuser and Heimfried Wolff (1999), *Future Report Demographic Change*, Bonn: Bundesministerium für Bildung und Forschung.

Pearson, Maggie (1996), *Experience, Skill and Competitiveness. The Implications of an Ageing Population for the Workplace*, Luxembourg: Office for Official Publications of the European Communities.

Performance and Innovation Unit (2000), *Winning the Generation Game: Improving Opportunities for People Aged 50–65 in Work and Community Activity*, London: The Stationery Office.

Prager, Jens U. and Ulrich Schoof (2006), 'Active aging in economy and society – a policy framework', in Bertelsmann Foundation (ed.), *Active Aging in Economy and Society*, Gütersloh, Germany: Bertelsmann Stiftung, pp. 26–37.

Productivity Commission and Melbourne Institute of Applied Economic and Social Research (1999), *Policy Implications of the Ageing of Australia's Population, Conference Proceedings*, Canberra: AusInfo.

Quinlan, M., C. Mayhew and P. Bohle (2001), 'The global expansion of precarious employment, work disorganisation and occupational health: a review of recent research', *International Journal of Health Services*, **31** (2), 335–414.

Reday-Mulvey, Geneviève (2003), 'Encouraging and extending working life – recent policies and best practice in Europe', Geneva Association, Etudes et Dossiers no. 268, Geneva.

Sennett, Richard (2006), *The Culture of the New Capitalism (Castle Lectures in Ethics, Politics & Economics)*, New Haven, CT: Yale University Press.

Sheen, Veronica (2000), *Older Australians A Working Future?*, vol 10, Melbourne: Council on the Ageing.

Sheen, Veronica (2001), *Investing in the Future: Australia's Ageing Workforce*, vol 11, Melbourne: Council on the Ageing.

Sutter, Hannelore (1989), *Training of Older Workers in the Federal Republic of Germany*, Geneva: International Labour Organization.

Taylor, Philip (2002), *New Policies for Older Workers*, Bristol: The Policy Press.

Taylor, Philip (2003), 'Age, labour market conditions and male suicide rates in selected countries', *Ageing and Society*, **23**, 25–40.

Taylor, Philip (2004), 'Age and work: international perspectives', *Social Policy and Society*, **3** (2), 163–70.

Taylor, Philip (2006), 'Employment initiatives for an ageing workforce in the EU-15', Luxembourg: Office for Official Publications of the European Communities, accessed 12 April, 2007 at www.eurofound.eu.int/publications/htmlfiles/ef0639. htm.

Taylor, Philip and Alan Walker (1994), 'The ageing workforce: employers' attitudes toward older workers', *Work, Unemployment and Society*, **8** (4), 569–91.

Taylor, Philip and Alan Walker (1996a), 'Intergenerational relations in employment', in Alan Walker (ed.), *The New Generational Contract*, London: UCL Press, pp. 159–86.

Taylor, Philip and Alan Walker (1996b), 'Combating age barriers in job recruitment and training: United Kingdom', European Foundation for the Improvement of Living and Working Conditions, working paper no. wp/96/44/EN, Dublin.

Thomas, Andrew, Maggie Pearson and Richard Meegan (1992), *Older Workers: Conditions of Work and Transition to Retirement, United Kingdom*, Geneva: International Labour Office.

Tros, F. (2004), 'Towards "flexicurity" in policies for the older workers in EU-countries?', paper prepared for the IREC Conference, Utrecht, August.

The Victorian, South Australian and Western Australian Equal Opportunity Commissions, and the Australian Employers' Convention (2001), *Age Limits: Age-related Discrimination in Employment Affecting Workers over 45*, Melbourne: Victorian Equal Opportunity Commission.

de Vroom, Bert (1996), 'Combating age barriers in job recruitment and training: United Kingdom', European Foundation for the Improvement of Living and Working Conditions, working paper no. wp/96/42/EN, Dublin.

Walker, Alan (1999), 'The principles and potential of active ageing', keynote introductory report for The European Commission Conference on Active Ageing, Brussels, 15–16 November, p. 2.

Walker, Alan (2002), 'A strategy for active ageing', *International Social Security Review*, **55**, 121–39.

Walker, Alan and Philip Taylor (1998), *Combating Age Barriers in Job-recruitment and Training: A European Portfolio of Good Practice*, Luxembourg: Office for Official Publications of the European Communities.

Working Group on the Implications of Demographic Change (2002), *The Challenge of Longer Life. Economic Burden or Social Opportunity?*, London: The Catalyst Forum.

World Bank (1994), *Averting the Old Age Crisis*, Washington, DC: World Bank.

World Health Organization (WHO) (2002), *Active Ageing: A Policy Framework*, Geneva: WHO.

Worsley, Richard (1996), *Age and Employment: Why Employers Should Think Again About Older Workers*, London: Age Concern England.

Yocum, Katherine L. (1992), *Older Workers: Conditions of Work and Transition to Retirement, USA*, Geneva: International Labour Office.

1. Looking forward to working longer in Australia

Sol Encel

OLDER WORKERS IN PROFILE

The ageing of the labour force has been the subject of an almost unbroken series of official, semi-official and academic reports since 1990, although its implications had attracted attention considerably earlier. In 1958, a seminar on mental health in the city of Melbourne was addressed by the executive director of the Victorian Employers' Federation, Mr S.M. Gilmour, who declared that 'men and women should be encouraged and enabled to work part or full time for so long as they are able and willing to do so'. He was supported by the secretary of the Trades Hall Council, who advocated a national approach to later life employment which would mean that 'age will become less a matter of any given time for retirement and more a matter of right and desire to either work or retire' (Stoller, 1960: 55, 64). Some years later, the abolition of compulsory retirement was advocated by the economist Ronald Henderson in a national report on poverty. Henderson noted the connections between age, poverty and unemployment (Henderson, 1976). An attempt to outlaw age discrimination was made in the following year by the New South Wales state government, but was defeated in the upper house of the state parliament. During the 1990s, however, both age discrimination and compulsory retirement were outlawed in all states, in the two territories (Australian Capital Territory and Northern Territory), and by Federal legislation in 2004 (Encel, 2001, 2004). Age discrimination, long-term unemployment and enforced early exit from the labour force were major themes in a series of reports from 1992 onwards. More recently, emphasis has shifted towards concern with the retention of older workers in the labour force, especially given the prospect of declining numbers of school leavers entering the labour market as the result of a low birth rate. (In 2005, the total fertility rate was 1.77.) The Australian Treasury has estimated that whereas the working population presently grows by approximately 170 000 persons per year, the projected growth for the entire decade 2020–30 will be no more than 125 000. More recently, the impact of an ageing population on the labour force has been examined in detail in a report by the Productivity Commission. (The Commission is a statutory agency which conducts inquiries into a broad range of economic and social issues, and advises the Australian Government on microeconomic policy and regulation.) The Commission's report makes the following points concerning labour force participation:

- Over the next 40 years, aggregate labour force participation rates (LFPR) are projected to fall by around eight percentage points from their current level of 63.5 per cent to 55.4 per cent by 2045.
- Average weekly hours worked per employee will drop by 10 per cent, reflecting the rising incidence of part-time work and the increasing labour market share of older workers, who have a greater tendency to work part-time than their younger counterparts.
- The negative effects of ageing on participation and average hours worked outweigh the positive influence of reduced unemployment.
- In the two years 2004 to 2006, the number of workers was estimated to grow by approximately 320 000 whereas it would take nearly the full 20 years from 2025 to 2045 for the same growth to occur.
- In the next 40 years, the pace of effective growth in labour supply will be slower than population growth, unlike the past.

The average age of employees is expected to rise over the next 40 years: two-and-a-half years for males and three years for females (Productivity Commission, 2005: 3.1). In 2005, within the overall participation rate of 63.5 per cent, there were substantial differences between men and women, and between age groups. A report by the OECD illustrates these differences in employment status, using 50 as the benchmark for older workers.

The overall employment share of older women is 19.5 per cent of employed women, compared with 22 per cent in the case of men. Older women are, however, underrepresented in industries such as the utilities (electricity, gas and water supply); finance and insurance; and retail trade. Although women make up the majority of employees in retail trade, retailing employs only 12 per cent of all older women. Older women are overrepresented in education (15 per cent of all older women) and health and community services (22 per cent). Older men are generally underrepresented in service-based industries such as hospitality, retailing and cultural and recreational services. They are overrepresented in education, public administration, and transport. The sectors which employ the largest shares of older men are manufacturing (14 per cent), property and business services (12.5 per cent) and construction (10.5 per cent). The OECD report notes that the share of older workers in total employment has increased,

Table 1.1   Employment status by age and gender, 2003 (percentages of total employment)

Age group	Non-casual employees	Casual employees	Self-employed
Men			
15–24	51.3	43.4	5.3
25–49	65.7	10.5	23.8
50–4	60.1	7.6	39.0
55–9	52.5	8.3	32.3
60–4	42.6	14.1	39.3
65+	18.9	18.0	63.1
Total	59.8	15.7	24.5
Women			
15–24	47.2	51.1	1.7
25–49	64.6	20.9	14.5
50–4	61.3	18.2	20.5
55–9	56.4	18.2	20.5
60–4	47.0	24.9	28.1
65+	31.7	26.4	41.9
All	59.6	26.3	14.1

Source: OECD, 2005, Ageing and Employment Policies: Australia, p. 45.

from 15 per cent in 1990 to 21 per cent in 2003. The increase is unevenly distributed between industries. For expanding industries, such as property and business services and health and community services, the LFPR of older workers has risen faster than the average for the workforce. By contrast, for declining industries such as manufacturing and agriculture, there has been a fall in employment shares of older workers. This suggests that 'older workers adjust well to changes in labour demand and that older workers are not trapped in declining industries' (OECD, 2005: 48). The optimism reflected in this statement is at odds with high rates of long-term unemployment among older workers, a feature of their labour market status discussed in detail later in this chapter. (See Table 1.1.)

COHORT EFFECTS

The Productivity Commission report examines the wide variation in labour market behaviour resulting from cohort effects. The variation is particularly marked in the case of women. Greater involvement in secondary schooling and tertiary education since the 1950s resulted in lower participation rates

Table 1.2   Projected participation rates, 2005–41

Age group	2005	2041
Men		
50–4	85	80
55–9	74	72
60–4	50	51
65–9	20	32
70+	6	8
Women		
50–4	70	81
55–9	48	72
60–4	30	40
65–9	18	32
70+	2	3

Source: Productivity Commission, 2005: 3.25.

for young women. As against this, the dip in participation associated with childbearing, the 'nappy valley', has become shallower and narrower. The peak level of LFPR for women is now in the age range 40–4, contrasting strongly with the situation before the 1914–18 war. The Commission concludes that the long-term effect will be to increase participation among women in their 50s. By contrast, male LFPR has dropped sharply with age. Thus, the LFPR for the 1896–1900 birth cohort was around 80 per cent for men aged 60–4, but had fallen to less than 50 per cent for the 1936–40 birth cohort. Using cohort analysis, the Commission projects participation rates for the period until 2041. The different projections for men and women are shown in Table 1.2.

EDUCATIONAL EFFECTS

The role of education in improving employment prospects is well known. A recent Australian review of vocational education and training carried out a systematic analysis of research in the area, as well as conducting a number of in-depth studies. Their conclusion was that skill development activities led to improved labour market outcomes for many mature workers, in terms of higher employment rates or increased wages. This was especially the case for women and for previously unemployed people. Labour market gains were greater for those who completed higher level qualifications. They concluded, ironically, that lower level qualifications or incomplete qualifications may

Table 1.3   Participation rates by education, gender and age, 2002

Age group	Education		
	Low level	Medium level	High level
Men			
25–49	87	95	96
50–64	65	79	85
Women			
25–49	62	61	80
50–64	40	66	70

Notes:
Low level = less than upper secondary education
Medium level = upper secondary education
High level = tertiary education.

Source: OECD, 2005, Ageing and Employment Policies: Australia, p. 49.

have a negative effect. The study also identified three main factors affecting skill development of older persons:

- attitudes and behaviour of employers and employees towards the employment of older persons and their acquisition of new skills;
- the personal circumstances and attitude to learning of older persons; and
- public policy in related areas such as retirement income policies, as these are linked to the time that individuals have to realize their investment in training.

The report emphasizes the need for public policies to address these factors, including more emphasis on vocational education and training, as well as the removal of disincentives, skill development activities tailored to suit the circumstances of particular groups of older workers, and measures to change the attitudes of employers (NCVER, 2005: 5–7). The relation between educational levels and employment levels is shown in Table 1.3.

THE UNEMPLOYMENT PARADOX

Despite the general decline in unemployment and the increased labour force participation rates of older workers, they continue to be disproportionately affected by joblessness. The OECD report notes that re-employment

Table 1.4   *Unemployment rates by education, gender and age, 2002*

Age group	Education		
	Low level	Medium level	High level
Men			
25–49	9.1	3.9	3.2
50–64	7.1	4.2	3.0
Women			
25–49	7.1	3.9	3.2
50–64	3.5	3.5	1.9

Source: OECD, 2005, Ageing and Employment Policies: Australia, p. 49.

chances decline with age. During 2003, for instance, 20 per cent of unemployed men aged 25 to 44 found jobs, compared with 15 per cent of men aged 60 to 64. Among women, the corresponding figures were 13 per cent and 9.4 per cent. The majority of women who found employment did so in part-time jobs, whereas the majority of men (apart from the 60 to 64 age group) found full-time jobs. The OECD report also analyses the high levels of 'inactivity' among older men and women. In the age group 25–49, inactivity rates in 2003 were 8.5 per cent for men and 26.4 per cent for women. For men aged 50–4, the rate rose to 13.6 per cent, increasing sharply to 26 per cent in the 55–9 age group, and to 51 per cent among those aged 60 to 64. For women, the rate was 29.9 per cent in the 50–4 age group, rising sharply to 49.7 per cent among those aged 55–9 and 75 per cent among those in the 60–4 age groups (OECD, 2005: 55–6). (See Table 1.4.)

Perhaps the most distressing feature of mature age unemployment is its duration, which has increased steadily, despite fluctuations, since the 1970s. In 1978, the average duration of unemployment for persons aged 55 and over was 36 weeks; in 1999, 104 weeks; and in 2004, 130 weeks. These rates are approximately double the long-term unemployment rate (LTU) for the population as a whole. Very long-term unemployment (VLTU), which is defined as being out of work for at least two years (104 weeks), involves a disproportionately large number of men over 55. The OECD report notes that in 2002, 53 per cent of unemployed persons aged 55–9 were LTUs, compared with 23 per cent of persons under 50 (OECD, 2005: 55). Similar figures were recorded by the Australian Bureau of Statistics in the following year. In the ABS Labour Force Survey for November 2003, 23 per cent of all unemployed people were LTU; among unemployed 45–64 year olds, the proportion was 40 per cent, and among these aged 55–64, it was 49 per cent. The ABS report goes on to observe that the severity of LTU among persons aged 45 to 64 means that they are likely to become discouraged and drop out of the labour force altogether. In September 2002, 53 per cent of those classified as 'discouraged jobseekers' were aged 45 to 64 years (ABS, 2004: 117). Realistically, the majority of LTU workers aged 55 and over are unlikely to find continuous employment again, whether full-time or part-time, before they reach pension age.

THE POLICY RESPONSE

Changes in the labour force have major consequences for the social security system, in particular the growth of part-time and casual employment. This growth is particularly related to the large-scale entry of women into the paid work force, which became evident in the 1960s and has accelerated since then. Between 1980 and 2000, the labour force participation rate of women increased from 47 per cent to 61 per cent (ABS, 2001). Particularly striking has been the rise in the proportion of married women in the paid work force, which rose from 30 per cent of all employed women in 1954 to more than 60 per cent at the present time. Married women account for almost 80 per cent of all part-time workers. This has led to expectations that women will have the ability to provide for themselves through employment, rather than being supported by the state through pensions and benefits if they do not have a husband to support them. This has, in turn, caused a re-examination of the expectations that underpinned the social security system, that is, that eligibility for pensions does not depend on prior labour force participation (Cass, 1994). Rising concern about the increasing proportion of older people in the population was reflected in widespread talk about a 'pensions crisis'. A report by the Government's Economic Planning and Advisory Council echoed the concerns expressed in a World Bank report of 1994 (Clare and Tulpule, 1994; World Bank, 1994). Government concern about the rising cost of pensions had, in fact, already led to the introduction of compulsory national superannuation, as described below. Although the Labor Government elected in 1983 was committed to social-democratic policies, these were accompanied by a neo-liberal approach to economic management popularly labelled 'economic rationalism'. This included a policy of reducing or containing government expenditure on social welfare. Neo-liberal economic management was fuelled by the prospect of rising costs to government of the growing numbers of older, retired persons relative to the population of working age (the so-called age dependency ratio). The preferred strategy was to retard the growth of old-age pension expenditure by encouraging alternative forms of saving for retirement, which would supplement or even replace the standard age pension, introduced in 1909 and paid for out of taxation.

NATIONAL SUPERANNUATION

Legislation introduced in 1992 provided for a compulsory national contributory retirement incomes system. This meant that a significant component of retirement incomes would move from public to private provision, although subsidized by tax expenditures. A second aim was to provide a large pool of capital for private sector investment. A third consequence was to establish a clear link between 'productive work' (defined as paid employment) and economic wellbeing outside the labour force (Rosenman and Warburton, 1997). The 1992 legislation introduced a Superannuation Guarantee Charge (SGC) which requires employers to contribute to a fully vested, portable superannuation scheme for each employee. Employer contributions were set originally at 3 per cent of an employee's earnings, but were to rise progressively to 9 per cent by 2000, with employee contributions of 3 per cent to be phased in from 1997. The 9 per cent level was reached in 2002. The scheme now covers more than 90 per cent of employees, and the superannuation funds have accumulated more than $A600 billion. However, until 2007, superannuation contributions were also taxed, at the rate of 15 per cent, a policy which was not particularly well-received. The Superannuation Guarantee has the following features:

- The scheme is fully funded through a number of 'approved' funds, whose trustees include both employer and employee representatives, with few restrictions on investment policy.
- Benefits take the form of defined contributions, fully vested and portable, preserved to age 55, which is due to rise to 60 in 2025. Early withdrawals are not permitted. The ultimate benefit may be taken in the form of a lump sum, pension or annuity with tax/transfer incentives.
- Coverage extends to all employees between 18 and 65 with earnings greater than $A450 per month. Self-employed persons are not covered.
- Employer contributions are tax deductible. Fund income (contributions and earnings) were taxed (until 2007) at the concessional rate of 15 per cent.
- The administration of the scheme is generally recognized to be complex, and has been the subject of numerous adjustments during its lifetime.
- The state pension remains as a 'safety net', available to all Australian residents aged 65 and over, subject to income and asset tests, and indexed to average weekly earnings (Bateman and Piggott, 1997, 1999).

The national superannuation scheme was set up as the 'third pillar' of a retirement income system whose other components are the non-contributory state pension and privately operated superannuation schemes. The World Bank report of 1994 gave Australia a nod of approval for establishing the three-pillar structure. At the time the national superannuation scheme was introduced, there was considerable expectation that it would largely replace the state pension, thus lightening the growing fiscal burden resulting from an ageing and increasingly long-lived population. This expectation now seems unlikely to be realized. Superannuation industry experts believe that the SGC will not provide an adequate level of retirement income for most elderly Australians. However the Government has backed away from any suggestion that it should follow the example of other countries and raise the age of eligibility for the state pension from 65. Because of the different labour market situations of men and women, the national superannuation scheme provides unequal benefits between the sexes. Disadvantages for women have been summarized as follows:

• Women's working patterns and lifelong earnings are compromised by interruptions to paid employment due to child-bearing, child-rearing and other family responsibilities. Time out of the workplace results in lower superannuation contributions and lower levels of retirement savings.

• Women live longer than men (the current life span is 82 for women and 78 for men). With this increased life expectancy, more and more women will have to rely on their own financial resources for long periods of time. Increasing longevity will aggravate the problems confronting older women.

• The increasing incidence of divorce and the low remarriage levels of divorced women indicate that expectations of financial security through access to a partner's superannuation or other retirement savings may not be realized.

• Superannuation fees and charges diminish retirement savings and women are disproportionately affected, as they tend to have small balances and multiple accounts.

• The superannuation system is complex and poorly understood by the public, and disadvantages women because investment options are based on male earning models which do not apply to women in part-time or casual employment (Olsberg, 2001).

A shift of emphasis by the Government was marked by the 'Intergenerational Report' issued by the Treasurer, Peter Costello, in 2002 as one of the national budget papers. The predominant theme of the report (discussed in more detail below) was the need to maintain 'fiscal sustainability'. Early in 2004, this theme was taken up in a series of speeches by Mr Costello and the

Prime Minister, John Howard, which foreshadowed moves designed to address the ageing of the work force and the rising costs of pensions and aged care. Mr Costello proposed changes to the national superannuation scheme to provide tax incentives which would encourage workers to access their superannuation assets while remaining employed, and to invest some of these funds in 'growth pensions'. Part-time work, combined with a part-pension, would keep people working longer. He also foreshadowed a tightening of rules governing the granting of disability pensions, pointing out that 3 per cent of the population was receiving disability benefits, compared with 1 per cent a generation ago. Mr Costello also foresaw the disappearance of full-time retirement, which would be replaced by a combination of part-time work and part-time retirement. He proposed the following changes in the relations between labour force participation and superannuation:

- liberalization of superannuation contributions so that anyone working full-time or part-time can continue contributing until age 65 (which was then not the case);
- liberalization of current restrictions on superannuation contributions for persons continuing in employment between ages 65 and 74;
- a provision that superannuation funds should be required to pay benefits to all persons aged 75 and over, instead of leaving superannuation assets to their estate; and
- a reduction of tax exemptions on superannuation contributions for wealthy persons.

These changes, implemented in 2004–5, are in line with recommendations made by the national Human Rights and Equal Opportunity Commission in 2000, following a review of age discrimination (HREOC, 2000).

THE NATIONAL AGEING STRATEGY

In March 2002, the Minister for Ageing, Kevin Andrews, launched a 'National Ageing Strategy', which was based on a series of discussion documents issued by the Government between 1999 and 2001. The document follows closely upon the range of issues identified in a number of reports by the OECD, including the reform of pensions and taxation systems to remove financial incentives to early retirement and financial disincentives to later retirement. This would involve the use of a mix of tax/transfer systems, funded systems, private savings and earnings, to achieve a better balance of burden-sharing between generations and greater flexibility in the making of retirement decisions. The report also follows the OECD's concern with the employability of older workers and the need for training and retraining. The report discusses four main issues:

- independence in later age through employment, lifelong learning and financial security;
- the delivery of quality health care;
- the improvement of public attitudes to older people and the need for appropriate provision in relation to physical safety, housing and urban design, transport, recreation and tourism, and the use of new communications and online technologies; and
- the encouragement of 'healthy ageing'.

The use of the term 'strategy' is political language which conveys the impression of a coordinated approach towards a clearly defined end. Braybrooke and Lindblom, in a critical discussion of the concept of 'strategy' in relation to public policy, concluded that policy decisions more commonly took the form of 'disjointed incrementalism' (Braybrooke and Lindblom, 1963). The 'National Ageing Strategy' did not actually commit the Government to any particular programmes, and avoids questions relating to government expenditure and fiscal policy. It may be seen as the fulfilment of an undertaking given by a previous Minister for Ageing during the International Year of Older Persons in 1999. The national strategy report was largely overtaken by the 'Intergenerational Report' issued by the Australian Treasurer, Peter Costello, as one of the documents attached to the national budget in May 2002. This report addressed itself to questions of fiscal policy and the impact of demographic change on Australian government finances. It identified seven priorities for ensuring fiscal sustainability:

- achieving budget balance and ensuring that government debt remains low;
- maintaining an efficient health care system, complemented by widespread participation in private health insurance;
- containing the growth of the Pharmaceutical Benefits Scheme (that is, government subsidies for expensive drugs approved by an expert advisory committee);
- developing an affordable and effective residential care system that can accommodate the expected growth in the number of very old people;
- a social safety net that encourages working age people to find jobs and remain employed;
- encouragement of mature age participation in the labour force; and
- a retirement incomes policy that encourages private saving for retirement and reduces future demand on the state pension.

The report avoided the language of 'crisis' and 'burdens' which characterizes much public discussion of the impact of an ageing population, but it also sidestepped any suggestion that extra revenue will be required to meet increases in aged care costs, which were estimated to rise from 0.7 per cent of GDP in 2000 to 1.8 per cent in 2041. It places strong emphasis on private saving and 'user pays' policies. The report reiterates the view that increased reliance on superannuation income will reduce pressure on the age pension, a view which is not universally shared, as we observed earlier. In spite of cost pressures, the report assumes throughout that revenue stability will be maintained throughout the period from 2000 to 2041 which is covered by the report, that is, no increase in taxation. The basic assumptions of the Intergenerational Report are criticized in a detailed analysis by two academic economists, which focuses on three main items:

- the effects of a fall in unemployment rates, predicted by the report to reach 4 per cent within the next 10–20 years, are understated;
- the potential for future increases in labour force participation is greatly underestimated; and
- future costs of health and aged care are predicted with excessive certainty.

As they observe, the report assumes that the expectation of life will continue to rise, but discreetly avoids the implication that this will involve increasing costs and therefore the need for extra revenue. It also avoids any discussion of policies that would increase work incentives, as opposed to early retirement disincentives, or incentives for women to return to the work force after having children. The projections made in the report assume that the labour force participation rate of women will rise to approximate male levels over the 40-year period, but ignore the probability that this will require policy measures such as subsidized child care and maternity leave. The same critique also queries the reliance on superannuation income as a solution to the problem of financial security on retirement. The case for superannuation would be much more plausible in circumstances of full employment and job security. As it is, the increase in part-time and casual jobs, and the continued use of downsizing to cut labour costs, means that a large section of the labour force is unlikely to accumulate significant retirement income through superannuation contributions, and will join the ranks of age pensioners (Dowrick and McDonald, 2002). In 2007, the Treasurer issued a second Intergenerational Report, which follows similar lines to its predecessor, but acknowledges that the costs of ageing estimated in the first report were exaggerated.

The subject of positive ageing and its synonyms: healthy ageing, productive ageing, active ageing and successful ageing has only recently become a significant item on the policy agenda in Australia. It is increasingly accepted that illness and disability in old age are not inevitable and that interventions can postpone, reduce or even prevent some of the problems associated with ageing. As a result, a number of policy statements advocating such interventions have appeared in the last 15 years, produced by both national and state governments, although not much in the way of concrete action has followed. Generally speaking, such declarations of policy are concerned with maintaining the health and well-being of older people after retirement from the paid labour force (Browning and Kendig, 2003). The role of employment in contributing to positive ageing has received comparatively little attention, although it was touched upon in one of the discussion documents produced during the preparation of the National Ageing Strategy (Bishop, 1999).

The National Ageing Strategy and the Intergenerational Reports were both concerned with the incidence of early exit from the workforce and stress the need to retain the skills and experience of older workers, especially in the light of skill shortages which are evident in a number of industrial sectors. Although enforced early exit, sometimes described misleadingly as 'involuntary retirement', is the more important factor, voluntary early retirement remains a reality. Both enforced early exit (often in the form of 'downsizing') and voluntary retirement were responsible for a decline in labour force participation during the 1980s and 1990s. A survey of retirement by the Australian Bureau of Statistics in 1997 found that between 1960 and 1995, the average age at which people left the workforce fell by four years for men and five years for women. The same survey also found that 71 per cent of men left employment between the ages of 45 and 64, and 53 per cent between 55 and 64. For women, the corresponding figures were 43 per cent between 45 and 64, and 21 per cent between 55 and 64 (ABS, 1997).

A more recent survey of retirement indicates that the trend to early exit has slowed, and participation rates for men over 60, in particular, have returned to the levels recorded in the 1980s (ABS, 2006). Several factors may be adduced for this shift, including a tight labour market and growing consciousness of the need to remain longer in the workforce in order to save for ultimate retirement. However as the OECD report suggests, these changes do not significantly alter the fact that participation rates for older workers in Australia are relatively low by international standards.

Until recently, pension and superannuation policies encouraged workers to retire early. A government economist, David Ingles, notes that community attitudes have been broadly supportive of early retirement for many years. In turn, these attitudes have been reflected in provisions governing access to superannuation and social security payments, and also in employer behaviour and workers' expectations. One effect of the pensions system has been to encourage people to retire early and to use up superannuation assets before pensionable age so that they can pass the pension means test (known as 'double dipping') (Ingles, 1999). A critical review of this argument points out that double dipping is only available to people with significant assets and accumulated superannuation payments. Nevertheless the author argues, policies that induce older people to leave the workforce are destructive in the long run. Retirement income policies should be complemented by strategies to encourage prolonged employment, and governments should adopt an integrated approach to rebuild a culture of longer working life (Perry, 2001).

EMPLOYMENT AND SOCIAL SECURITY

Since 1990, there have been notable shifts in government policy which are gradually reshaping the employment/retirement/social security nexus. National occupational superannuation was one step in this direction. A further step was to raise the pension age for women from 60 to 65, over a ten-year period commencing in 1995. This has been a significant factor in raising the labour force participation rate among women aged 60–5. Another amendment to pensions policy was the Pension Bonus Scheme, introduced in 1998, which provides for an additional payment of 9 per cent on top of the standard pension for those remaining in employment beyond age 65. In 2002, this was supplemented by providing for a lump sum payment of $A30 000 in lieu of the pension increase. So far, take-up has been modest, and the most likely reasons appear to be that the financial incentive is not great enough to tempt large numbers. The relations between employment and the social security system were examined by a 'reference group' set up by the Federal Government in 1999. The resulting report, *Participation Support for a More Equitable Society*, was published in 2000 and is generally known as the McClure Report after the chairman of the reference group. The key theme of the report is 'participation', seen as the answer to welfare dependency. The Government's response was given in the budget for 2001–2, which announced a programme entitled 'Australians Working Together'. The AWT programme contains a section dealing specifically with mature-age persons, defined in this case as people aged 50 and over. A number of special benefits are provided in this programme, in particular the 'Transition to Work' scheme aimed at people aged 50 and over. A statement by the Minister for Employment and Workplace Relations, Kevin Andrews (previously Minister for Ageing), outlines the benefits available under this scheme:

Transition to Work builds self-esteem and addresses confidence issues of mature
age workers. It improves participants' prospects of obtaining paid employment
through assessment, skills training, support and advice on how to get into the
jobs market . . . This strategy over 4 years will provide additional and focused
assistance to both mature age job seekers and those already in work but considering retirement. (Andrews, 2004)

The Transition to Work programme has three elements, known as Jobwise
Outreach, the Mature Age Industry Strategy and the Mature Age Workplace
Strategy. Apart from improving job-search skills for the older unemployed,
the programme aims to increase job opportunities in industries where opportunities for their employment appear to exist, including retail trade, business
services, and hospitality. The programme also aims to encourage employers
to recognize the value of reliable and experienced older workers. Despite the
sentiments expressed in launching these projects, the actual funding is quite
modest, amounting to $A12.1 million in the budgetary year 2004–5. The
Government has also endeavoured to raise consciousness among employers
about the value of older workers. Apart from rhetoric, a positive movement in this direction was the introduction of the Mature Age Employer
Champion Award, conferred for the first time in 2005 on the firm of Coates
Hire Ltd, which provides street barriers used to direct traffic during road-
works and building construction. The award noted that 18 per cent of
Coates' staff were aged over 50. The need to change employers' attitudes is
also canvassed in two reports published by the Business Council of Australia
in 2003. (The BCA represents the 100 largest corporations in Australia.) The
first report, entitled *Age Can Work*, examines policies in Australia and a
number of other countries. It recommends that public attitudes to workforce
participation by older people need to be addressed, and suggests a policy of
working with employers and their associations to improve retention rates for
older employees through family-friendly policies, employer support for
retraining, and improved services and support for older persons. A second
report, also entitled *Age Can Work*, argues that 'cultural change is essential'.
It requires the tackling of entrenched attitudes and organizational cultures
which undervalue the contribution of mature age workers. The report stresses
the value of diversity in the workforce and the need for business corporations
and government to work together (Encel, 2003). It should be noted that the
Age Can Work report was jointly commissioned by the BCA and the
Australian Council of Trade Unions (ACTU). The ACTU's national congress in 2003 adopted, for the first time, a policy regarding older workers,
opposing age discrimination and supporting the rights of workers to continue in employment after the 'normal' retiring age. Other employer groups
have produced similar statements. The Australian Chamber of Commerce
and Industry, which represents small and medium-sized enterprises, has

suggested that the Government pay employers a 'learning bonus' to encourage older workers to undertake formal training and improve their skills. The chief executive of the Australian Industry Group, which mainly represents manufacturing industry, has proposed tax-based incentives like the changes to superannuation announced by the Government early in 2004 (*Sydney Morning Herald*, 28 October 2004). Other employment and training measures have been introduced which are aimed directly or indirectly at improving labour market prospects for older people. They include a Training Account, designed to assist job-seekers to gain work related skills; the Vocational Education and Training Priority Places Program; the Basic IT Enabling Skills programme; and training credits, available to job-seekers who have completed certain minimum requirements. In 2005, the Government also introduced a tax incentive scheme, the Mature Age Worker Tax Offset, available to workers aged 55 and over with annual earnings of up to $A58 000. The tax cuts are expected to apply to an estimated 750 000 workers, and would cost $A1 billion over four years. The scheme is designed to persuade older workers to remain in employment. Announcing the programme, Prime Minister John Howard claimed that the tax incentive would counter the trend to early retirement, which he has criticized a number of times, calling for an end to the 'cult of early retirement'. Following the general election of 2004, Howard created the new ministerial portfolio of Workforce Participation, responsible for administering the tax offset programme.

STATE-BASED PROGRAMMES

Although the Federal Government bears the main responsibility for labour market policy, the state governments have also been active in the area. The first government at any level to introduce an active labour market programme aimed at older workers was the state government of New South Wales, which established its 'Mature Workers Program' in 1989. The objectives of the MWP were to maximize the retention of mid-life and older workers in the labour force and to facilitate the entry of older persons into the labour force. During its lifetime, the MWP was able to place more than 30 000 older workers in jobs, with a high rate of retention (Perry, 2002). In 2004, as a result of budget stringency, the MWP was abolished, despite widespread public protests. In Victoria, the 'Community Business Employment Program' has placed several thousand job seekers aged 45 and over into work since it was established in 2000. Following a report in 2002 on the impact of an ageing population, the state government announced a programme to encourage best practice schemes in the public sector, and the promotion of 'Age Aware Employer Champions'. The largest state-based labour market programme was set up in Queensland in 1998, with the aim of creating 56 000 employment opportunities over a six-year period. The programme was not originally targeted at older workers, but in 2001 it was decided to focus more intensively on this group. Smaller programmes have operated in South Australia and Western Australia. Apart from incentives to employers, the South Australian government supports a community organization, DOME (Don't Overlook Mature Expertise) which provides specialist employment assistance to mature age persons. In Western Australia, the government launched a programme entitled 'Profit from Experience' in 1999. After a three-year trial period, the programme was integrated into the broader framework of state government employment policies.

CONCLUSION

As the labour force continues to age, governments will come under increasing pressure to introduce active labour market strategies to retain and retrain older workers. One important factor will be the progressive exit of the baby boom generation from the labour force, whose effects are beginning to be felt. As described above, the full impact of an ageing labour force, combined with low fertility rates, is expected to arrive in the decade following 2020. As that date moves closer, governments will be constrained to take more concerted action, rather than the 'disjointed incrementalism' which has so far characterized policy in this area.

REFERENCES

Andrews, K. (2004), address by Minister for Employment and Workforce Relations Kevin Andrews to the annual conference of the Recruitment and Consulting Services Association, Canberra, 3 August.

Australian Bureau of Statistics (ABS) (1997), *Retirement and Retirement Intentions*, catalogue no. 6238.0, Canberra: ABS.

ABS (2001), *Australian Social Trends 2001*, catalogue no. 4102.0, Canberra: ABS.

ABS (2004), *Australian Social Trends 2004*, catalogue no. 4102.0, Canberra: ABS.

ABS (2006), *Retirement and Retirement Intentions*, catalogue no. 6238.0, Canberra: ABS.

Bateman, Hazel and John Piggott (1997), 'Private pensions in OECD countries – Australia', OECD Labour Market and Social Policy occasional papers no. 23, Paris: Organisation for Economic Co-operation and Development.

Bateman, Hazel and John Piggott (1999), 'Mandatory retirement provision: the Australian experience', *Geneva Papers on Risk and Insurance*, **24** (1), 95–113.

Bishop, Bronwyn (1999), 'Employment for mature age workers', Minister for Ageing discussion paper, Canberra.

Braybrooke, David and Charles E. Lindblom (1963), *A Strategy of Decision*, New York: Free Press.

Browning, Colette and Hal Kendig (2003), 'Healthy ageing: a new focus on older people's health and well-being', in Paul Liamputtong and Heather Gardner (eds), *Health, Social Change and Communities*, Melbourne: Oxford University Press, pp. 182–205.

Cass, Bettina (1994), 'Social security policy into the 21st century', in Julian Disney and Lynelle Briggs (eds), *Social Security Policy: Issues and Options*, Canberra: Australian Government Publishing Service, p. 10.

Clare, Ross and Ashok Tulpule (1994), '*Australia's ageing society*', Economic Planning and Advisory Council background paper 37, Canberra.

Costello, Peter (2002), *Intergenerational Report 2002–03*, Canberra: Commonwealth of Australia.

Dowrick, A. and P. McDonald (2002), 'Critique of the intergenerational report', Centre for Economic Policy Research occasional paper, Australian National University, Canberra.

Encel, Sol (2001), 'Age discrimination in Australia: law and practice', in Zmira Hornstein (ed.), *Outlawing Age Discrimination*, Bristol: Policy Press, pp. 12–30.

Encel, Sol (2003), *Age Can Work*, Melbourne: Business Council of Australia/ Australian Council of Trade Unions.

Encel, Sol (2004), 'Age discrimination in law and in practice', *Elder Law Review*, **3**, 1–14.

Henderson, Ronald F. (1976), *Final Report of the Poverty Inquiry*, Canberra: Australian Government Publishing Service.

Human Rights and Equal Opportunity Commission (HREOC) (2000), 'Age matters', report by HREOC, Canberra, pp. 43–4.

Ingles, D. (1999), 'Structural ageing, labour market adjustment and the tax-transfer system', Centre for Economic Policy Research conference paper, Australian National University, Canberra.

National Centre for Vocational Education and Research (NCVER) (2005), *The Mature-Aged and Skill Development Activities: A Systematic Review of Research*, Adelaide: NCVER.

Olsberg, Diana (2001), *Missing Out? – Women and Retirement Savings*, Sydney: Research Centre on Ageing and Retirement, University of New South Wales.

Organisation for Economic Co-operation and Development (OECD) (2005), *Ageing and Employment Policies – Australia*, Paris: OECD.

Perry, Julia (2001), *Early Retirement – What is the Problem?*, Sydney: Social Policy Research Centre, University of New South Wales.

Perry, Julia (2002), *Too Young to Go*, Sydney: Ministerial Advisory Committee on Ageing.

Productivity Commission (2005), *Economic Implications of an Ageing Society*, Canberra: Productivity Commission.

Rosenman, Linda and Jeni Warburton (1997), 'Retirement, retirement incomes and women', in Allan Borowski, Sol Encel and Elizabeth Ozanne (eds), *Ageing and Social Policy in Australia*, Cambridge: Cambridge University Press, pp. 137–56.

Stoller, Alan (ed.) (1960), *Growing Old*, Melbourne: F.W. Cheshire, pp. 55, 60.

Sydney Morning Herald (2004), 'Welfare state of mind to change', 28 October.

World Bank (1994), *Averting the Old Age Crisis*, New York: Oxford University Press.

2. Japan: towards employment extension for older workers

Masato Oka

INTRODUCTION

This chapter evaluates recent developments in policies for the employment promotion of older workers in Japan. The first section provides a profile of older workers in the national labour market context. The second summarizes the development of public policies for older workers, in particular, focusing on the 2004 Amendment Law on Stabilization of Employment of Older Persons. The third section analyses firms' behaviour in response to public policies. Concluding remarks will offer suggestions for a new Japanese-style personnel management system, which may provide a means of achieving age-free employment.

OLDER WORKERS IN PROFILE

Demographic Change and Workforce Ageing

Japan has been experiencing the most rapid population ageing in the world. The percentage of those aged 65 or over was 7 per cent in 1970, 14 per cent in 1994, and is estimated to be 25 per cent in 2014 (National Institute of Population and Social Security Research, hereafter NIPSSR, 2002). The causes can be seen in declining fertility rates and increasing longevity. The fertility rate decreased dramatically from 3.65 in 1950 to 1.29 in 2003, and may decrease further. On the other hand, life expectancy increased by approximately 20 years from 1950 to 2000 (Statistics Bureau, Abridged Life Table). It will increase further, to 79.8 for men and 87.5 for women by 2025. Recent statistics show that the size of the Japanese population peaked in 2005 at 130 million, and is estimated to decrease in the following decades (NIPSSR, 2006).

Figure 2.1 shows the age structure of the labour force from 1980–2004 (Statistics Bureau, various) and the estimated figures for 2015 and 2025

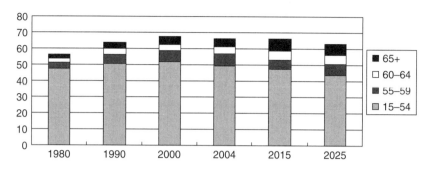

Source: Statistics Bureau, various. MHLW for 2015, 2025.

Figure 2.1   Labour force by age groups (millions)

Table 2.1   Men's labour force participation rates by age groups (%)

Year	1990	1995	2000	2004
50–4	96.3	97.3	96.7	95.7
55–9	92.1	94.1	94.2	93.2
60–4	72.9	74.9	72.6	70.7
65+	36.5	37.3	34.1	29.2
All	77.2	77.6	76.4	73.4

Source: Statistics Bureau, various.

(Cabinet Office, 2005). It points to rapid labour force ageing as well as labour shortages in the near future. The 'Year 2007 problem', as it is described, is the starting year of mandatory retirement of the post-war baby-boomers born from 1947–9. Concerns about the loss of accumulated skills and experiences of this large cohort have been discussed widely (Higuchi *et al.*, 2004).

Labour Market Context and Work Status of Older Workers

Among men aged in their 50s, labour force participation rates are above 90 per cent, declining sharply to 70 per cent among the 60–4 age group and 30 per cent after age 65 (Table 2.1). With regard to women, the rate for those aged in their 50s exceeds the average for all ages by approximately 15 percentage points, declining markedly after age 60 (Table 2.2). The unemployment rate of the 60–4 age group exceeds the average for all ages, this

Table 2.2　Women's labour force participation rates by age groups (%)

Year	1990	1995	2000	2004
50–4	65.5	67.1	68.2	68.4
55–9	53.9	57	58.7	59.6
60–4	39.5	39.7	39.5	39.7
65+	16.2	15.6	14.4	12.9
All	50.1	50	49.3	48.3

Source:　Statistics Bureau, various.

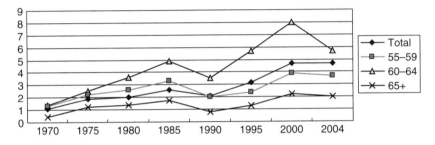

Source:　Statistics Bureau, various.

Figure 2.2　Unemployment rates (both sexes, %)

difference widening in the 1990s, but narrowing in the early years of the twenty-first century (Figure 2.2).

With regard to changes in the working status of persons around the age of 60, some particular features can be observed. These are: first, a move from large firms to smaller ones in terms of labour force size; second, a move from manufacturing towards the service sector; and third, a move from full-time to part-time employment and self-employment. There is a clear tendency towards a diversification in the type of work undertaken as workers age (Table 2.3).

The percentage of non-working persons increases after age 60. However more than half of non-working men aged 60–4 want to work. Thus, there is a wide gap between supply and demand in the labour market for ageing men. As for ageing women, their need for work is less but still considerable. It is also reported that the majority of working men (75.9 per cent) and women (65.5 per cent) aged 55 and over want to continue in work until at least 65 years old (MHLW, survey report, 2000). These figures demonstrate that Japanese older persons' motivation to work is high.

Table 2.3   Work status of older men and women in the year 2000

Age group	55–59	60–64	65–69
Men			
Total of working people	89.9	66.5	51.6
Full time employee	61	25.7	12.5
Part time employee	1.6	9.4	8
Employment status n.a.	0.3	0.3	0.2
Executive	10.6	9.1	7.1
Self-employed	14.1	17	17.6
Family work	0.7	1.4	2.4
Voluntary work	1	3	3.2
Piece work	0.2	0.4	0.3
n.a. about work status	0.4	0.2	0.3
Total of non-working people	10.1	33.5	48.4
Non-work and want to work	6.7	18.4	18.1
Non-work and not want to work	3.4	14.9	29.9
n.a. about desire to work	0	0.2	0.4
All men	100	100	100
Women			
Total of working people	59.7	41.5	28.7
Full time employee	24.7	8.9	3.4
Part time employee	13.2	10.2	5.3
Employment status n.a.	0.3	0.2	0
Executive	2.4	2.6	1.8
Self-employed	8.1	7.7	7.1
Family work	6.6	7.8	5.9
Voluntary work	2.2	2.2	2.9
Piece work	0.4	0.3	0.1
n.a. about work status	0.4	0.3	0.1
Total of non-working people	40.3	58.5	71.3
Want to work	14.1	20.2	15
Not want to work	26	37.9	55.3
n.a. about desire to work	0.2	0.4	1
All women	100	100	100

Source: MHLW, 2000.

Mandatory Retirement System

The above-mentioned patterns can be explained, in part, by the organization of Japan's retirement system, and in particular, the mandatory element, known as *Teinen*, and the public pension component (Kimura and

Oka, 2001). *Teinen* refers to a chronological age at which labour contracts are ended automatically. Currently, for a large majority of workers, this age is 60. It has been closely associated with the employment practices of large Japanese firms, the so-called lifetime employment contract and age-oriented pay and promotion system. The latter was introduced at the end of 19th century in order to extend years of service of employees to cope with labour shortages of skilled workers in modern industries (Hagiwara, 1988).

This employment practice, together with company welfare and fringe benefit arrangements, has been effective in maintaining the loyalty of employees. However it has a built-in problem, implying a heavier payroll burden with increasing years of service (Oka and Kimura, 2003). The *Teinen* rule was introduced in order to cope with this problem, as well as refreshing firms' organizational structures. At the beginning of twentieth century *Teinen* age was 50 or 55.

The rule was introduced widely in large firms in the period between the World Wars. From the 1970s it became popular in small-to-medium-sized firms. After *Teinen*, lives of ageing workers are widely diversified. Some seek jobs by themselves, others are reemployed by the same firm, while some choose to retire from the labour market. Thus, *Teinen* does not necessarily mean an end to working life. However it is an important life event at which steps towards complete retirement commence.

Public Pension System

The public pension system is another key factor determining the retirement behaviour of older workers. The Japanese system for employees is comprised of two elements: a fixed sum portion called the basic pension and an earnings-related portion.

The basic pension benefit is paid to an insured person and their spouse, and varies only according to the length of contribution years. As of 2004 the model pension benefit for a couple was 233 000 yen per month. It comprised 101 000 yen of the earnings related portion and 132 000 yen of the full basic pension portion for a couple who had paid premiums for 40 years. The replacement rate was approximately 60 per cent.

Figure 2.3 shows the income structure of older persons' households, which consisted of people aged 65 or over and, if any, unmarried children aged 18 or younger. As of 2003, the amount of the public pension accounted for 72 per cent of total income. It was far greater than the share of work earnings, 18 per cent. By comparison, in 1980 the share of income accounted for by the public pension was approximately the same as that of work earnings. It is clear that the role of public pension for older households has become increasingly important in recent times. Older households' income

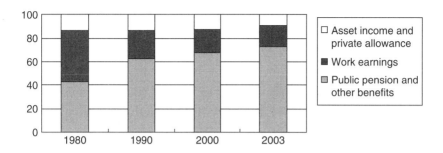

Source: Cabinet Office, various.

Figure 2.3   Income structure of older persons' households (%)

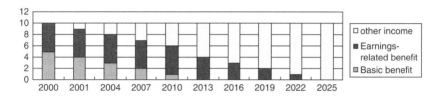

Figure 2.4   Changes envisaged from employee pension reform for the 60–64 age group

per capita is almost the same as the average of all households (Cabinet Office, 2000).

Successive pension reforms have been made since the mid-1980s in order to cope with the predicted solvency crisis in the system caused by rapid population ageing. The major elements of the reforms have been increasing premium and pensionable ages and reducing benefit levels. As for the latter, the 2004 Amendment of the Employee Pension Law aimed at reducing the replacement rate gradually from 60 per cent to 50 per cent of the average disposable income of premium payers by 2023. With regard to the pensionable age, the 1994 Amendment of the Employee Pension Law aimed at raising this gradually from 60 to 65, between 2001 and 2025 for men and between 2006 and 2030 for women (MHLW, various).

Figure 2.4 outlines the two stages of the scheme. In the first, between 2001 and 2013, the above-mentioned basic benefit for the 60–4 age group will disappear. In the second stage, between 2013 and 2025, the earnings-related portion will also disappear gradually. Roughly speaking, the pension benefit for those aged in their early 60s will be halved by 2013, and will completely disappear by 2025; although an actuarially reduced benefit will be available from age 60. The intention is that the decreasing pension benefit will be replaced by other income sources, mainly earnings from employment. One of the main aims of the reform is to extend employment to age 65.

PUBLIC EMPLOYMENT POLICIES FOR OLDER WORKERS

A Brief History

Successive Japanese governments have consistently developed a positive employment policy for older people since the early 1970s. The process can be divided into two periods.

The first was between 1971 and 1986, and aimed at extension of *Teinen* age from 55 to 60. The intention of the 1971 Law Concerning Stabilization of Employment of Older Persons (hereafter, the Older Workers Law) was to promote the employment of workers aged 45 and over. From the mid-1970s, the policy focus was on the extension of *Teinen* age from 55 to 60 by means of subsidies for firms, and the quota rule for the employment of older persons in 1976, requesting firms' best efforts to raise the percentage of regular employees aged 55 and older by up to 6 per cent or more (Campbell, 1992: 162). The 1986 Amendment of the Older Workers' Law was called the 'Age 60 Teinen Act'. It was the completion of the initial policy target, although the duty of employers was limited to making their best efforts. A *Teinen* age of less than 60 was legally prohibited in 1998, when the rule metamorphosed from firms' practice to statutory order.

The second period started in the mid-1980s, aiming at further employment extension up to age 65. The trigger was debates concerning the pension reform of 1985. It was argued that re-extension of *Teinen* might be necessary in order to cope with the inevitable rise of the pensionable age to 65 in the near future. In 1990, the Older Workers' Law was amended in order to encourage employers to make efforts for continued employment up to age 65. In 1994 the Government announced officially the schedule of pension reform from 2001 to 2013. The 2000 Amendment of the Older Workers' Law formally declared that employers should make best efforts to actualize continued employment until age 65.

The 2004 Amendment of the Older Workers' Law

This law was epoch-making. The contents were divided into three pillars:

1. statutory employment security up to age 65;
2. provisions for assisting in the reemployment of older persons; and
3. provisions for securing diversified job opportunities for older persons.

With regard to the first pillar, which is the mainstay of the 2004 Amendment, employers are obligated to endeavour to: (a) raise *Teinen* age; (b) introduce or improve the continuous employment system after *Teinen* until a worker reaches age 65; or (c) abolish the *Teinen* rule entirely. The obligatory age of employment is 62 from April 2006 to March 2007, 63 from April 2007 to March 2010, 64 from April 2010 to March 2013 and 65 after April 2013. This schedule is synchronized with the rise of pensionable age. The above-mentioned employment security measures should be applied in principle to all *Teinen* retirees who wish to continue work.

There are many controversial points in the law, which may be described as loopholes, resulting from compromises among the stakeholders. First, firms are exempted from the principle of retaining all applicants if management and unions reach an agreement on exceptions and can justify this.

Second, when agreement on the standards of a continued employment scheme cannot be reached by management and labour, the employer will be allowed to impose these, subject to employment regulations. This measure is effective for three years in large firms, until March 2009 and five years for small and medium-sized firms, until March 2011.

Third, penalties against violation of the law are absent. The government shall give assistance, advice and instruction to insubordinate employers. If employers refuse to take any positive action, the government shall make a recommendation as an administrative sanction, which may include publicity of the name of companies violating the law. This shows that its success is dependent largely on the sense of social responsibility of firms.

The second pillar of the 2004 Amendment Law is a provision for promoting the re-employment of older persons. It is reported that older job seekers are seriously affected by age discrimination. In a survey conducted in 1998–99, more than 70 per cent of unemployed persons aged 50 and over stated that the reason for their unsuccessful job-search activity was the difference between their age and the age requirements mentioned in situations-vacant advertisements (MHLW, 2001).

In response, the Employment Measures Law was amended, and since October 2001 companies have been requested to carry out recruitment and hiring activities without reference to age. This measure has been supplemented by guidelines to abolish age discrimination, although these specify a number of circumstances under which age limits in recruitment are permitted. Also, the law does not impose any penalty for violation (Taylor *et al.*, 2002).

However the Government took a further step in the 2004 Amendment of the Older Workers Law. This requires employers to state the reason why they set an age limit in a recruitment advertisement, although it does not apply after the age of 65 years. The law also stipulates that, in cases where persons aged 45–65 lose their jobs due to dismissal, and when they want re-employment, 'their employers shall endeavour at all times to take necessary measures to assist in re-employment of said older persons'.

The third pillar of the 2004 Amendment Law is a provision for securing diversified job opportunities for older persons. It has strengthened the function of Silver Human Resource Centres (SHRC), which have aimed to provide temporary and short-term jobs for older persons aged 60 and over since the mid-1970s. The original image of SHRC members was a kind of paid volunteer engaging in useful activities in their community, for example, cleaning public parks and so forth (Bass and Oka, 1995). Its current membership is about 750 000 nationwide (SHRC, website). The activities of SHRC have been strictly separated from the conventional labour market, although the demarcation line has gradually blurred. Under the long recession since the early 1990s, SHRCs took on the role of job provider for older workers, because of their poor prospects elsewhere. With regard to the 2004 Amendment Law, the function of SHRCs has been further expanded to include acting as a temporary labour exchange for older workers engaging in specific occupations defined by the law. This suggests that SHRCs may become a comprehensive job centre serving older people in future.

Policy Measures for Promoting the Employment of Older Persons

The Government has developed various policy measures for promoting employment among older workers. These include subsidies and grants for employers and older workers (MHLW, website; OECD, 2004: 118–19).

First, a measure exists to encourage employers to continue employing their older workers. 'The subsidy for promotion and establishment of continued employment' is provided to employers who increase *Teinen* age or implement a continued employment scheme to age 65 or over, and those who set up a new business in order to promote the employment of older persons in large numbers. It also subsidizes employers who carry out training of workers aged 55 or over in order to open up new career paths for them.

Second, encouragement is provided to employers to assist workers who are scheduled to be retrenched and needing to find alternative employment. 'The subsidy for assisting job-seeking activities of older workers' is provided to employers who grant paid holidays for job-search activities or vocational training to employees aged 45–64. It also subsidizes employers who succeed in finding new jobs for their redundant employees through employment agencies. The subsidy is also available for an employers' association of small and medium-sized firms that arranged measures supporting the re-employment of older workers.

Third, employers are also encouraged to hire older workers. 'The subsidy for employment development for specified job-seekers' is provided to employers who hired persons aged 60–4 through the public labour exchange or private job centres. It subsidizes one-quarter (one-third for small and medium-sized firms) of the wage of the worker for the first six months of employment. 'The subsidy for urgent employment development for middle-aged and older persons' is for employers who provide opportunities for trial employment to job-seekers aged 45–59 for a set period. The amount of subsidy per recruit is 100 000 yen per month for a maximum of three months.

Fourth is a measure to improve workplaces for older workers. 'The subsidy for improving employment environment for older workers' is provided to employers who increase numbers of employees aged 60–4 through workplace improvements. 'The subsidy for barrier-free workplaces for older employees' is provided to employers who make comprehensive efforts to introduce measures to move towards barrier-free workplaces. A low interest loan called 'The loan for improving work environment of older workers' is available for such arrangements through the Japan Public Policy Investment Bank for employers with five or more full-time workers aged 60 and over.

The amount of these subsidies depends on firm size and contents of the scheme. The Japan Organization for Employment of the Elderly and Persons with Disabilities (JEED) has engaged in various related services for the above-mentioned subsidies as well as other supportive arrangements like advisory and counselling services. JEED is an independent administrative institution established in 2003 with functions transferred from government, the Japan Association for Employment of Persons with Disabilities (JEAD, founded in 1971, renamed in 1986), and the Association of Employment Development for Senior Citizens (AEDSC, founded in 1978). The budget of JEED for older workers in 2006 was 56 billion yen. It is a considerable amount; however, no detailed information on policy evaluation is available.

A range of measures are targeted directly at older workers. 'The grant for continued employment of older persons' is aimed at workers aged 60–4 whose wages have decreased to a certain level. Prior to a revision in 2003, the maximum amount of the grant was 25 per cent of the new wage, which was paid after *Teinen* retirement, if the new wage was less than 85 per cent of pre-*Teinen* wage. Due to the high cost of the scheme, the above-mentioned figures were revised to 15 per cent and 75 per cent respectively in 2003, representing a considerable reduction in the value of the benefit. 'The in-work employee pension' may be considered as a kind of subsidy supplementing low wages from second career jobs. It is a partial employee pension benefit for workers who continue work from age 60 and over with wages less than a certain amount.

'The grant for a joint job creating scheme of older persons' exists to assist in the establishment of a small business consisting of three or more persons aged 45 and over, who jointly start a new business and create job opportunities for other older workers. This is a new approach.

The effects of these measures on labour force participation of older persons are arguable, though the Government insists that they have positive effects. A systematic evaluation is needed.

FIRMS' EMPLOYMENT POLICIES AND PRACTICES TOWARDS AGEING WORKERS

Sketch of the Current Situation

The 1990 Amendment of the Older Workers Law demonstrated the Government's priority for employment extension to age 65. The Japan Federation of Employers' Associations (*Nikkeiren*) strongly resisted this policy and published a report entitled 'Japanese style management in the new era' in 1995. This addressed the need to review the traditional lifetime employment model as well as the age-oriented pay and promotion system and move towards a flexible, diversified, and merit-oriented employment system. In this new strategy, the roles of older workers were not clearly defined. The report assumed that most *Teinen* retirees should be rejected from the core workforce and could be re-employed as temporary workers. It seemed to be reflective of the severe business environment caused by the burst of the bubble economy from 1992 as well as rapid globalization of the economy. *Teinen* retirement of baby boomers anticipated in the early 2000s might also be an important reason.

Figure 2.5 shows the progress of continued employment practice in firms with 30 or more employees. The number of firms which have introduced some kind of continued employment scheme to age 65 increased from 52 per cent to 67 per cent between 1992 and 2004. However progress towards a scheme for all applicants until age 65 has been stagnant, at around 20 per cent in the 1990s, which reflected the above-mentioned employer attitude. Recent progress, between 2000 and 2004, may be the result of the 2000 Amendment of the Older Workers Law as well as the increase in pensionable age, which commenced in 2001.

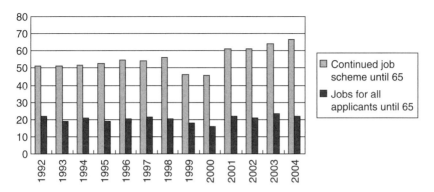

Source: MHLW, Employment Management Survey, each year.

Figure 2.5 Schemes for continued employment up to age 65

The Ministry of Health, Labour and Welfare conducted a survey on the progress of employment extension to 65 as of 1 January 2006 when the enforcement of the 2004 Amendment of Older Workers Law was approaching in April. The sample was taken from firms with 300 or more employees. According to the press release, 23.7 per cent had already introduced a continued employment system up to age 65 for all applicants. Another 74.2 per cent reported they were ready to implement proper measures in the near future. Therefore, a total of 97.9 per cent of firms had responded positively to the requirements of the law. Breaking down the responses, an overwhelming majority (93.6 per cent) operated some kind of reemployment scheme up to age 65, while *Teinen* extension to age 65 accounted for 5.9 per cent. Schemes for *Teinen* abolition formed only 0.5 per cent (MHLW, press release, 27 January 2006). In a further survey carried out by the Japan Business Federation (*Nippon Keidanren*), 11.9 per cent of responding firms stated that they had already satisfied the new requirements of the law, and 80.4 per cent replied that they would adopt or expand their continued employment system (JIL, 2006).

These studies indicate that firms' preparations for the legal enforcement of the 2004 Amendment of Older Workers Law had almost been completed by early 2006. However it must be noted that the Government's survey only sampled large and medium-sized firms. It is reported that 18 per cent of smaller firms with less than 300 employees were not ready for fulfilling the new legal requirements as of 1 June 2006 (MHLW, press release, 13 October 2006). Five years' grace until March 2011 will be insufficient for substantial progress to be made.

There are also many detailed questions to be considered: pay and working conditions, quality of work, and so forth. These will be answered through selected case studies and more expansive research. As a first step, two case studies are presented below. The first is a large local municipality (hereafter Y City), which will show a typical, and arguably obsolete, provision for coping with the 2004 Amendment of the Older Workers Law. The second is the case of Toyota Motor Corporation (hereafter Toyota), which may point the way to age-free employment.

Case of Y City

Y City has a typical organizational structure for a public sector organization. Though efforts have been made in recent years to introduce some elements of a merit-oriented pay and promotion system, it is still basically of the traditional age-oriented variety. This is shown clearly in the age-wage profile (Figure 2.6).

Most administrative personnel may be promoted to rank 4, which is the goal of the rank and file. If they pass examinations for higher positions, they may be able to climb the promotion ladder up to rank 10, which is the top rank for the chief of a bureau. *Teinen* age is 60, when an advantageous lump-sum payment is available.

Traditionally, the majority of senior officers were positioned for new well-paid jobs in related organizations prior to their *Teinen* retirement. This practice is known as *Amakudari* (golden parachutes). As for rank and file employees, 50 per cent of *Teinen* retirees took up new jobs elsewhere in the public or private sectors. For those to whom new, outside, jobs were not available, part-time jobs were offered in a department of Y City. However pay and working conditions were relatively poor.

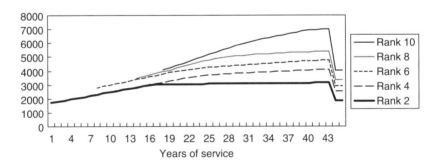

Source: Y City Personnel Division.

Figure 2.6   Age-wage profile of Y City (100 yen)

In 2001, Y City introduced a new measure known as 'reappointment scheme' for *Teinen* retirees. Its main purpose was to cope with the increase of full pension age, as well as a rapid increase in the number of *Teinen* retirees. A shortage of *Amakudari* positions because of the long recession since 1992, and criticism by taxpayers of 'privileged' public servants might also be important background factors.

The reappointment scheme is applied to those aged between 60 and the full pension age, which was 62 as of 2006, rising gradually to age 65.

Figure 2.7 shows the changing annual incomes of rank and file personnel. The annual salary of reappointed personnel working 31 hours a week (80 per cent of standard weekly hours) is 3.25 million yen, or 40 per cent of pre-*Teinen* salary. However adding the earnings-related benefit of the public servants' pension, the total income is 4.9 million yen, or 60 per cent of pre-*Teinen* salary. After retirement from this job, a full pension benefit of 2.8 million yen, or 35 per cent of the pre-*Teinen* salary is available.

From 2004–5, 60 per cent of *Teinen* retirees of Y City were offered the reappointment contract. The remaining 40 per cent included those who got jobs elsewhere in related organizations, those who chose full retirement, and those who received a poor job evaluation in the pre-*Teinen* years. It is notable that even a municipality was not ready to accept the request of central government for job security for all applicants among Teinen retirees up to age 65.

According to a personnel officer, treatment of former senior officers might become a serious issue in the near future. Formerly, attractive *Amakudari* jobs were easily available for all of them. However nowadays, increasing numbers cannot be found positions. The personnel section has commenced consideration of this issue.

The pay and working hours of the reappointment scheme are comparable to those in the private sector. However the quality of reappointment

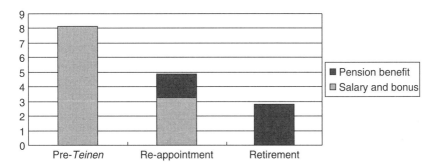

Source: Y City Personnel Division.

Figure 2.7 Income change after Teinen *at Y City* (million yen)

jobs seems poor. The personnel section pieces together jobs from various sections of Y City in order to offer them to reappointed workers.

Surveys of reappointed workers indicate that this practice tends to be a cause of disunity between them and pre-*Teinen* workers, the former viewed as outsiders by the latter. It is also reported that most reappointed workers are transferred to a different assignment in a different workplace, wasting skills and experience. Some complain that such a transfer is stressful, and the practice is being reviewed by the personnel management section.

The reappointment scheme may be effective in providing supplementary income, making up for the loss of benefit caused by the pension reform. However it seems that there is no substantial progress towards age-free employment. The *Teinen* rule and age-oriented personnel management system remain, acting as barriers to older workers' employment. Such behaviour is also observable in the private sector.

Case of Toyota

Toyota's personnel management policy towards older workers in the 1980s can be characterized as 'reject and retain'. Workers aged in their mid-50s were divested of their managerial positions and treated as 'half-retirees' until age 60 *Teinen*. Their pay level was lowered and their roles ambiguous. This was a legacy of the former *Teinen* retirement rule which was applied at age 55 (see Oka and Kimura, 2003).

Since the 1990s Toyota has engaged in successive reforms of its personnel management system. The background factor to these reforms has been the presence of a large cohort of employees recruited in the 1960s and early 1970s approaching age 50. A number of issues need to be tackled. The financial aspect of the problem can be seen in a heavy payroll burden due to the company's age-oriented pay system. An insolvency crisis for the company pension scheme and retirement lump-sum payment have also been projected. Another challenge for the personnel management strategy was that Toyota became unable to respond to employee expectations of promotion to management positions due to reducing numbers of such positions and an increasing staff age profile. Toyota has been concerned about loss of morale as a consequence of ambiguous job roles among older employees.

According to a personnel officer interviewed in 2003, Toyota has appreciated the long-term employment system for the stable industrial relations climate it provided, as well as further improvement of the lean production system. Toyota believes that its business model depends on high levels of skills and experience among its workforce, which might be accumulated through ongoing on-the-job training as well as off-the-job activities such as the so-called Quality Control Circles. Aiming at improving productivity while responding to the challenge of a potential payroll burden and declining morale among employees, Toyota introduced a new personnel strategy named 'the Challenge Programme' (1996) and 'the Professional Human Resource Development Programme' (1999). The latter is a career development scheme for younger employees in their first 10 to 15 years of service. It aims to equip staff with high level professional skills and a wide vision. It may be called a period for cultivating human resources, in which rich training opportunities and quasi-age-oriented pay and promotion are guaranteed for all employees.

After this process, successful employees are promoted to a higher level known as *Kikan-shoku* or Skeleton Position, who provide the management core of the organization. The Challenge Programme applies to such staff. In this scheme, features of age-oriented pay and promotion system disappear completely. Decision-making on promotion, pay level and other issues is based solely on a competency assessment.

There are two kinds of categories or assignments for those in the Skeleton Position: the 'Management Position' and the 'Expert Position'. The former refers to employees assigned to a management role, for example, head of a sales division. The latter refers to employees assigned to a staff role, for example, a researcher, consultant, or in another professional area.

The elements and weights of competency assessment are different between the two categories. With regard to the 'Management Position', the composition is capability for creative thinking on a new challenging agenda (20 per cent), ability to complete business objectives (30 per cent), skills in organization management (20 per cent), skills in utilizing human resources (20 per cent), and popularity among his/her colleagues and staff (10 per cent). Regarding the 'Expert Position', the share of knowledge and skills on his/her speciality (for example accountancy, market research, and so on) accounts for 50 per cent. Other elements of competency assessment are the same as that for the 'Management Position', but the weight of each element is reduced to 10 per cent on average. The result of this assessment is the sole basis for decisions on pay and promotion of individual senior managers (Katayama, 2005).

The message from this new personnel system is that the company aims to prevent a decline of morale among non-managers as well as declaring the end of the traditional age-oriented personnel management system for those in Skeleton Positions. As a logical consequence, Toyota abolished the resignation rule from management positions at age 57 in 1998, substantially removing age barriers for staff. This may be evaluated as a progress towards an age-free employment system.

Together with the 'Challenge Programme' Toyota introduced a new personnel system which offered middle managers with 15 or more years of service the opportunity to enrol in the so-called 'Challenge Career Programme'. This appears to be an advantageous early retirement scheme, with benefits including retraining, outplacement, and a generous lump-sum payment (Taylor *et al.*, 2002). According to a recent survey, an annual average of approximately 300 managers have enrolled in the scheme, and 30 of them have taken up the offer of second career jobs provided by the scheme.

With regard to employment extension to age 65, Toyota's efforts have continued over a considerable period of time. In 1991, it launched a re-employment scheme for *Teinen* retirees on an experimental basis. This aimed to respond to labour shortages in the booming bubble economy at that time as well as to offer opportunities for healthy and able *Teinen* retirees to work in manual jobs on annually reviewed contracts. However Toyota did not accept further *Teinen* extension, against the Government's expectation. The reason given by a personnel officer was that worker capability varies widely after age 60. In practice, the majority of applicants were re-employed in 1991. Pay was low, but approximately 60 per cent of income level at age 60 was guaranteed with the inclusion of the company pension and the public in-work pension.

In the mid-1990s the re-employment scheme was temporarily discontinued due to a drop off in labour demand in the wake of the severe Japanese recession. The 2000 Amendment of the Older Workers Law requested that firms endeavour to offer continuous employment up to age 65. Toyota restarted the re-employment scheme in 2001 when the full pension age rose to 61.

However Toyota did not accept the Government's request to continue employment for all applicants until age 65. The scheme was limited to manual workers under age 63. The selection process took account of recommendations by the applicant's former supervisors and colleagues as well as health status and the 'strong will to work with a cooperative spirit' of the applicant.

In 2002 there were about 1000 *Teinen* retirees. Approximately 300 of them applied for a reemployment job, and Toyota selected 100. These figures show that the re-employment scheme was not attractive to *Teinen* retirees, and it was difficult for those that did apply to find jobs. Reemployed workers could choose full-time or part-time employment. In the case of full-timers, they were paid approximately three million yen a year, or one-third of their wage at *Teinen* retirement. It was almost the same level as new college graduates. However total income, including in-work pension and company pension, was approximately 60 per cent of pre-*Teinen* pay. Most of Toyota's fringe benefits were available. The duties and workplace for re-employed workers were usually the same as that of pre-*Teinen* days.

Toyota's response to the 2004 Amendment of the Older Workers Law was initially tough. As the number of *Teinen* retirees between 2007 and 2009 was projected to be approximately 2000 each year, Toyota has been seriously concerned that re-employment of all these people might damage its competitiveness. As the 2004 Amendment Law allows firms to decide how they implement the re-employment scheme Toyota has continued negotiations with the trade union.

In March 2006, Toyota made a dramatic decision, to extend the re-employment scheme gradually up to age 65, and in principle to retain all applicants, including white-collar personnel (*Asahi Shin Bun*, 20 March 2006). It was the most positive response to the 2004 Amendment of Older Workers Law from a leading enterprise. It was also a friendly response to the request of the Toyota trade union. The company's excellent business performance since 2002 might have influenced its response. Since Toyota's esteem in the Japan Business Federation (*Nippon Keidanren*) is high, the new scheme may be a major step forward in achieving the Government's strategy.

Other Notable Case Examples

Arguably one of the worst cases can be seen in a re-employment scheme of a large power company. Employees who wish to continue to work beyond age 60 are obliged to retire from the mother firm at age 57. They are expected to abandon their right to job security until *Teinen* at 60, and are then allowed to apply for a new job which they will retain up to age 65 in a firm belonging to the mother firm group. The annual basic pay in the re-employment post is about one-third of that at age 57. Bonus pay is available, depending on merit and performance (*Yomiuri Shin Bun*, 15 March 2006). This scheme aims to decrease total payrolls between age 57 and 65 by cutting wage costs in the pre-*Teinen* years and distributing the remainder into the re-employment period. This scheme could be viewed as ageist, even if it may provide a modicum of job security over the longer-term.

There are only a few cases of *Teinen* extension to age 65. A heavy manufacturing company recently extended *Teinen* age from 60 to 63 in order to cope with labour shortages resulting from a large number of *Teinen* retirements projected to occur between 2007 and 2009. Although wages are halved after age 60, employment status is not that of a temporary worker but a regular worker, to whom all fringe benefits and job security are guaranteed. It is reported that approximately 80 per cent of *Teinen* retirees join the scheme. This case may provide a good example for proponents of the

Government's current strategy, though its rapid take-up elsewhere seems unlikely (*Asahi Shin Bun*, 13 March 2006).

With regard to the quality of reemployment jobs, a large gas company appears to have overcome this problem successfully. It has a long history of reemployment schemes since the1970s. Recently, about half of the *Teinen* retirees applied to join its current scheme and 90 per cent were reemployed. It is reported that ageing workers' roles are as mentors and trainers of younger employees. Apparently, they appreciate the opportunity to engage in meaningful activities (Ibid.).

CONCLUDING REMARKS

The year 2006 was the commencement of the semi-final stage of the Government's strategy towards employment security up to age 65. It should be concluded by 2013, when the basic benefit of the employee pension is scheduled to disappear for the 60–4 age group. At this time, the final stage will commence, to be concluded by 2025, when the earnings-related benefit of the employee pension will finally disappear for the 60–4 age group.

The current target is March 2011. By then all firms should have implemented some continuous employment scheme, in principle, for all *Teinen* retirees up to age 65. It will be a bitter trial for employers to cope with the mass *Teinen* retirement of the baby-boomers born from 1947–9. Equally, it seems that extending *Teinen* to age 65 will be no less difficult for some.

Employer attitudes are widely differentiated between negative and positive attitudes in terms of progress towards age-free employment. Generally speaking, employers would like to retain their power of selecting re-employed workers with close-to-illegal measures notwithstanding the legal requirements of the 2004 Amendment of Older Workers Law. It is crucial to introduce effective penalties aimed at preventing such negative behaviour. At the same time, trade unions should play their proper role, since the Older Workers Law permits exceptional cases if employers reach an agreement with trade unions.

The pay and working conditions of these schemes appears to be poor on the whole. In many cases, pay is halved, status reduced, while working hours and assignments are almost the same as they were pre-*Teinen* according to a recent report of an extra-governmental organization (JEED, 2005, website).

The quality of work of *Teinen* retirees also often appears poor. It seems likely that most post-*Teinen* schemes will not fulfil the needs of older workers, as their roles will be ambiguous and unimportant in many cases.

Arguably, a potential step forward towards age-free employment can be observed in the case of Toyota. Although at this time, no commitment to extend or abolish the *Teinen* rule has been made explicitly, the company has introduced a genuine merit-oriented personnel management system for senior employees, thereby removing the potential payroll burden caused by workforce ageing of employees which would have occurred under the previous age-oriented pay system. It may also remove age barriers from employment, at least from a theoretical point of view. Those with high job capability may be continuously employed regardless of their age.

At the same time Toyota highly values the so-called lifetime employment system, because of the opportunity it provides to create a team of highly skilled workers through long-sighted programmes of employee development, while maintaining stable industrial relations. Toyota could be characterized as a hybrid of the Japanese-style long-term employment system and the Western-style merit-oriented system. This may become the new Japanese personnel management system in the future. Although the age 60 *Teinen* rule has been maintained so far, it would be relatively easy for Toyota to raise it to 65, or even abolish it altogether, in the years of labour shortages projected in the future.

Constructing an active ageing society based on job security, regardless of age, may well be one of the major challenges facing Japan in the coming decades. Examples like Toyota could point the way ahead for Japanese industry.

REFERENCES

Asahi Shin Bun (2006), 2 February and 13 March.

Bass, S. and M. Oka (1995), 'An older worker employment model: Japan's Silver Human Resource Centres', *The Gerontologist*, **35** (5), 679–82.

Cabinet Office (*Naikaku-Fu*) (various), *Kokumin Seikatsu Kiso Chosa* (*Basic Survey on the National Life*), Tokyo: Gyousei.

Cabinet Office (various), *Korei Shakai Hakusho* (*White Paper on Ageing Society*), Tokyo: Gyousei.

Campbell, John C. (1992), *How Policies Change: The Japanese Government and the Aging Society*, Princeton, NJ and Oxford: Princeton University Press.

Hagiwara, M. (1988), *Teinensei no Rekishi* (*History of the Teinen System*), Tokyo: Nihon Rodo Kyokai.

Higuchi, Y. and the Ministry of Finance Policy Research Institute (eds) (2004), *Dankai Sedai no Teinen to Nihon Keizai* (*Retirement of the Baby-boomer Generation and the Japanese Economy*), Tokyo: Nihon-Hyoron-Sha.

Japan Federation of Employers Associations (*Nihon Keieisha Dantai Renmei: Nikkeiren*) (1995), *Shin Jidai no Nihon-teki Keiei* (*The Japanese Style Management in the New Era*), Tokyo: JFEA.

Japan Organization for the Elderly and Persons with Disability (JEED) (2005), *Korei Shakai Tokei Yoran* (*Statistical Abstract on the Aged society*), Tables 9-6 to 9-9.

Japan Institute for Labour Policy and Training (*JIL: Nihon Rodo Kenkyu Kikou*) (2001), 'Guidelines to abolish age limits in the revised employment measures law', *Japan Labour Bulletin*, **40** (11), 4–5, accessed at www.jil.go.jp/

Japan Institute for Labour Policy and Training (2005), 'The law concerning stabilization of employment of older persons: provisional translation by the specialist', accessed 12 April, 2007, at www.jil.go.jp/ english/laborinfo/library/documents/llj_law16.pdf.

Japan Institute for Labour Policy and Training (2006), 'Employers now obligated to employ workers up to age 65', *Japan Labor Flash*, **60**.

Katayama, O. (2005), *Toyota wa Ikanisite Saikyou no Shain wo Tsukuttaka* (*Toyota's Human Resources Development System*), Tokyo: Shodensha.

Kimura, Takeshi and Masato Oka (2001), 'Japan's current policy focus on the longer employment for older people', in V. Marshall, W. Heinz, H. Kruger and A. Verma (eds), *Restructuring Work and the Life Course*, Toronto, Buffalo, NY and London: University of Toronto Press, pp. 348–59.

Kimura, Takeshi, Ikuro Takagi, Masato Oka and Maki Omori (1994), 'Japan: Shukko, Teinen and re-employment', in Frieder Naschold and Bert de Vroom (eds), *Regulating Employment and Welfare; Company and National Policies of Labour Force Participation at the End of Worklife in Industrial Countries*, Berlin and New York: Walter de Gruyter, pp. 247–307.

Ministry of Health, Labour and Welfare (*MHLW: Kosei-Rodo-Sho*) (various), *Rodo Keizai Hakusho* (*White Paper on Labour Economics*), Tokyo: Nihon Rodo Kenkyu Kikou (JIL).

Ministry of Health, Labour and Welfare (various), *Kani Seimei Hyo* (*Abridged Life Table*), Tokyo: MHLW.

Ministry of Health, Labour and Welfare (various), *Koyo Kanri Chosa Kekka no Gaiyou* (*Summarized Report on the Employment Management Survey*), Tokyo: MHLW.

Ministry of Health, Labour and Welfare (2000), *Heisei 12 Nen Konenreisha Shugyo Jittai Chosa Hokoku* (*Survey Report on the Reality of Employment of Older Persons*, conducted in 2000), Tokyo: Zaimu-sho Insatsu-kyoku (*Ministry of Finance, Stationery Office*).

Ministry of Health, Labour and Welfare (2001), *Rodo Keizai Hakusho* (*White Paper on Labour Economics*), Tokyo: Japan Institute for Labour Policy and Training.

Ministry of Labour (1998), *Heisei 8 Nen Konenreisha Shugyo Jittai Chosa Hokoku* (*Survey Report on the Reality of Employment of Older Persons*, conducted in 1996), Tokyo: Okura-sho Insatsu-kyoku (*Ministry of Finance, Stationery Office*).

Miura, F. (ed.) (1995–2001), *Zusetsu Koreisha Hakusho* (*Illustrated White Paper on the Older Persons*), Tokyo: Zenkoku Shakai Fukusi Kyogikai (*National Council of Organizations for Social Welfare*).

National Institute of Population and Social Security Research (NIPSSR) (2002), *Nihon no Shorai Jinko Suikei 2001–2050* (*Population Projections for Japan, 2001–2050* based on 2000 Census), Tokyo: NIPSSR, accessed at www.ipss.go.jp/pp-newest/02.pdf.

National Institute of Population and Social Security Research (NIPSSR) (2006), *Nihon no Shorai Jinko Suikei* (*Population Projections for Japan* based on 2005 Census), NIPSSR, accessed at www.ipss.go.jp/ pp-newest/03.asp.

Oka, M., and T. Kimura (2003), 'Managing the ageing work force: the interplay between public policies and the firm's logic of action', *The Geneva Papers on Risk and Insurance*, **28** (4), 596–611.

Organisation for Economic Co-operation and Development (OECD) (various), *Employment Outlook*, Paris: OECD, accessed at www.oecd.org.

OECD (2004), *Ageing and Employment Policies, Japan*, Paris: OECD.

Shimizu, T. (1991), *Koreisha Koyo Taisaku no Tenkai* (*The Progress of the Employment Policies for Older Persons*), Tokyo: Rodo Horei Kyoukai.

Silver Human Resource Centre (SHRC) (Zenkoku Silver Jinzai Centre Kyokai) (2006), 'Statistical abstract', accessed at www.zsjc.or.jp/.

Statistics Bureau, Ministry of Internal Affairs and Communications (Somu-sho, Tokei-Kyoku, formerly Management and Coordination Agency, Statistics Bureau) (various), *Rodo-ryoku Chosa* (*Labour Force Survey*), Tokyo, accessed at www.stat.go.jp/data/roudou/3.htm.

Tuylor, P., S. Encel and M. Oka (2002), 'Older workers – trends and prospects', *The Geneva Papers on Risk and Insurance*, **27** (4), 512–33.

Yomiuri Shin Bun (2006), 15 March.

3. Work and retirement in Canada: policies and prospects

Julie McMullin, Martin Cooke and Terri Tomchick

INTRODUCTION

As in other Western countries, the demographic ageing of the Canadian population is a key issue in public policy debates and one that is generally thought to present a challenge that can be addressed through careful policy making (McMullin and Cooke, 2004; PRI, 2004). In an effort to do this, several arms of Canada's Federal Government have been actively engaged in research and outreach activities (for instance, roundtable and workshop sessions) in which academics and government officials are invited to comment on working papers. Through these initiatives, 'life-course flexibility' and 'active ageing' have emerged as concepts that could be utilized by policy makers to develop policies that would more effectively deal with the challenges of population ageing.

With specific regard to workforce ageing, policy discussions of 'life-course flexibility' and 'active ageing' have focused primarily on extending the length of time that Canadians spend engaged in paid employment (PRI, 2004). Yet, it is unclear whether the aim of adjusting policies to extend the working lives of Canadians has been realized and whether new policies would be able to effectively deal with issues of diversity. As such this chapter addresses three questions. First, in light of the national and international pronouncements of the importance of 'active ageing' and 'life course flexibility' (OECD, 2000; PRI, 2004), to what degree has Canada developed policies that effectively encourage labour force participation of older workers? Second, to what extent do such policies benefit older workers who have lost their jobs and who are finding it difficult to re-enter the labour market. And, third, do these policies recognize the variability among Canadians, in terms of their social and economic characteristics and preferences or ability to continue working?

These questions are particularly important because along with population ageing and the potential labour shortages that may result, Canada has faced countervailing pressures of international trade and globalization. Competition and trade with the United States are major economic forces in Canada, and have led to the relocation of Canadian employers to the US in order to take advantage of lower labour costs. The 1994 North American Free Trade Agreement (NAFTA) included Mexico, as well as Canada and the US, and led to numerous plant closures and lost jobs in Canada, particularly in manufacturing (CLC, 2004). This economic globalization may have had disproportionate effects on older workers in Canada (Cooke *et al.*, 2006), many of whom may have been made redundant, or have taken early retirement. Notably, Canada has also experienced job growth as jobs are relocated from the USA to Canada. The problem is that there is a skills mismatch at the micro level between the jobs gained and the jobs lost which often places individuals in precarious labour market situations.

Furthermore, Canada, in order to minimize work disincentives, offers a generally low level of employment security when compared with other Western countries. According to Esping-Andersen (1999), Canada, along with the United States and the United Kingdom, is classified as a 'liberal' welfare state in which there is relatively little employment protection and employers are free to dismiss employees with two weeks' notice. Although Canadians are unionized at a higher rate than the United States, mainly because of a relatively larger state sector, the rate of unionization declined during the 1980s and 1990s (Lipset and Meltz, 2004). Collective agreements in Canada are typically negotiated at the firm level, rather than industry or sector level. Finally, there is little direct involvement of governments or other organizations in labour negotiations in Canada, unlike some European countries where 'social partners' play a large role (de Vroom, 2004; Teipen and Kohli, 2004).

To examine whether Canada has developed policies that effectively encourage labour force participation among older workers and whether these policies take diversity into account, this chapter describes and critically evaluates some of the key measures taken in Canada to alter the labour market experiences of older workers. Before turning to the specifics of these policies, we provide a profile of older workers and review some of the particular concerns that have been raised in Canada over the potential effects of the ageing of the labour force. Next, we argue that the response to these concerns has been threefold and has involved invoking the 'life-course flexibility' and 'active ageing' concepts, revising public policies that are seen to push older workers out of the labour market, and developing policies that encourage continued employment of older workers. We conclude with a discussion of the paradox of the public policy framework in Canada which, on the one hand, aims to encourage labour force participation among highly skilled older workers while, on the other hand, is not effective in reintegrating older, displaced workers into the labour market.

PROFILE OF OLDER WORKERS

Labour Force Participation Rates

Since the 1970s Canada's labour force has grown because of both an influx of women into the labour market and the entrance of a large 'baby boom' cohort into paid employment. Assuming that age specific labour force participation or immigration rates do not dramatically change, this growth is soon expected to slow and then reverse. Estimates suggest that the current total labour force participation rate of 67 per cent will drop to as low as 57 per cent by 2025 (Statistics Canada, 2004). This is due, in large part, to the retirement of older workers in the baby boom cohort.

As Table 3.1 shows, between 1976 and 2001 the labour force participation rates of workers between the ages of 45 and 59 increased, while the

Table 3.1   Labour force participation rates by age and gender

Age	1976	1981	1991	2001
All				
45–9	72.3	76.5	83.6	85.4
50–4	67.6	71.0	76.1	79.6
55–9	60.5	59.7	61.0	62.7
60–4	44.8	43.4	35.6	37.0
65 and over	9.1	7.9	6.7	6.0
Men				
45–9	93.8	94.1	92.8	91.2
50–4	90.6	90.9	87.9	86.6
55–9	84.1	82.3	76.0	72.4
60–4	66.5	64.0	47.8	47.0
65 and over	15.2	12.9	11.1	9.4
Women				
45–9	50.8	58.6	74.3	79.7
50–4	45.5	51.0	64.2	72.5
55–9	38.3	38.8	46.0	53.2
60–4	24.7	25.0	24.1	27.4
65 and over	4.2	4.1	3.4	3.4

Source: The Labour Force Participation Survey Table 282-0002, Statistics Canada.

rates of workers over the age of 60 decreased. In 1976, 72.3 per cent of the Canadian population aged 45–9 participated in the workforce, but by 2001 the participation rate had climbed to 85.4 per cent. A similar increase occurred for those between the ages of 50 and 54, from 67.6 per cent in 1976 to 79.6 per cent in 2001. However during the same period, a much smaller increase in labour force participation is observed for those workers age 55–9 (from 60.5 per cent in 1976 to 62.7 per cent in 2001), while this trend is reversed for workers aged 60–4 and for those aged 65 and older. The labour force participation rate for 60- to 64-year-olds decreased from 44.8 per cent in 1976 to 37 per cent in 2001 and for those aged 65 and over it decreased from 9.1 per cent in 1976 to 6.0 per cent in 2001.

Trends in overall labour force participation rates mask very significant differences in the labour force participation rates of older men and women. The labour force participation of older men has declined dramatically since the mid-1970s. In 1976, 84.1 per cent of men between the ages of 55 and 59 participated in the labour force. However by 2001 their rate of participation had dropped to 72.4 per cent. Over the same time period, the labour force participation rate of men between the ages of 60 and 64 dropped even more from 66.5 per cent to 47 per cent and for those aged 65 and older the rate dropped from 15.2 per cent in 1976 to 9.4 per cent in 2001. A recent study of labour force inactivity among men over the age of 55 found that retirement, regardless of reason, was what mainly accounted for this decrease in labour force participation (Habtu, 2002).

Unlike men, the labour force participation rates of older women have increased. In 1976, 50.8 per cent of women aged 45–9 and 45.5 per cent of women aged 50–4 were in the labour force. By 2001 these percentages increased to 79.7 per cent and 72.5 per cent respectively. Similarly, in 1976 38.3 per cent of Canadian women aged 55–9 participated in the workforce but by 2001 their participation rate had climbed to 53.2 per cent. Interestingly, the participation rate of women between 60 and 64 years of age did not change that dramatically between 1976 and 2001 (24.7 per cent and 27.4 per cent respectively). Notably, although women's participation rates have increased compared with their male counterparts, older women are still considerably less likely than men to be employed (Statistics Canada, 2003).

Figure 3.1 presents the percentage of the population aged 55–64 in the labour force for Canada and all OECD countries combined. As Figure 3.1 shows, the decline in labour force participation among older men was steeper in Canada than it was in the OECD as a whole. As in other countries, the move towards earlier labour force withdrawal by Canadian men has been offset somewhat by the entrance of Canadian women into the labour force. The trend towards lower labour force participation and earlier

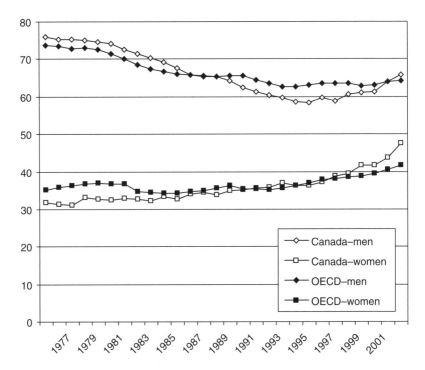

Source: OECD, Labour Force Surveys.

Figure 3.1   Percentage aged 55–64 in the labour force: Canada and OECD
countries, 1976–2001

retirement of older workers appears to have turned around in Canada in recent years, as it has in other countries (Quinn, 2003). However the reasons behind this change, and whether it marks real reversal of the long-term trend, remain unclear (Maltby, de Vroom, Mirabile and Øverbye, 2004: 3).

EARLY RETIREMENT

While Canada does not have a statutory retirement age, age 65 remains the most common age at which to retire (Kieran, 2001). The reason for this is twofold: Canada's retirement income system stipulates that individuals become eligible for full benefits at age 65, and corporate policies or collective agreements in Canada often mandate that workers must retire at age 65. Although age 65 is still the most common age at which Canadians retire the median retirement age declined from age 65 in 1976 to close to age 62 for men and age 61 for women in 2004 (Kieran, 2001; Statistics Canada, 2005a, b) and there is significant variability across occupations and industries (MacKenzie and Dryburgh, 2003). This trend towards early retirement had been led, in large part, by government downsizing in the public sector during the mid-1990s, which encouraged many older workers to take early retirement packages. This resulted in the overall early retirement rate (that is, the number of early retirees as a percentage of recent retirees) climbing to 46 per cent in 1997. However the trend towards early retirement appears to be turning around because by 2000 the early retirement rate had dropped to 40 per cent (Kieran, 2001). Indeed, there seems to be much ambivalence and uncertainty about retirement and early retirement in Canada (MacGregor, 2006). For instance, a recent General Social Survey suggests that one third of working age Canadians either do not plan to retire or do not know when they will retire planned to work beyond age 65 (Statistics Canada, 2003).

In discussing early retirement, it is important to note that many Canadians who are classified as 'retired' may be displaced or unemployed older workers who have given up looking for a job or who define themselves as retired because of the stigma attached with being labelled 'unemployed'. In fact, a recent Canadian study showed that only 51 per cent of men and 30 per cent of women defined their job exit as retirement by the age of 65 (Rowe and Nguyen, 2003). Others exited jobs to take on new positions and, as Rowe and Nguyen suggest, 'in many cases, the job separation that ultimately ended a career must have been a layoff, an illness or disability, or a family related event' (Rowe and Nguyen, 2003: 56). LeBlanc and McMullin (1997: 291) note that there may be a multitude of reasons for early exits from the labour force ranging from 'greater ideological acceptance of early retirement, company restructuring (such as downsizing) due to a poor economic climate, and the growing use of early retirement packages by employers'.

UNEMPLOYMENT

In 2003, the nationwide unemployment rate was 7.6 per cent and for Canadians aged 25 and older it was 6.4 per cent (see Table 3.2). As Table 3.2 shows, Canadian unemployment rates vary by age.

Unemployment among workers aged 25 to 34 was 7.3 per cent, while those between the ages of 35 and 44 experienced unemployment at the rate of 6.6 per cent. Interestingly, in comparison with all other age groups, Canadians between the ages of 45 and 54 experienced the lowest rate of

Table 3.2   Unemployment rates by age, 2003

	Unemployment rate
All	7.6
25 and over	6.4
25–34 years	7.3
35–44 years	6.6
45–54 years	5.7
55–64 years	6.3

Source: Labour Force Survey, CANSIM, Table 282-0002, Statistics Canada.

unemployment at 5.7 per cent while the self-reported unemployment rate for those between the ages of 55 and 64 increased slightly to 6.3 per cent.

Although rates of unemployment for older workers tend to be lower than average rates, a recent study of long-term unemployment shows that compared with younger workers older workers experience greater difficulty when it comes to reintegrating into the workforce. In 2003, older workers (defined in this study as those aged 45 and over) made up 35 per cent of the labour force and posted a 17 per cent incidence of long-term unemployment. This led one commentator to conclude that, compared with all other age groups, older workers 'consistently posted the highest incidence of long-term unemployment' (Dubé, 2004). The possible reasons for long-term older worker unemployment are many and include the fact that they 'experience greater labour market difficulties since they are concentrated in traditional industries, many of which experienced zero or negative growth; have held jobs requiring limited qualifications, low levels of education and training; and look for jobs that offer similar wages to those they used to receive' (Forum of Labour Market Ministers and HRDC, 2002).

CONCERNS ABOUT POPULATION AND LABOUR FORCE AGEING IN CANADA AND THE EMERGENCE OF 'ACTIVE AGEING'

Population and labour force ageing have been significant concerns in Canada since at least the early 1980s. The growing proportion of older people, relative to the working age population, is linked to projections of increased costs for health care and pensions, and a smaller tax base. However the Canadian Government has made changes to contribution rules for the public pension systems that will guarantee funding for the next few decades (Mérette, 2002). Despite the solvency of public pension plans, some organizations, such as the Canadian Taxpayers Federation have argued that the age of full eligibility for benefits should be raised to 69, in order to relieve pressure on pension plans (Turchansky, 2004; Milke, 2004). It is important to note that if these changes were adopted, it would make the full pensionable age in Canada older than even the USA, where it is gradually being raised to 67 (Cooke, 2003).

It is unclear how the ageing of the population will affect health service utilization and cost. Unlike the United States, Canada has a universal public health care system. There have been claims of a 'crisis' in the funding of Canadian health care since the 1980s, and these claims often refer to an increase in demands on the health care system due to an older population. However there is evidence that these concerns may also be overstated. For example, Carrière (2000) has found that previous projections of the health care costs related to the hospital-based care of the elderly have been high, and that although the ageing of the population is cited widely in debates about Canada's health care system, the effects of an ageing population have not yet been felt. There is also some concern expressed over the fact that there will be fewer children in the future to care for ageing parents, placing additional demands on children and on the state (Stone *et al.*, 1998). However these concerns may also be overblown. At least in Canada, the proportion of older people who do not have any children for support continues to be small, and most older Canadians continue to live independently, rather than with their offspring (Connidis, 2001: 35).

In addition to concerns about the expense of an older population, there are concerns that an older and smaller labour force may mean inefficiencies and slower economic growth (Robson, 2001). Within many industries and occupations the retirement of members of the baby boom cohort is linked to the fear that a large number of workers will leave the workforce within a short time span, resulting in a shortage of workers with job-specific skills (McMullin and Cooke, 2003). Employer and industry groups have identified skills shortages as an ongoing problem, and one which threatens Canada's economic growth (Canadian Labour and Business Centre, 2001). Suggested solutions to the problems of skills shortages include increasing immigration and the recognition of immigrant training credentials, as well as increasing the labour force participation of older workers (McMullin and Cooke, 2003).

The response to concerns over population and labour force ageing has been threefold. In the first place, Canadian policy makers and think tanks have increasingly invoked the terms 'life-course flexibility' and 'active ageing' in delineating their policy programmes and in stressing the need for social change. Second, policies that have served to push older workers out

of the labour market are being revised. Third, policies that encourage continued employment of older workers are being developed. The next section
considers each of these responses in turn.

THE 'ACTIVE AGEING' CONCEPT

In general, there is a strong Canadian policy focus on increasing labour
force participation among older workers which has been driven, at least
in part by the Policy Research Initiative (PRI). The PRI is a cross-
departmental federal government research organization that conducts
research in support of Canada's policy agenda. A key goal of the PRI is to
transfer knowledge to appropriate policymakers within the various federal
departments. Importantly, the PRI is a part of Canada's Privy Council
Office which serves the Prime Minister of Canada and acts as the Cabinet
Secretariat. Through its research programme entitled 'Population Aging
and Life-Course Flexibility' the PRI has been instrumental in bringing the
active ageing concept to the forefront of Canadian public policy agenda.
Indeed, this concept has been widely promoted by Peter Hicks, who was the
Senior Project Director with the PRI on the population ageing research
project between 2002 and 2004, and who, incidentally, spent the preceding
six years with the OECD (at the time the OECD was developing the active
ageing idea). Peter Hicks is now the assistant deputy minister in the policy
and strategic direction division of Social Development Canada, and interestingly, active ageing is a policy research theme that is taking on height-
ened significance within that department.

In one of PRI's publications, entitled 'Population aging and life-course
flexibility: the pivotal role of increased choice in the retirement decision'
(PRI, 2004), lengthening working life, mainly by postponing retirement, is
singled out as the policy direction with the most potential for reducing the
potential macroeconomic effects of population ageing. In particular, the
potential of slower economic growth is identified as the most serious public
policy challenge associated with population ageing (PRI, 2004: 5). This and
other similar PRI papers follow on the work of Hicks (2003) by suggesting
that it would be possible to extend working life by allowing more 'flexibility'
at earlier ages to take longer parental leave or to take training leave, to
pursue 'lifelong learning'. However the policy mechanisms through which
such initiatives would be realized remain unclear. Projecting average annual
hours worked, these papers show the potential for such changes to counter
the effects of an ageing workforce, under certain assumptions.

The PRI report also presents survey results showing large proportions
of recent retirees who would have liked to have remained at work under

different conditions. 'Flexibility' in retirement and providing older workers with better work options is a key part of their policy prescriptions, as well as better allocating non-work time throughout life. According to the PRI, lifelong learning would allow older workers to get better jobs, and would encourage return to the labour force after the loss of a job. Allowing more time for caring work in earlier stages of the life course would relieve pressure on public health systems (PRI, 2004).

However despite advocating 'flexibility' and 'choice' over the life course, the PRI paper ignores some key issues. For one, the report does not focus at all on the incomes of older workers themselves. In order for older workers to truly have 'flexibility' or a 'choice' about work or retirement, neither option should result in a serious risk of poverty or social exclusion. Furthermore, the paper ignores the structural barriers to continued work by older people, including ageism on the part of employers. For instance, they assume that providing training leave will result in the greater employability of older workers, and that employers' attitudes will change with labour market conditions (PRI, 2004: 18). At a more fundamental level, the PRI does not give serious consideration to the wide variety of life courses that people experience (Marshall and Mueller, 2002).

PUBLIC POLICIES THAT PUSH OLDER WORKERS OUT OF THE LABOUR MARKET

Mandatory Retirement

Despite the current rhetoric around active ageing and extensions of working life, there are several policies in Canada, including provisions for mandatory retirement that discourage the labour force participation of older workers. Mandatory retirement is not enforced by law in Canada. However corporate policies or collective agreements often dictate that workers must retire at age 65. Canadians have been debating whether to outlaw mandatory retirement since at least the early 1970s and over the years this issue has been brought in front of the Supreme Court of Canada several times, with contradictory rulings (Klassen and Gillin, 1999). One of the key issues in these court cases revolves around equity provisions in Provincial and Federal Human Rights Codes. As many of them stand, age 65 is the upper age limit for protection against age discrimination in employment (MacGregor, 2006). A second key issue has to do with the tension between individual human rights and societal benefit. The rulings in several of these court cases suggested that mandatory retirement was not discriminatory because it 'is functional for society as a whole because forcing older workers to retire creates job opportunities for younger workers' (Gillen and Klassen, 2000: 61).

In 1986, the Federal Government abolished mandatory retirement for federal public servants. However six years later, when the Federal Government attempted to abolish mandatory retirement for all other Canadians, the bill (Bill C-108) did not reach Second Reading in the House of Commons (Canadian Human Rights Act Review Panel, 2000). As a result, there are significant differences among the provinces in mandatory retirement. Four provinces, Alberta, New Brunswick, Nova Scotia and Prince Edward Island, have removed age 65 as the upper age limit for protection against age discrimination in employment but allow contracts to be negotiated with mandatory retirement provisions. British Columbia, Newfoundland and Saskatchewan allow mandatory retirement by stipulating an upper age limit of 65 in their human rights codes. Ontario has passed legislation that ended mandatory retirement as of December 2006, joining Quebec and Manitoba which had already done so (Ontario Ministry of Labour, 2005; Gunderson, 2004).

Canadians seem to be increasing their opposition to mandatory retirement. In a recent telephone poll conducted by Decima Research in 2003, 33 per cent of respondents voiced opposition to mandatory retirement compared with 20 per cent in 1996 (CBC News, 2004). Mandatory retirement has become a hotly debated issue in Canada's most populous province, Ontario. The round of debates that culminated in the banning of mandatory retirement began in April of 2003 when the Government of Ontario led by Premier Ernie Eves called for its abolition. In its 'Speech from the Throne' the Government promised to 'introduce legislation that would allow more seniors to remain active in the workforce – retiring at a time of their own choosing, not an arbitrary, government-appointed time' (Hewitt Research Advisory, 2003: 1). Bill 68, the Mandatory Retirement Elimination Act, was introduced shortly thereafter. The bill faced heavy opposition from the New Democratic Party which argued that eliminating mandatory retirement would weaken public support for pensions as well as violate contractual agreements. Employer groups, such as the Canadian Vehicle Manufacturers Association and the Toronto Board of Trade, also voiced their opposition. Ultimately, the Bill was not passed as an election was called and the Tories were defeated by the Liberals before it received a Second Reading (MacGregor, 2006). However on 29 January 2004, the newly elected Liberal Government announced that they would also seek to abolish mandatory retirement, with Premier Dalton McGuinty stating that 'the policy thrust is the correct one' (Benzie and Brennan, 2004). The legislation came into force on 12 December 2006 (CBC News, 2006).

Union representatives have also come out against abolishing mandatory retirement. Buzz Hargrove, the president of the National Automobile, Aerospace and Agricultural Implement Workers Union of Canada (CAW-Canada) Union argues that banning mandatory retirement 'gives corporations – and governments, by the way – who fund pension plans . . . an argument to put less money in because they say you can work longer and make an equal amount of money' (Benzie and Brennan, 2004). Invoking intergenerational equity debates, Hargrove also argued that 'the longer people work, the less opportunities there are for young people' (Benzie and Brennan, 2004)

In a report published by the C.D. Howe Institute in March 2004, entitled *Banning Mandatory Retirement: Throwing Out the Baby with the Bathwater*, Morley Gunderson (2004: 6) argues that 'mandatory retirement should not be regarded as blanket age discrimination, but as part of a mutually agreed company personnel policy or collective agreement, generally negotiated by individuals with reasonable individual or collective bargaining power'. Gunderson states that although the age cap should be removed from the human rights codes, exemptions for legitimate pension plans and collective agreements should be made. Ultimately, he purports that banning mandatory retirement entirely 'throws out the baby – mutually agreed private contracts – with the bathwater – age discrimination' (Gunderson, 2004: 7).

At the federal level, support for eliminating mandatory retirement policies has been voiced by several high profile politicians including the Canadian Prime Minister Paul Martin (Martin, 2004). Support for the idea that mandatory retirement amounts to age discrimination has also come from a report commissioned by the Department of Justice. The report, *Promoting Equality: A New Vision*, reviewed the Canadian Human Rights Act and addressed the issue of mandatory retirement. In the panel's view, mandatory retirement policies remove the choice of when to retire from the older worker and are thus, discriminatory. The report also acknowledges the negative impact that these policies may have on recent immigrants and women, noting that these workers may have insufficient funds for retirement due to a shorter period of employment (Canadian Human Rights Act Review Panel, 2000; Gillin and Klassen, 2000).

Public Pension System

Linked to issues of mandatory retirement are the rules and regulations of Canada's two-tiered public pension system. The first tier is the Old Age Security (OAS) and the second is the Canada Pension Plan (CPP). The Old Age Security (OAS) programme has been the foundation of Canada's retirement income system since 1952 (HRDC, 2004a). The OAS programme encompasses the basic OAS pension, the Guaranteed Income Supplement, and the Allowance.

To be eligible to receive an OAS pension individuals must have reached their 65th birthday, be a Canadian citizen or legal resident, and lived in Canada as an adult (over the age of 18) for a minimum of ten years. The OAS is not dependent on a person's employment history and is designed to provide Canadians aged 65 and over with a minimum income (Government of Canada, 2004). An individual's benefit rate is based on the personal income of the individual in the year prior to applying for the OAS. The maximum amount of annual income for which a person may claim full benefits is $57 879. In other words, if an individual's income exceeds $57 879[1] in the year prior to applying for the pension their OAS benefits would be reduced. An applicant is not eligible for the OAS if their annual income exceeded $94 530 in the year prior to their application (Government of Canada, 2004).

The Canada/Quebec Pension Plan (C/QPP) is the second tier of Canada's retirement income system. The C/QPP is a contributory, earnings-based pension plan which is funded by compulsory employee and employer contributions. It is paid to those individuals who have contributed to the plan and benefit rates are determined by how long and how much the contributor has paid into the plan. To begin collecting benefits an individual must be either 65 years of age, or between 60 and 64 and be either no longer working or earning less than the current monthly maximum C/QPP retirement pension payment[2] ($814.17 in 2004) (HRDC, 2002; HRDC2004b). The plan, which was introduced in 1966, was designed to replace 25 per cent of the earnings on which a person's contributions were based.

In keeping with the movement towards allowing for flexible retirement, the C/QPP allows for both early and late retirement. Under the plan, Canadians may retire between 60 and 70 years of age. This presents an opportunity for older displaced workers to begin collecting benefits between the ages of 60 and 64 (LeBlanc and McMullin, 1997). However it should be noted that individuals are penalized for drawing benefits before the age of 65 and rewarded for retiring later. Depending on the timing of retirement, benefits are permanently adjusted by 0.5 per cent for each month before or after their 65th birthday. For instance, when compared with a person who retires at age 65, a person retiring at age 60 will receive payments that are 30 per cent lower, whereas a person who retires at age 70 will receive pension payments that are 30 per cent higher (HRDC, 2002b).

On the surface, the C/QPP removes the incentive to retire early and encourages later retirement. Yet, individuals are often better off claiming pension benefits at age 60 with a 30 per cent reduction in their full benefit than waiting to claim their full benefit at age 65. This is because they are able to draw benefits for five additional years and the actuarial reduction under current CPP provisions is not large enough to be 'actuarially fair'. The CPP allows individuals to work on a full- or part-time basis after retirement benefits commence. However CPP pension regulations do not allow persons to claim benefits and contribute to the plan simultaneously. In 2004, only 8 per cent of Canadians aged 65 and older worked for pay (Statistics Canada, 2005a). If the system allowed people to continue contributing to the CPP, with corresponding increases in their benefits, more individuals might be drawn to partial retirement (SDC, 2004).

POLICY EFFORTS DIRECTED AT RETAINING OLDER WORKERS IN THE LABOUR MARKET

Phased Retirement

Phased retirement has been identified as an important means of increasing the labour force participation of older workers, but one that is not yet common in Canada (OECD, 2000: 91). According to Fourzly and Gervais (2002: 168), there are two different forms of 'phased retirement'. Gradual retirement entails a gradual reduction in hours or days of work, before retirement takes places. Deferred retirement refers to continuing part-time work by pensioners who wish to remain employed. Whereas gradual retirement was most often encouraged in the 1990s by Canadian companies seeking to downsize their workforces, more recently a few employers, most notably institutions of higher education, are implementing deferred retirement as a means of retaining older workers (Fourzly and Gervais, 2002). Canada does not have a formal programme to promote gradual or phased retirement, including the gradual reduction of working hours.

Provincial governments have also started adopting phased retirement programmes. Saskatchewan has adopted a programme to allow its civil servants to reduce their hours as they approach retirement age, while Nova Scotia has implemented a phased retirement programme for its teachers (Buckler, 2003). As of January 2004, the province of New Brunswick allows hospital nurses to take advantage of a phased retirement programme. That programme has been adopted to improve retention and recruitment of nurses and will be evaluated for its effectiveness within two years of implementation. Because the median age of retirement for nurses in Canada hovers at around age 56 (McMullin and Cooke, 2004), this programme allowed those eligible to apply for phased retirement at the age of 56 in

2004. In 2005, the age of eligibility dropped to 55. The programme allows nurses to reduce their hours to 50 or 60 per cent and to supplement their incomes by accessing their occupational pension (Buckler, 2003; Office of Human Resources, 2003). Nevertheless this programme may still be effective in lengthening the time that nurses remain engaged in the labour market, at least on a part-time basis.

One of the pitfalls of phased retirement programmes for employees is the possibility of having their occupational pension payments reduced. Pension plans often base their payments on the last five years that an employee works. Under this type of plan individuals electing to participate in a phased retirement programme will receive reduced pension payments. However it should be noted that, recognizing this pitfall, many Canadian companies have changed their pension plans to calculate pension payments based on the employee's five highest earning years (Buckler, 2003). A second problem with phased retirement is that Canadian tax laws do not allow an employee to be both a contributor and a beneficiary of a pension plan at the same time. In an attempt to offset this, some Canadian employers base their share of the employee's pension payment on their full-time salary, even if they work reduced hours (Buckler, 2003).

Training and Active Labour Market Policies

Until recently, older displaced workers in Canada have received very little support from the Canadian Government. In a report entitled *Older Worker Adjustment Programs: Lessons Learned*, Human Resources Development Canada acknowledged the lack of programmes for older workers (HRDC, 1999: 4). Furthermore, the report notes that this population tends to be underrepresented among clients of the major Canadian employment programmes (HRDC, 1999: 16–17). The Canadian Jobs Strategy (CJS) is an example of how the needs of displaced older workers are not being met by a major employment strategy of the Canadian Government. Not only were they not included as one of the many groups targeted under this training employment programme, displaced older workers were also underrepresented as participants (LeBlanc and McMullin, 1997).

The shift from a focus on compensation programmes to active labour market programmes is indicated by the termination of the Program for Older Worker Adjustment (POWA) in March of 1997. At the time, POWA was Canada's only programme for displaced older workers. A joint provincial and federal initiative, the POWA programme provided financial assistance to workers over age 55 who had been laid off, and who had worked the necessary number of years in specific industries (LeBlanc and McMullin, 1997). In June 1999 the Canadian Government announced $3 million in funding for the Older Workers Pilot Project Initiative (OWPPI). A joint initiative between federal and provincial/territorial governments, it funds active labour market projects targeted at workers between the ages of 55 and 64 who were displaced or who are threatened with displacement (Treasury Board of Canada Secretariat, 2003). The programmes that were implemented around the country were diverse and the industries to which they were applied included the construction industry, the non-profit and community service sector, and agriculture, as well as others. They encompassed a variety of measures that had been identified as ways to improve the employment situation of older workers. Many of the pilot projects incorporated employment subsidies with the purpose of encouraging employers to hire and retain older workers. Most of the projects provided some form of guidance and training for the older workers themselves. Additionally, many of the programmes included campaigns to increase awareness among employers of the need to retain older workers. Evaluations of these pilot projects are currently under way.

In Canada, active labour market policies tend to be targeted at younger workers or are age neutral (Leblanc and McMullin, 1997). The initiatives under the OWPPI are the only ones currently targeted towards older workers. Although older workers are also eligible for other programmes, as described above, they tend to be less well served by them. The OWPI initiatives are far from comprehensive, however, and do not provide a uniform set of services or programmes across the country. As a pilot programme, funding is limited and not guaranteed to be ongoing. In March 2003, the OWPPI initiative received a one year extension and benefited from an additional $15 million in funding (Treasury Board of Canada Secretariat, 2003). At that time, the OWPPI was officially scheduled to end in March 2004. However in May 2004 the Minister of the recently restructured Human Resources and Skills Development Canada (HRSDC) announced additional funding for 2004–5 for those provinces already participating in the OWPPI (HRSDC, 2004c). As well, Ontario, Alberta and British Columbia, provinces that represent a majority of the Canadian population, are not currently participating in the project. The result is that these programmes have thus far helped to reintegrate only a relatively small number of older workers into the labour market (Treasury Board of Canada Secretariat, 2004).

Despite their use in other countries, it should be noted that active labour market programmes that target older workers exclusively may have negative consequences. Programmes that give wage subsidies to firms hiring older workers may actually make age more salient in the workplace, and contribute to ageism (Taylor, 2002; McMullin, 2003). Furthermore, in the context of concerns over 'generational equity', programmes and policies that might be seen as unfairly benefiting older workers over younger ones may heighten a 'politics of age'. It should also be remembered that the definitions of 'older workers' that are applied in these programmes are often entirely arbitrary (Taylor, 2002), and do not recognize that the age at which workers are considered 'old' varies widely (McMullin and Cooke, 2003).

CONCLUSIONS

As in other countries, most of the Canadian policies that have been developed to deal with ageing labour forces have been aimed at increasing the labour force participation of older workers which is linked to the discourse on active ageing. For the most part, the current policy approaches in Canada have not been very effective in this regard. This is, in part, because there has not yet been a holistic approach taken to such policy development in Canada and, in part, because there are a number of barriers to the continued employment of older workers that need further consideration.

As shown above, the structure of the public pension system and provisions for mandatory retirement remain significant barriers to continued employment of older workers in Canada. There have not been the needed changes to Canada's pension system that would encourage both flexibility and income security in retirement. And, with mandatory retirement still in place in certain jurisdictions, flexibility in the age at which people may retire is further limited. The goal of all programmes should be to enhance the choices that are available to older workers, a point with which most, even those who are against abolishing mandatory retirement, would agree. Furthermore, Canadian policy approaches tend not to focus on the diversity of older workers' situations and experiences. Indeed, the few policy changes that have been made in Canada seem to have been driven much more by concerns about the economic consequences of population ageing than by concerns for the well-being of older Canadians themselves. The lack of attention to programmes that would increase the labour force integration of older workers, or actively promote phased or flexible retirement attests to the low priority given to providing older workers with real choices regarding retirement and work.

Unlike some European countries, there are no institutionalized pathways to early retirement in Canada that can be closed off in order to retain older workers in the labour force. And, employers are free to offer early retirement packages and to dismiss older workers during downturns. Clearly, there is room for Canada to enact policies and programmes that would discourage employers from looking to older workers as the way to deal with falling demand. To date, no such policies have been implemented that would do so. Furthermore, because labour market reintegration programmes do not serve the needs of older workers well, there is a paradox between the policy goal of keeping highly skilled older workers in the labour market and the reality of many older workers who need to work but for one reason or another cannot find suitable employment.

The PRI research programme on population ageing and life-course flexibility offers some promise towards significant and positive social change. Although this research programme has not yet reached the stage of solid policy recommendations, several aspects of its approach already seem to be identifiable in the existing Canadian policies. However it must be stressed that there is no indication that the policy changes that have been made in Canada have been the result of a coherent policy framework for addressing the challenges of population ageing. Rather, individual policies have been made by different departments, and different levels of government, with little evidence of coordination.

Nonetheless the PRI initiatives are well founded. We must be cautious, however, because the increasing privatization of income in retirement combined with little employment protection suggests that older Canadians may have less income and job security in the future. Policy makers must keep in mind that job dissatisfaction, lack of control at work, and too many job demands increases the likelihood of early retirement (Turcotte and Schellenberg, 2005). Thus, policies that would encourage employers to offer jobs that have more autonomy, good jobs, would go a long way towards increasing the length of time workers engage in paid employment.

NOTES

1. Based on 2004 information.
2. Through the CPP all workers who are unable to continue working because of a mental or physical ailment may collect a disability benefit. In order to qualify for benefits, an applicant must be under the age of 65, disabled, and not currently receiving a retirement pension. Eligibility also hinges on whether the person has made sufficient contributions to the plan. To be classified as disabled and therefore eligible for the plan, one must have 'a physical or mental disability which is both severe and prolonged' (HRSDC, 2004c). According to the plan, 'severe' is defined as any condition that prevents an individual from working regularly at any job, while 'prolonged' is defined as a condition that is long term or may result in death (Social Development Canada, 2005).

REFERENCES

Benzie, R. and R. Brennan (2004), 'Mandatory retirement's days are numbered', *The Toronto Star*, 30 January, p. A7.

Buckler, G. (2003), 'Easing into retirement', *Globeandmail.com*, 12 November, accessed 12 April, 2007 at www.globeandmail.com.

Canadian Human Rights Act Review Panel (2000), *Promoting Equality: A New Vision: The Report of the Canadian Human Rights Act Review Panel*, Ottawa.

Canadian Labour and Business Centre (CLBC), Canadian Labour and Business, and Industry Training and Apprenticeship Commission (2001), *Where Did All the Workers Go? The Challenges of the Aging Workforce*, Ottawa, Ontario: Canadian Labour and Business Centre Industry Training and Apprenticeship Commission.

Canadian Labour Congress (CLC) (2004), 'NAFTA-North American Free Trade Agreement: NAFTA-the social dimensions of North American economic integration', accessed at http://action.web.ca/home/clcpolicy

Carrière, Yves (2000), 'The impact of population aging and hospital days: will there be a problem?' in Ellen M. Gee and Gloria M. Gutman (eds), *The Overselling of Population Aging: Apocalyptic Demography, Intergenerational Challenges, and Social Policy*, Toronto, Ontario: Oxford University Press, pp. 26–44.

CBC News (2004), 'Opposition to mandatory retirement growing: poll', *CBC News Online*, accessed 1 March at www.cbc.ca/stories/print/2004/03/01/business/mandatoryretire_040301

CBC News (2006), 'In depth: retiring mandatory retirement', accessed 20 August, 2007 from www.cbc.ca/news/background/retirement/mandatory_retirement.html.

Connidis, Ingrid Arnet (2001), *Family Ties and Aging*, Thousand Oaks', CA: Sage.

Cooke, M. (2003), 'Population and labour force ageing in six countries', University of Western Ontario Workforce Aging in the New Economy Project working paper (#4), London, Ontario.

Cooke, M., W. Lehmann and J. McMullin (2006) 'Job disruptions of older workers in Canada in the 1990s', paper presented at the Canadian Association on Gerontology meetings, Montreal, October.

de Vroom, Bert (2004), 'The shift from early to late exit: changing institutional conditions and individual preferences: the case of the Netherlands' in Tony Maltby, Bert de Vroom, Maria Luisa Mirabile and Einar Øverbye (eds), *Ageing and the Transition to Retirement: A Comparative Analysis of European Welfare States*, Aldershot, UK: Ashgate, pp. 120–53.

Dubé, V. (2004), 'Sidelined in the labour market', *Perspectives on Labour and Income*, **5** (4), 5–11.

Esping-Andersen, G. (1999), *Social Foundations of Postindustrial Economies*, Oxford: Oxford University Press.

Forum of Labour Market Ministers and Human Resources Development Canada (2002), 'Older workers in the labour market – employment challenges, programs and policy implications', *Workplace Gazette*, **5** (3), 56–7.

Fourzly, M. and M. Gervais (2002), 'Collective agreements and older workers in Canada', Ottawa: Human Resources Development Canada Labour Program.

Gee, E.M. and Gloria M.Gutman (eds) (2000), *The Overselling of Population Aging: Apocalyptic Demography, Intergenerational Challenges, and Social Policy*, Toronto, Ontario: Oxford University Press.

Gillin, C.T. and Thomas R. Klassen (2000), 'Retire mandatory retirement', *Policy Options*, July–August, 59–62.

Gillin, C.T., David MacGregor and Thomas R. Klassen (eds) (2005), *Ageism, Mandatory Retirement, and Human Rights in Canada*, Toronto: Canadian Association of University Teachers and Lorimer Press.

Government of Canada (2004), 'Old age security. Seniors policies and programs database: a collaborative federal/provincial/territorial government initiative', accessed 1 April at www.sppd.gc.ca/sppd-bdppa/english/details.jsp?PROGRAM_ID=204.

Gunderson, Morley (2004), *Banning Mandatory Retirement: Throwing Out the Baby with the Bathwater*, Ottawa: C.D. Howe Institute.

Habtu, Roman (2002), 'Men 55 and older: work or retire?', *Perspectives on Labour and Income*, **3** (12), 27–34, accessed at www.statcan.ca/english/studies/75001/archive/2002/2002-12-03.pdf.

Hewitt Research Advisory (2003), 'Ontario proposes elimination of mandatory retirement', *Hewitt Research Advisory Canadian Research Group Newsletter*, accessed 1 April at www.hewitt.com.

Hicks, Peter (2003), 'New policy research on population aging and life-course flexibility', *Horizons*, **6** (2), 3–6.

Human Resources Development Canada (HRDC) (1999), *Older Worker Adjustment Programs: Lessons Learned – Final Report*, evaluation and data development strategic policy SP-AH093-12-99E, (December), Ottawa: HRDC.

HRDC (2002), *Canada Pension Plan: Retirement Pension*, Ottawa: HRDC.

HRDC (2004a), 'Overview: old age security and Canada Pension Plan', accessed 31 March at www.hrsdc.gc.ca/asp/gateway.asp?hr=/en/isp/pub/overview/oasprog.shtml&hs=ozs.

HRDC (2004b), 'Canada Pension Plan (CPP) – payment rates', accessed 18 April at www.hrsdc.gc.ca/en/isp/pub/factsheets/rates.shtml.

Human Resources and Skills Development Canada (2004c), 'Employment Insurance (EI) and regular benefits', accessed 22 April at www.hrsdc.gc.ca/asp/gateway.asp?hr=en/ei/types/regular.shtml&hs=tyt.

Kieran, Patrick (2001), 'Early retirement trends', *Perspectives on Labour and Income*, **13** (4), 7–13.

Klassen, Thomas R. and C.T. Gillin (1999), 'The heavy hand of the law: the Canadian supreme court and mandatory retirement', *Canadian Journal on Aging*, **18** (2), 259–76.

LeBlanc, L.S. and J.A. McMullin (1997), 'Falling through the cracks: addressing the needs of individuals between employment and retirement', *Canadian Public Policy*, **23** (3), 289–304.

Lipset, S.M. and N.M. Meltz (2004), *The Paradox of American Unionism: Why Americans Like Unions More Than Canadians do, but Join Much Less*, Ithaca, NY: ILR Press.

MacGregor, David (2006), 'Editorial: neglecting elders in the workplace: civil society organizations, ageism, and mandatory retirement, *Canadian Journal on Ageing*, **25** (3), 243–6.

MacKenzie, A. and H. Dryburgh (2003), 'The retirement wave', *Perspectives on Labour and Income*, **4** (2), 5–11.

Maltby, Tony, Bert de Vroom, Maria Luisa Mirabile and Einar Øverbye (eds) (2004), *Ageing and the Transition to Retirement: A Comparative Analysis of European Welfare States*, Aldershot, UK: Ashgate.

Marshall, Victor W. and Margaret M. Mueller (2002), 'Rethinking social policy for an aging workforce and society: insights from the life course', Canadian Policy Research Networks discussion paper no. W/18, Ottawa.

Martin, Sandra E. (2004), 'Mandatory retirement debate far from decided', *National Post*, accessed 1 April at www.canada.com/components/printstory/printstory4.aspx?id=824307ba-218b-,49e7-9.

McMullin, J.A. (2003), 'Workforce aging, older workers and ageism', paper presented at the symposium on New Issues in Retirement, Statistics Canada, Ottawa.

McMullin, J.A. and M. Cooke (2003), 'Workforce ageing: an examination of the age composition of occupations and industries in Canada', paper presented at the annual meetings of the European Sociological Association, Murcia, Spain, September.

McMullin, J.A. and M. Cooke with R. Downie (2004), *Labour Force Ageing and Skill Shortages in Canada and Ontario*, Canadian Policy Research Networks research report W/24, Ottawa.

Mérette, M. (2002), 'The bright side: a positive view on the economics of aging', *IRPP Choices*, **8** (1).

Milke, M. (2004), *Fair Pensions for Future Generations: Tripled Tax Rates & Prospects for Reform. A Taxpayer's Guide to the Canada Pension Plan*, Ottawa: Canadian Taxpayers Federation, accessed 17 August, 2005 at www.taxpayer.com/pdf/Fair_Pensions_For_Future_Generations_March_2004.pdf.

Organisation for Economic Co-operation and Development (OECD) (2000), *Reforms for an Ageing Society*, Paris: OECD.

OECD (2004), 'Labour force survey data', accessed at www1.oecd.org/scripts/cde/default.asp

Office of Human Resources (2003), 'Phased retirement option approved for hospital nurses', Fredericton, NB: Government of New Brunswick, accessed 14 April, 2004 at www.gnb.ca/cnb/news/ohr/2003e0521oh.htm.

Ontario Ministry of Labour (2005), *FAQ: mandatory retirement*, accessed 14 December at www. labour.gov.on.ca/english/news/2005/05-141faq.html.

Policy Research Initiative (2004), 'Population aging and life-course flexibility: the pivotal role of increased choice in the retirement decision', discussion paper.

Quinn, J. (2003, September), 'Main patterns in older workers' emerging responses to recent changes in their environments involving retirement', paper presented at the Statistics Canada Symposium on New Issues in Retirement, Ottawa.

Robson, W.B.P. (2001), *Aging Populations and the Workplace: Challenges for Employers* and *A BNAC Statement*, Winnipeg, Manitoba: The British-North American Committee, accessed 12 April, 2007 at www.cdhowe.org/pdf/BNAC_Aging_Populations.pdf.

Rowe, G. and H. Nguyen (2003), 'Older workers and the labour market', *Perspectives*, catalogue no. 75-001-XPE, (Spring), 55–8.

Social Development Canada (2004), 'Canada Pension Plan (CPP) retirement pension', accessed 29 March at www.sdc.gc.ca.

Social Development Canada (2005), 'Canada Pension Plan disability benefits', catalog no. ISPB 153-10-05E, accessed 16 August, 2007, from www1.servicecanada.gc.ca/en/isp/pub/cpp/disability/benefits/disability.pdf.

Statistics Canada (2003), 'Fact Sheet on Retirement', *Perspectives on Labour and Income*, **4** (9).

Statistics Canada (2004), 'The near-retirement rate', *Perspectives*, (February), 18–22.

Statistics Canada (2005a), 'Labour force participation rates by sex and age group', CANSIM 282-0002, accessed 21 December at www.statcan.ca.

Statistics Canada (2005b), 'Labour force survey estimates, retirement age by class of worker and sex', CANSIM II 282-0051, accessed 13 December at http://dc2.chass.utoronto.ca.

Stone, L.O., C.J. Rosenthal, I.A. Connidis (1998), 'Parent-child exchanges of supports and intergenerational equality', Statistics Canada, cat. no. 89-557-XPE, Ottawa: Ministry of Industry.

Taylor, Philip (2002), *New Policies for Older Workers*, Bristol: Policy Press.

Taylor, Philip (2004), 'A "new deal" for older workers in the United Kingdom?', in Tony Maltby, Bert de Vroom, Maria Luisa Mirabile and Einar Øverbye (eds), *Ageing and the Transition to Retirement: A Comparative Analysis of European Welfare States*, Aldershot, UK: Ashgate, pp. 186–204.

Teipen, Christine and Martin Kohli (2004), 'Early retirement in Germany', in Tony Maltby, Bert de Vroom, Maria Luisa Mirabile and Einar Øverbye (eds), *Ageing and the Transition to Retirement: A Comparative Analysis of European Welfare States*, Aldershot, UK: Ashgate, pp. 93–119.

Treasury Board of Canada Secretariat (2003), 'Older Workers Pilot Projects Initiative (OWPPI)', accessed 15 April, 2004 at www.tbs-sct.gc.ca/rma/eppi-ibdrp/hrdb-rhbd/h005_e.asp.

Treasury Board of Canada Secretariat (2004), 'Older Workers Pilot Projects Initiative (OWPPI)', accessed 15 April at www.tbs-sct.gc.ca/rma/eppi-ibdrp/hrdb-rhbd/owppi-ippta/2002-2003_e.asp.

Turchansky, Ray (2004), 'Raising the CPP eligibility age won't fly', *Canada.com News*, accessed 11 March, at www.canada.com.

Turcotte, Martin and Grant Schellenberg (2005), 'Job strain and retirement', *Perspectives*, Statistics Canada, cat. no. 75-001-XIE, Ottawa: Statistics Canada.

Underhill, S.C., V.W. Marshall, and S. Deliencourt (1997), 'Options 45, HRDC survey final report, executive summary', *One Voice*, Ottawa.

4. Sing if you're glad to be grey. Working towards a happier older age in the United Kingdom

Philip Taylor

> I'm coming up to that age but it's funny, as you get older you become more and more interested in the future. You live for your family and future generations.
>
> **Margaret Thatcher***

INTRODUCTION

Students of the field of age and work would, of course, reflect on the irony of the above quote from Margaret Thatcher, who led a Conservative administration at a time when public policy was overtly aimed at excluding older workers from the labour market, their future, at least concerning paid work, apparently viewed as less important than that of the generations that followed. There is, in fact, a longer history of consideration of the issue of the employment of older workers in the United Kingdom, going back at least as far as the 1950s when post-war labour shortages encouraged debate about increasing their participation. In the present, the national debate concerns the so-called pension crisis brought about by an ageing population and a lack of investment in retirement income systems. Add to the mix strong economic growth over the last decade with concerns about labour shortages, and what was a discussion about the disadvantages facing older workers in the 1980s and 1990s has been transformed into one about how to extend working lives. Observing the changing fortunes of older workers in recent times, it is easy to be somewhat sceptical that a lasting change is under way, yet it does appear that their status is improving, underpinned by public policy reforms and buttressed by economic growth.

This chapter considers the changing status of older workers in the labour market over the last two decades. This is important because understanding

---

* Comment concerning retirement made as she opened a new housing development for older people in 1988. Accessed at www.margaretthatcher.org/speeches/displaydocument.asp? docid-107205.

something of the history of older workers' employment may provide pointers to their likely future status.

OLDER WORKERS: LABOUR MARKET INDICATORS

It has been recognized in British policy circles for some time that population ageing will have a profound effect on the composition of the labour market. From the end of the 1980s the share of younger people in the labour force began to decline. At the same time, 'prime-age' adults began to make up an increasing share of the working age population. Between 1990 and 2000, the average age of the working age population increased by 1.3 years from 37.5 to 39.0 (Dixon, 2003). Population and labour force projections show a further ageing of the labour force. The average age of the working age population is projected to increase by around 0.7 years in the decade to 2010, and 0.5 years in the following decade according to Government Actuary's Department population projections from 2002. By 2010, the proportion of working age people between 50 and 64 years old will be greater than at any time since the mid-1970s. It was predicted that from 2005 the proportion of prime-age adults (30–49) would begin to decline. By contrast, the proportion that are older adults (50–64) is predicted to increase from 27 per cent in 2000 to 32 per cent by 2020 (Dixon, 2003). Thus, roughly one-third of the labour force will be aged 50 or over by the year 2020.

The trend towards a reduction in the length of working life which is observed elsewhere has also taken place in the UK. It should be noted however, that while employment rates have fallen over the last two decades, by comparison with a number of other Member States, these have remained relatively strong in the UK. It is also important to note a reversal of the trend towards early exit from the labour market. Employment rates among older workers have been increasing for some time, with levels not seen since the early 1980s (see also National Statistics website, 2005). As a consequence, the gap in employment rates between younger and older workers is also closing to levels comparable with the 1980s. Also notable is that in recent years the employment rate for the over 50s has increased somewhat faster than the overall employment rate (Table 4.1). This leaves the UK having achieved the Stockholm target for employment rates among older workers for some time. This even applies to men aged 60–4 (53.9 per cent), but not women (31.9 per cent). A remarkable fifth (19.4 per cent) of men aged 65–9 are in some kind of paid work, though rather fewer women (10.6 per cent).

*Table 4.1   Employment rates among 50- to 69-year-olds and overall rates
              (Spring) (per cent)*

Year	50–69	16-State Pension Age	Difference
1999	50.1	73.7	23.6
2000	50.7	74.4	23.6
2001	51.9	74.5	22.7
2002	52.3	74.3	22.1
2003	53.7	74.6	20.9
2004	54.1	74.7	20.6
2005	54.7	74.6	19.9
2006	55.2	74.4	19.2

Source: Labour Force Survey, Great Britain.

Left out of official statements is an explanation for this apparent change in older workers' relationship with the labour market. Hotopp (2005) shows that while the employment rate for workers aged 50 and over has been increasing since 1993, this effect has been stronger for women, reflecting changes in society. She also associates the upward trend with improved economic prosperity and a strong labour market. Her analysis indicates that it may also, to an extent, be driven by increasing participation among ethnic minorities in this age group, being interpreted as a cohort effect.

It is also clear that older workers are a group with complex and interrelated labour market disadvantages. By far the most important issue when considering the position of older workers (and men somewhat more than women) is that of disability, or perhaps more accurately, the claiming of disability benefits, as this seems to be associated with the existence of employment opportunities. According to the Department for Work and Pensions (2006), 1.17 million individuals aged between 50 and state pension age were claiming Incapacity Benefit, the main benefit for those with disabilities, although it should be noted that those classified as economically inactive due to illness, sickness or disability has declined somewhat since 1999. By comparison, only 157 000 were claiming benefits related to unemployment. This is a remarkable figure on its own, but added to this, a substantial proportion of those older people on IB are long-term claimants. As Table 4.2 shows, in 2003 over 660 000 people aged over 50 had been claiming Incapacity Benefit for more than five years alone. Overall, over one million people aged 50 or over had been claiming IB for one year or more in 2003, suggesting that most would have a less than tenuous relationship with the labour market. However the Government has pointed to the

Table 4.2   Number of claimants of Incapacity Benefit in February 2003, by age, sex and duration of benefit (thousands)

	All	Up to 1 month	Over 1 month up to 3 months	Over 3 months up to 6 months	Over 6 months up to 1 year
All Ages	2387.9	41.8	89.0	125.1	179.9
Under 20	41.7	2.7	5.3	8.6	7.8
20–4	107.0	4.2	9.6	13.0	16.1
25–9	119.8	3.9	7.9	11.8	14.8
30–4	179.1	4.5	9.2	13.4	18.6
35–9	226.7	4.4	9.2	13.6	21.0
40–4	255.8	4.8	9.9	13.2	20.3
45–9	287.5	4.4	9.5	–	19.6
50–4	369.1	5.5	10.7	–	22.2
55–9	487.6	4.7	12.3	–	26.5
60–4	313.6	2.7	5.4	7.8	13.1
65 and over	–	–	–	–	–
Men					12.4
					14.0
All Ages	1467.3	25.9	55.1	74.7	17.4
Under 20	21.2	1.3	2.4	3.7	3.6
20–4	59.1	2.5	5.9	7.3	8.9
25–9	71.5	2.6	5.0	7.6	9.0
30–4	106.4	2.7	6.0	8.6	11.7
35–9	133.2	2.9	5.5	8.5	12.3
40–4	143.7	2.8	5.8	7.1	11.2
45–9	153.4	2.5	5.3	6.5	10.3
50–4	192.8	3.0	6.3	7.3	11.5
55–9	272.7	2.8	7.5	10.5	15.6
60–4	313.3	2.7	5.4	7.7	13.0
65 and over	–	–	–	–	–
Women					
All Ages	920.6	15.9	33.9	50.4	72.8
Under 20	20.5	1.4	2.9	4.9	4.2
20–4	47.8	1.7	3.7	5.7	7.2
25–9	48.3	1.4	2.9	4.2	5.7
30–4	72.7	1.7	3.2	4.7	6.9
35–9	93.5	1.4	3.7	5.1	8.7
40–4	112.2	2.0	4.1	6.0	9.1
45–9	134.1	1.9	4.2	5.9	9.3
50–4	176.4	2.5	4.4	6.7	10.7
55–9	214.9	1.8	4.8	6.9	10.9
60–4	0.3*	–	–	0.1	0.1
65 and over	–	–	–	–	–

Ageing labour forces

Table 4.2   (continued)

	Over 1 year up to 2 years	Over 2 years up to 3 years	Over 3 years up to 4 Years	Over 4 years up to 5 years	Over 5 years
All Persons					
All Ages	275.1	228.7	195.0	168.4	1,085.0
Under 20	8.3	5.6	3.4	–	–
20–4	25.4	12.9	8.9	9.1	7.7
25–9	21.0	15.7	11.9	9.4	23.5
30–4	26.3	21.4	16.0	13.2	56.5
35–9	29.6	23.6	20.8	17.1	87.5
40–4	31.1	25.9	21.4	18.0	111.3
45–9	31.1	28.2	23.2	21.9	137.2
50–4	35.9	32.9	29.4	26.6	192.0
55–9	42.6	39.2	37.9	31.9	275.2
60–4	23.7	23.4	22.1	21.3	194.2
65 and over	–	–	–	–	–
Men					
All Ages	163.6	137.8	117.1	97.1	688.9
Under 20	4.7	3.2	2.3	–	–
20–4	13.7	7.4	4.8	4.5	4.1
25–9	12.6	10.0	6.8	4.8	13.2
30–4	16.4	12.6	9.4	7.1	31.8
35–9	16.9	14.7	12.2	9.6	50.6
40–4	16.9	14.1	11.8	10.0	64.0
45–9	16.5	14.3	11.4	10.6	76.0
50–4	18.4	16.4	15.6	12.6	101.7
55–9	23.8	21.8	20.7	16.6	153.4
60–4	23.6	23.4	22.1	21.3	194.2
65 and over	–	–	–	–	–
Women					
All Ages	111.5	90.9	77.8	71.3	396.1
Under 20	3.6	2.4	1.1	–	–
20–4	11.7	5.5	4.1	4.6	3.6
25–9	8.4	5.7	5.1	4.6	10.3
30–4	9.9	8.8	6.6	6.2	24.7
35–9	12.8	8.9	8.5	7.5	36.9
40–4	14.1	11.9	9.6	8.1	47.2
45–9	14.6	13.9	11.8	11.2	61.2
50–4	17.5	16.5	13.8	14.0	90.3
55–9	18.8	17.4	17.2	15.2	121.8
60–4	–	–	–	–	–
65 and over	–	–	–	–	–

Source: http://www.statistics.gov.uk/StatBase/ssdataset.asp?vlnk=3993&Pos=2&ColRank=1&Rank=272.

significant proportion of Incapacity Benefit claimants aged over 50 who express an interest in re-entering the labour force (28.9 per cent of men and 24.1 per cent of women in 2006).

Also notable is evidence that older people have fewer qualifications than their younger counterparts: 20.9 per cent of those aged 50 to state pension age have no formal qualifications, compared with 13.4 per cent of those aged between 16 and state pension age. There are also important gender differences. Among those aged over 50 to state pension age, women are more likely to have no qualifications; 13.5 per cent of men versus 17.1 per cent of women, but the picture is reversed for those aged under 50. Older employees are also less likely to have received work training in the last three months. In 2006, approximately a quarter (25 per cent) of those aged between 50 and state pension age compared with almost a third (31.4 per cent) of those aged 24–49 had received training. The incidence of training falls off dramatically after state pension age (DWP, 2006).

A recent Chartered Institute of Personnel and Development survey: *Who Trains at Work* (2005) found a significant gap between the training 'haves' and the 'have-nots' with older workers less likely to be trained by their employers. Analysis of the UK Labour Force Survey indicates that the key factor constraining older workers' training activities is a lack of opportunities provided by employers rather than disinterest among older workers (Taylor and Urwin, 2001; see also Trinder, 1992).

While unemployment rates among older people are lower than those for younger workers, once they lose a job, this is much more likely to become a long-term situation. In 2006, almost one-third (32.8 per cent) of the unemployed aged 50 to state pension age had been unemployed for a year or more, compared with a quarter (24.3 per cent) of so-called 'prime-age' workers (age 25–49). Men aged 50–4 were at particular risk, with 44.2 per cent classified long-term unemployed. This disadvantage is highly gendered. Almost two-fifths (39.7 per cent) of men aged between 50 and state pension age were long-term unemployed, compared to a fifth of women (20.2 per cent) in 2006 (DWP, 2006).

Additionally, the disadvantage facing older workers is differently manifested by geographical region, with employment rates in 2006 among those aged between 50 and state pension age varying from 76.2 per cent in the South East Region to 62.9 per cent in the North East Region, and the percentage of those categorized as inactive due to sickness, disability or injury varying from approximately 60 per cent in the North East and Wales, to around 33 per cent in the Eastern region and the South East. Actual claimants of disability-related benefits vary similarly. The percentage of claimants of Invalidity Benefit or Severe Disablement Allowance, at 8.2 in the South East and 9.1 per cent in the Eastern region, is less than half that of the North East and Wales (20.7 per cent and 21.5 per cent respectively) (DWP, 2006).

EMPLOYER BEHAVIOUR

Numerous employer surveys over many years point to widespread age discrimination in the British labour market. While these have collected much useful data, they have adopted different methodologies and have been carried out at different points in the economic cycle, making an assessment of trends in attitudes and practices impossible. A recent major study was carried out by Metcalf and Meadows (2006) among a representative sample of employers with at least five members of staff. Respondents were the most senior person with an overview of HR issues. The survey considered policies and practices concerning age and those which might be age-related. It was found that age was recognized as an issue in many organizations but that discriminatory practices were widespread. For instance, while 72 per cent of establishments had a policy concerning equal opportunities, only 56 per cent had one which mentioned age. Monitoring of workforces with respect to age was occurring in 49 per cent of cases, but only 5 per cent had acted as a result. Regarding recruitment, 49 per cent of establishments had a maximum recruitment age. Eight per cent of establishments stated that certain ages counted against applicants. In the case of older workers, age 60 was an important threshold. Notable was the finding that only 1 per cent of establishments had age as a criterion for training. This is in stark contrast to the findings on training presented earlier. Turning to employer attitudes, one-fifth (21 per cent) of respondents believed that certain jobs were more suitable for some age groups than others.

Recently, extensive case study research was carried out among mostly large British employers as part of a wider European study examining practices concerning older workers and on managing age more generally (Naegele and Walker, 2006; Taylor, 2006). The primary drivers of policy in these organizations were a desire to retain the expertise and experience of older employers or the need to recruit staff to meet labour shortages. Occasionally, 'positive' aspects were referred to, for instance, improving the atmosphere in work groups. Public policy and the actions of professional bodies has also played a role, for example, in terms of requirements for parts of the National Health Service to implement programmes concerning lifelong learning and career development.

Among the case organizations, Denso Manufacturing, a vehicle parts manufacturer, has taken a comprehensive approach. It has raised the level of support available to tackle occupational health issues, particularly those affecting older employees. It has redesigned the working environment to reduce physical stresses and strains. The result has been reduced sickness absence and injury and improved productivity. Denso has taken steps to show that it values older employees' expertise and experience. There is also a programme for older staff lacking numeracy and literacy skills.

First Group, a transport company, has a programme that is relatively new. This has several aims: to allow drivers to extend their working lives beyond age 65, to give flexible working opportunities to those aged 60 to 70; and to raise awareness of financial and physical health issues among its employees.

Newham Health Authority, a trust in the National Health Service, has implemented three initiatives concerning recruitment, health and well-being, and awareness raising. It has run an initiative with a recruitment agency, which has helped to orientate older candidates returning to work. The trust has also been examining the value of having doctors and therapists 'on the spot' so that employees can access them whenever they have health or well-being problems. Finally, regarding awareness raising, recent national initiatives have been influential in changing HR practices and policies within the NHS, but the trust believes that more information about these should be disseminated to its workforce and has developed its own communication strategy.

Among the cases, the most positive results have been in the area of health and well-being. There has been an increased emphasis on both voluntary and organization-instigated actions in relation to health. The effect has been to prolong the working lives of some employees in their 50s and early 60s, particularly through occupational health support. However overall, among the case studies there was a lack of quantifiable evidence in the public domain on the numbers taking part and on outcomes.

An exception is a particularly interesting example of policy design in the form of British Telecom's programme on flexible working and retirement. Unfortunately, take-up has been rather less than BT would have liked. The five options were:

- Wind Down: working part-time or job sharing;
- Step Down: reducing work commitments by taking a position with a lower level of responsibility;
- Time Out: taking full- or part-time sabbaticals;
- Helping Hands: participating in volunteering or community work; and
- Ease Down: gradually reducing working hours and/or responsibilities, particularly in the last 12 months prior to retiring.

There was also little evidence, overall, that age positive initiatives were impacting on those aged over 60. BT had only recent abandoned its normal retirement age of 60 and so it was too early to assess the impact of that measure. Several organizations were concerned about the loss of corporate knowledge resulting from the departure of older staff but specific measures were taking time to be devised and implemented.

A difficulty with most studies that have considered employer behaviour and attitudes is that of who was surveyed. Such studies provide few insights because it is generally HR managers who participate. While they may accurately report on policy the actual behaviour of their management colleagues may be quite different. Thus, a proper understanding of the nature of age discrimination in the labour market is still lacking. Despite this basic deficiency, public policy has endeavoured to engage employers around the issue of age and work. It is to public policy that this chapter now turns.

PUBLIC POLICY

Present day attitudes stand in stark contrast to those of the 1980s and early 1990s. Current discussions about working until age 68 and beyond would have been unthinkable then, when an alliance of policy makers, trade unions, and employers focused their efforts on securing the future of young labour market entrants, older workers fairing poorly during the harsh recessions of this period. Voices speaking up for the right of older people to work were rare. Nevertheless, there was not quite the same deliberate engineering of early retirement that took place in other European countries at this time. So, to quote Margaret Thatcher again, in a letter to a fellow Member of Parliament in 1980, responding to a particular comment regarding the value of early retirement in combating unemployment: 'I cannot accept that it is right that any adult should be disqualified from taking work which may be available because of their age, sex or marital status' (www.margaretthatcher.org/speeches/displaydocument. asp?docid= 104465), although the same letter refers to the continued availability of the Job Release Scheme, which had originally been introduced by the previous Labour administration as a temporary, limited measure, to alleviate youth unemployment by providing allowances for older workers if they gave up their jobs to younger ones (Taylor and Walker, 1996).

A lowering of the state pension age was specifically ruled out in a reply to a Labour Member of Parliament's question concerning why the male state pension age could not be reduced to 60 in order to create work for the unemployed in a Parliamentary debate in 1981. To quote the then Prime Minister once again:

> We already have a limited job release scheme for those who retire early – I think at the age of 64. Their places are taken by young persons on the register. It would be financially difficult to reduce the pension age to 60. There are already about 9 million pensioners. The national insurance scheme is financed on a pay-as-you-go basis, namely, that contributions put in this year are paid out in pensions and benefits this year. The main reason is the enormously increased pension that would be paid out as many more people took advantage of much earlier retirement. That cost would have to be met by much larger contributions, both from employees and employers. The sums involved would be very large. (www.margaretthatcher.org/speeches/displaydocument.asp?docid=104561)

What is apparent in these quotes is that there was a less interventionist approach on the part of the government at that time concerning early retirement options than was the case in other European economies. However despite rhetoric concerning the right to work, regardless of age, the Job Release Scheme, perhaps unwittingly, legitimized the position that older labour was expendable and indeed, that younger labour was preferable.

This is clear from a further statement in Parliament by Margaret Thatcher, also in 1981. After describing a range of measures aimed at helping younger workers to gain skills and jobs she turns to assistance for the older unemployed. The contrast is stark:

> Fifthly, I turn to the job release scheme. Exceptionally large numbers of people will be reaching normal retirement age in the mid-1980s. By bringing forward that peak of retirement we can release jobs so that they may be taken by people who are at present unemployed. Our fifth proposal, therefore, is to lower the age for the job release scheme until March 1984 from 64 to 63 this November and to 62 from February next year – [interruption.] This will cost about £150 million in a full year. Sixthly, as my right hon. Friend [Patrick Jenkin] the Secretary of State for Social Services announced last week, those aged 60 and over who are unemployed and have been drawing supplementary benefit for a year or more will from November be able to retire on the higher long-term rate of supplementary benefit. This will cost about £20 million in a full year. (www.margaretthatcher.org/speeches/displaydocument.asp?docid=104694)

JRS was indeed expanded, reaching its peak, along with unemployment, in 1984–5 when some 90 000 older people were claiming an allowance (Taylor and Walker, 1996).

Now, after their participation slipped year after year in the 1980s and 1990s, older workers have been revealed by policy makers as critical to Britain's future economic success. Once viewed as career blockers as labour markets contracted, they have now undergone a metamorphosis in the policymaker's mind, being keepers of valuable knowledge and wisdom, filling the gaps left by the dwindling numbers of young labour market entrants. The necessity of early retirement has been superseded by an activation rhetoric.

Given that this transformation has taken place over a very short space of time, it might be concluded that earlier policies were misguided. However while it is true that a marked policy shift really only got underway after the election of a Labour Government in 1997, a new emphasis on extending working lives can be traced back as far as the late 1980s, when influential voices began to warn of an impending 'demographic timebomb'. Thus, what was then known as the Employment Department produced a guide to *Training Older Workers* (Employment Department, 1991). However it should be pointed out that the recession of the early 1990s meant that there was no discernible improvement in older workers' labour market position at that time. Also, as already noted, early retirement as it emerged in continental Europe, with substantial public intervention, was never a feature in the UK. Eschewing such an approach may have avoided the development of a culture of early retirement, arguably an unfortunate legacy for other European countries now trying to extend working lives, although it inevitably was the cause of great hardship to British older workers, needing to remain economically active, but for whom new economy jobs did not materialize (Walker, 1985; Westergaard *et al.*, 1989).

Turning then to the recent history of older workers, a rather more interventionist approach has been apparent since 1997, though this has had limits. A particular characteristic of policy development has been extensive consultation and public review of reforms, backed up by extensive official, quasi-official and independent programmes of research. This has meant that it has been possible with some certainty to judge the effects of policies. Various official and independent reports have also built a powerful case for prolonging working lives. In recent years, numerous official reports have considered the economic implications of population ageing and have emphasized the importance of reactivating older workers and tackling age barriers in the labour market (for instance, Cabinet Office Performance and Innovation Unit, 2000; Department for Education and Skills, 2001; Foresight Ageing Population Panel, 2000; House of Lords, Select Committee on Economic Affairs, 2003 a, b). Such efforts have been underpinned by a marked increase in scientific interest in the relationship between age and the labour market (for instance, Glover and Branine, 2001; Hirsch, 2003).

Perhaps principal among official reports was *Winning the Generation Game*, published by the Cabinet Office's Performance and Innovation Unit (2000). This set out a number of recommendations for the development of policies towards older people. Those aimed at government as follows:

- set out its vision of the role and value of older people;
- increase contact with and job-search assistance for people on sickness and disability benefits;
- provide careers information and advice to older displaced workers;
- raise the minimum age at which an immediate pension is payable;
- increase the transparency of occupational pension schemes by showing the cost of early retirement in company accounts;
- promote the advantages of diversity and flexibility in working practices through a group of 'champion' employers; and
- each Civil Service department to review the case for increasing its retirement age to 65.

Recognizing that age discrimination impacts on many areas of policy, the Government created a Ministerial Group on Older People to coordinate work across departments. The Secretary of State for Work and Pensions became the Government Champion for Older People and the Department for Work and Pensions, the lead department for older people. DWP has responsibility for monitoring progress across government by means of updates from other departments and for liaising with them on the development and expansion of a strategic approach to tackling older people's issues. However a recent report concluded that there was an 'outstanding need to provide an overall framework for work across government affecting older people because, despite progress in joining up policymaking, there remains a lack of coordination in some areas' (Comptroller and Auditor General, 2003: 8). The report suggested that this might be assisted by publication of the Government's older people strategy, which recently occurred.

The re-election of the Labour Government in 2001 brought with it a renewed emphasis on productive welfare policy which places employment at the centre of both social and economic policies (Walker, 2002). The election manifesto contained specific commitments in this field. to raise the employment rate from 50 per cent to 70 per cent, to tackle discrimination, to extend New Deal 50 plus (see below) and to examine ways in which occupational pensions could be combined with part-time work in order to encourage flexibility in retirement.

A range of government measures on age and work can be summarized as concerning pension reform, employment programmes, education and awareness raising and legislation. Tackling issues associated with the employment of older workers has proved highly contentious, with a vocal age lobby pushing for the widest possible access for older people, but at the same time, a trade union movement sceptical of pension reforms, in particular, and employers, resisting legislation to tackle age discrimination and anxious to retain the right to dismiss workers on grounds of age. This has meant that the Government has proceeded with extreme caution, seeking to balance these different points of view, and occasionally refusing to act. There have also been disputes between different parts of government.

The main thrust of policy has been to push employment rates upward, to open up a degree of retirement flexibility, to promote better practice among business and to protect workers from discrimination on grounds of age. Among the industrialized nations, Britain acted earlier and more broadly than many and was helped somewhat by never having developed large scale early retirement pathways. Nevertheless, the process of reform has been far from smooth, with considerable debate over the speed and extent of progress.

The Government's vehement adoption of a later exit agenda is probably to do with the following factors:

- a powerful age lobby campaigning for the right of older people to work;
- the Government's Welfare to Work agenda;
- concerns about the future sustainability of pension schemes; and
- labour shortages.

Added to this, there may be increasing public pressure for older workers to be given the opportunity to work on. A recent Age Concern/ICM survey (www.ageresource.org.uk/AgeConcern/news_869.htm) found that 76 per cent of workers were opposed to being forced to retire at a fixed age and cited more flexible working arrangements as the main incentive to carry on working. A recent review concluded that older people wanted choice about working arrangements in the run up to retirement and the option of working beyond state pension age (Loretto *et al.*, 2005). McNair (2006) in surveys of older people found interest in paid work on a flexible basis after retirement among the economically active, although among the inactive there was little interest in work. The potential for mobility also seemed to be higher among those from higher socioeconomic groups. It is difficult to know what can be read into such studies as prospective questioning is notoriously unreliable. Importantly, recent research points to higher levels of well-being among those older people in paid employment, the poorest among unemployed job-seekers, with the retired in between (Robertson *et al.*, 2003). The implication is that work is preferable, but retirement is better than unemployment.

Moreover, although employment flexibility for older workers is promoted as a means of them maintaining a relationship with the labour market and the principle has been strongly endorsed by policy makers, those practising it may be at significant risk. For instance, research among older freelance workers in the media industry (Platman, 2003) found that they were vulnerable to job insecurity and financial problems due to diminishing networks and skills. A reducing flow of work limited choice and control. In the following sections, major elements of policy are outlined and evaluated.

REFORM OF RETIREMENT INCOME SYSTEMS

There has been a gradual shift towards an extension of working life in the last decade. For example, in 1989 the then Conservative Government abolished the earnings rule, which restricted the amount a person could earn and still receive their state pension. Disney and Smith (2001) found that it had increased the working hours of older male workers by four hours per week but had no effect on the working hours of women. A further reform of the Conservative Government in 1995 was to equalize the state pension ages of men and women at 65 over a ten-year period beginning in 2010 (Blake, 2003, www.pensions-institute.org/wp/wp0107.pdf).

The Blair Government's manifest position on older workers is neatly summarized in its Pensions Green Paper (DWP, 2003) where it set out proposals for reforming the retirement income system. Here, it sought views on the following issues:

- providing additional help for those aged 50 and over to help them return to work and piloting measures to help recipients of disability-related benefits return to work;
- treating men and women between 60 and women's state pension age as active labour market participants when women's state pension age rises from 2010;
- maintaining the state pension age at 65, while providing generous increases for those deferring claiming their pension,
- implementing by December 2006 age legislation covering employment and vocational training, in which compulsory retirement ages are likely to be unlawful unless they can be objectively justified;
- allowing people to continue working for their employer while drawing their occupational pension, raising the earliest age from which a pension may be taken from age 50 to age 55 by 2010, and consulting on best practice to ensure that occupational pension rules do not discourage flexible retirement; and
- changing public service pension scheme rules, for new members initially, to make an unreduced pension payable from 65 rather than 60.

These proposals were important because they accepted:

- the need for an extension of working life;
- the need to support disability benefit claimants to return to employment;
- the importance of employment income for older people, in addition to income from a pension; and
- the value of promoting a gradual withdrawal from employment.

A number of commentators went further, recommending that the age at which people could start to draw their state pension be increased. It has been argued, for example, by the National Association of Pension Funds and the Institute for Public Policy Research, that it should be increased to 67 or 70 for both men and women. Publicly, the Government has been committed to a default retirement age of 65, though in 2006 a review body, the Turner Commission, recommended a staged, long-term, increase in the state pension age to 68.[1]

The logic of the argument is that an increase could change attitudes and encourage more people to work into later life. But the Government points out that there is not a straightforward relationship between the state pension age and when most people actually stop working. For example, two-thirds of men have stopped working by the age of 65. In its Green Paper the Government stated its view that increasing the state pension age was not necessary to ensure that the goal of extending working life is achieved. It went further, arguing that given its proposals on the deferral of claiming a state pension, the notion of a single fixed state pension age might start to seem anachronistic if, as intended, people will start drawing their state pension at a range of ages starting at 65.

Moreover, the Green Paper stated that while increasing the state pension age would reduce long-term public expenditure, it would disproportionately affect lower-income people who rely more on state benefits in retirement. Also, the same people tend to have lower life expectancies, and so, with fewer years in retirement, they would see a disproportionate reduction in their income. The effect might be particularly severe on those who had done manual work in heavy industries for long periods.

In its Pensions Green Paper the Government stated that it has already begun to address the issue from its perspective as an employer. A recommendation of the report *Winning the Generation Game* (Cabinet Office Performance and Innovation Unit, 2000) was that public sector employers should review their retirement ages and examine the case for allowing those who want to work on to age 65 to do so. According to the Government 75 per cent of civil servants can do this already and the number able to serve beyond age 60 is expected to increase. But most public service pension schemes still allow a normal pension to be taken at age 60 or under, or allow an earlier pension for those with longer service. The Green Paper proposed to change the rules of public service pension schemes as they applied to new members to make an unreduced pension payable from age 65 rather than 60. Government proposals regarding reform of public sector pension ages have been strongly criticized by civil service trade unions and have been shelved.

Finally, the notion of partial or gradual retirement is now being promoted. Until recently Inland Revenue rules allowed people to work and draw an occupational pension, but only if they were no longer employed by the company paying the pension. However since April 2006 occupational pension schemes are allowed to offer people the opportunity to continue working for the sponsoring employer while drawing their pension. Linked to this, the Government has announced that it will increase the minimum benefit age from 50 to 55 by 2010.

COMBATING AGE DISCRIMINATION AND PREJUDICES – FROM EDUCATION TO LEGISLATION

For many years throughout the 1990s successive Conservative and Labour administrations ruled out legislation proscribing age discrimination in employment on the grounds that it was 'bad for business'. In the early 1990s, it was the then Conservative Government's view that age discrimination legislation would not discourage employers from discriminating against older workers. It commissioned an international review of policies and practices (Moore *et al.*, 1994) which, it claimed, showed 'no conclusive evidence that anti-age discrimination legislation had been successful in improving either the economic activity rates of older workers or their employment prospects' (Employment Department press release, July 1994). However comparisons were made without taking into account differences in employment and social welfare policies between the countries studied, rendering them meaningless.

Meanwhile, in the run up to the 1997 general election it had been Labour Party policy to implement legislation. But just prior to the election this commitment was dropped, much to the consternation of age lobby groups. Instead, the now Labour Government stated that it was persuaded of the merits of an awareness raising campaign among employers. This was not the first time this had been attempted. The Conservative Government launched the 'Getting On' campaign in 1993 with the aim of educating employers about the value of recruiting older people. This high profile campaign aimed to make employers more aware of the issue and better informed about the qualities of older workers. The campaign included the production of a booklet, sent to 165 000 employers with over 75 workers in 1994, advising them, with examples of best practice from major companies, how to avoid discriminating against older people. The Government also produced a leaflet for staff in Job Centres, *What's Age Got to do with It?* which provided them with information about age discrimination.

An evaluation of 'Getting-On' produced disappointing results. A survey of 100 employers who had attended presentations as part of the campaign's activities found that many had done so out of professional interest, rather than in the capacity of an employer, suggesting, according to the report, that the presentations were not always reaching their target audience. Additionally, when asked about their prior knowledge of the campaign, only three out of ten of those attending were aware of it and even then, not in much detail. Moreover, even among what the researchers recognized was a self-selected, interested group, less than a third had taken any action subsequently (Hayward *et al.*, 1997).

Unperturbed, following consultation (Department for Education and Employment, 1998) the now Labour Government's Code of Practice on Age Diversity was launched in June 1999 and accompanied by a media campaign. The Code took a not dissimilar approach to the previous 'Getting On' campaign, though as the name implies, aimed to tackle age barriers more generally. Tens of thousands of copies have been issued. The Code sets out principles of non-age biased employment practices, provides guidance on the application of these and contains examples of best practice (Education and Employment Committee, 2001).

Any expectations officials might have had that they would do better at the second attempt should have been dampened by subsequent research. A preliminary and small scale evaluation of the Code three months after its launch indicated that awareness amongst business was low (Employers' Forum on Age, 1999). Among 430 businesses surveyed, 30 per cent were unaware of its existence, less than 10 per cent intended to make any changes in the way they recruited or trained, and 60 per cent stated that the Code would make no difference to the way they ran their businesses. Similarly the CBI's Employment Trends Survey 2000 found that, although half the employers surveyed were aware of the Code, only 9 per cent were using it (Education and Employment Committee, 2001: viii).

More recent findings confirmed that it was having a limited effect. Government commissioned research (Goldstone and Jones, 2001) found that over the three waves of an evaluation of the impact of the Code, awareness of it increased from 23 per cent to 37 per cent of respondents. However a very small number of respondents, 9 per cent at wave three, had seen a copy. Many more representatives of larger companies had seen one. A very small number, 2 per cent at wave three, of companies stated that they had changed policies as a result of the Code.

In addition to publishing its code of practice on age diversity the Government banned upper age limits in recruitment advertisements in official job centres. In 1998 it also committed itself to publish annual key indicators showing the position of older workers in the labour market (Education and Employment Committee, 2001). A further initiative is the Age Positive website (www.agepositive.gov.uk/). Launched in 2001, it comprises a variety of features including employer case studies and advice and guidance.

Turning now to the shift in favour of anti-age discrimination legislation, following the publication of the European Equal Treatment Directive there was substantial debate in the UK around its form and content. As a first step, the Government consulted about the issues the directive raised for the UK. Initial proposals were presented in 2001 (Cabinet Office, 2001). Then, in the consultation document *Equality and Diversity: Age Matters* the Department of Trade and Industry (2003) set out the Government's more detailed proposals. While in the development phase, Department of Trade and Industry deadlines for consultation slipped considerably and a proposal to put the legislation before Parliament by the end of 2004 was delayed. This meant that an intention to give employers, training providers, and others with new obligations under the directive two years to complete their preparations was not achieved.

In 2001 the Government established an Age Advisory Group and, more recently, an Age Task Force, the membership of which has included representatives from industry, government, trade unions, lobby groups and training providers. This group has advised on age legislation and provided support in developing accompanying guidance.

Unsurprisingly, there were major differences of opinion along the way. The issue of a default retirement age for companies was particularly controversial. The Government's advisory body on pensions argued that there should not be a default age at all, but if there was, this should be set significantly higher than 65. Others such as the Confederation of British Industry preferred a default retirement age of 65 (*Financial Times*, 23 June 2004). There was also conflict between the two Government departments most involved with age and employment issues, the Department of Trade and Industry and the Department for Work and Pensions. On the one hand, the DWP was promoting greater flexibility in retirement and arguing that mandatory retirement ages were not appropriate, while at the same time, the DTI said that no decision has been made on the future of retirement ages (*Financial Times*, 24 and 26 April, 2004). The DTI, along with business groups such as the Confederation of British Industry and EEF, the manufacturers' organization, was said to favour a default retirement age of 65, while the Department for Work and Pensions and the Trades Union Congress favoured having no mandatory retirement ages. The outcome was a somewhat cumbersome system involving a default age of 65, thereby backtracking on earlier proposals, whereby an individual wishing to stay on could request this of the employer, who could decline. The Government has made a commitment to review this arrangement in time.

The Employment Equality (Age) Regulations finally came into force on 1 October 2006, making illegal unjustified age discrimination in employment and vocational training, including pay and pensions. It is clearly too early to offer an assessment of the regulations' impact, although there were reports that, in the run up to their introduction, employers were deliberately dismissing older workers (http://news.bbc.co. uk/2/hi/uk_news/ 5333100.stm).

The Government has also announced that The Commission for Equality and Human Rights (CEHR) (DTI, 2004) will replace current bodies and take responsibility for the new legislation on workplace age discrimination. It will have responsibility for enforcing equality laws and promoting good practice in equality and diversity. It is the Government's view that the new commission will offer a cross-cutting and strategic approach and provide a single access point for employers.

EMPLOYMENT PROGRAMMES AND LEARNING

Recently, a range of measures have been focused on non-working older people. New Deal 50 Plus has been the flagship programme for older workers. Before launching into a detailed discussion however, a note of caution should be sounded. The Trades Union Congress (2003) listed the amount of government expenditure on various New Deal employment programmes, and reported that New Deal 50 Plus received a tiny fraction of that spent (2.1 per cent); less than New Deal for Lone Parents (10.3 per cent) and New Deal for Disabled People (3.4 per cent). Older workers do not appear high in the policy pecking order.

Nevertheless, this particular measure has been utilized by large numbers, although those on 'inactive' benefits have been less likely to participate. Given that these represent a far greater number of the client group, this points to weaknesses in the Government's strategy. Participation rates among older people have also been declining for some time, suggesting that the effectiveness of the programme has not been sustained.

If sustainability of employment is considered, New Deal 50 Plus has been a success. However a significant minority of clients feel demeaned by low pay and unskilled work, with occupational downshifting apparent. The programme also benefits clients in terms of improved self-confidence (although for many confidence appears to remain low throughout), increased motivation and more effective job-search behaviour (Moss and Arrowsmith, 2003).

Central to the Government's vision for the future of the welfare state is the reactivation of those not currently in work. In its Pensions Green Paper it stated that from 2003 it would progressively introduce a new package of more intensive back-to-work help for people aged 50 and over and guidance to employers on the benefits of recruiting and training older workers. It would extend the support available through New Deal 50 plus so that individually tailored help for each client could be drawn from a range of possible options: personal advice, training, work trials, volunteering opportunities and an in-work training grant. It would be available to all people aged 50 and over who had been on specified benefits for six months or more, and their dependent partners aged 50 and over.

The Government has also implemented Pathways to Work pilots, focusing on incapacity benefit claimants (DWP, 2004). Main features included:

- specialist personal adviser support;
- a series of work focused interviews during the first 12 months of a claim;
- greater responsibility and power for personal advisers to manage clients via easier access to government programmes;
- a financial incentive for claimants to return to employment; and
- involvement of other local stakeholders, for instance, employers and general practitioners.

In 2005, The Rt Hon Alan Johnson MP, Secretary of State for Work and Pensions, spoke at the Institute for Public Policy Research to the title: 'Fit for purpose – welfare to work and Incapacity Benefit'. His presentation summed up the Government's approach. Excerpts follow:

[S]ince 1997, we have begun to transform the welfare state from the passive one-size-fits-all inheritance to an active service that tailors help to the individual and enables people to acquire the skills and confidence to move from welfare to work . . .

But there is more to do. Last week I launched our Five Year Strategy: 'Opportunity and security throughout life'. Central to which is a reform of Incapacity Benefit that builds on our investment in the New Deal and Jobcentre Plus and focuses on what people can do rather than what they can't.

Our goal is genuine inclusion, stamping out the discrimination and disadvantage that prevents people from fulfilling their potential – and denies society the skills and contributions of those who want to work, but who remain outside the labour market.

We know that perhaps a million incapacity benefit claimants would like to work if they were given the right help and support. Indeed, nine out of ten people coming onto IB expect to get back to work in due course.

What's more, there is growing medical evidence that for many conditions working is much healthier than being inactive . . .

What is clear is that failing to help those on incapacity benefit who want and expect to get back to work is not just bad for the economy but bad for the people on IB themselves . . .

But the problems with the current incapacity benefit have been well documented . . .

It focuses on what people can't do and incentivises them to stay on the benefit by increasing it with time. These mixed messages mean confusion, uncertainty and risk aversion for both individuals and potential employers.

What's more, incapacity benefit classifies those receiving it as incapable of working, even before they have had a formal medical examination.

And when they've had this examination – the Personal Capability Assessment – those who are entitled get no appraisal of their likely future ability to return to work. It makes no distinction between whether the case is one of terminal cancer or back pain.

. . . a radically reformed version of incapacity benefit . . . will provide a basic benefit below which noone should fall. A speedy medical assessment linked with an employment and support assessment. Increased financial security for the most chronically sick; and more money than now for those who take up the extra help on offer. (http://www.dwp.gov.uk/aboutus/2005/07_02_05_ippr.asp)

Such efforts are laudable, but given, as already noted, the huge number of current long-term incapacity benefit claimants aged over 50, it seems unrealistic to expect that more than a relatively small proportion will re-enter the labour force via this approach. However if as is implied, this aims to be a preventive measure, in time it might begin to benefit older claimants if the duration they spend on the benefit can be reduced.

Additionally, under new proposals to make provision to job-seekers more flexible and responsive to client and local needs, the Government has announced a menu of options available to official Job Centre Plus offices, including wage subsidies to provide incentives to employers to take on those they might not normally consider (DWP, 2004).

Turning to skills and learning, in its recent Skills White Paper (DfES, 2005) and its national strategy for an ageing society (HM Government, 2005) the Government proposed developing better websites and guidance to older people making decisions about careers and skills. It also stated that its primary initiative for supporting training in the workplace – the National Employer Training Programme – would cater for the needs of older people. In Employer Training Pilots,[2] older people appeared to benefit significantly. On the other hand, elsewhere, the Government commented on trials of its new Adult Learning Grant (ALG) which have been piloted in certain areas, paying up to £30 per week for full-time learners, although only those aged between 19 and 30 were eligible. However, this ceiling was subsequently partially lifted (Pound *et al.*, 2007). Meanwhile, trials of adult apprenticeships have been carried out with evidence that they can help some people aged over 25. Therefore the Learning and Skills Council (LSC) made available £16.7 million in 2007–08 to fund 8000 additional places for this age group (House of Commons Hansard, 2007). It is notable, however, that the Government's primary measures of success in its recently published skills strategy document mainly referred to young people.

Additionally, the Government announced in its Skills White Paper that it was giving Sector Skills Councils the remit of considering future labour supply issues, including responding to demographic trends, noting, for example, that some such as Skillsmart, operating in the retail sector, are already working with employers who are targeting older workers to meet staffing requirements. The Skills White Paper also contained announcements on careers information, advice and guidance services for adults and a skills coaching service aimed at low-skill benefit claimants, which might benefit older workers indirectly.

A recent review of 'what works' for clients aged over 50 has been carried out by the Department for Work and Pensions (DWP). Moss and Arrowsmith (2003) identified a number of success factors and issues related to job-placement and training for older workers. The research brought together a review of previously published literature on policies and programmes with administrative data analysis of the back-to-work help available to people aged over 50. Key findings were as follows:

- Although a range of assistance is available to clients, and many programmes are open to both 'active' and 'inactive' clients, take up is mostly among the former.
- Lack of take up among the much larger group of 'inactive' clients, many of whom want to work, reflects their very infrequent contact, until the introduction of the new Jobcentre Plus initiative, with those able to refer them to programmes.
- A number of approaches are particularly effective for older clients, including personal adviser (PA) support, flexible training, financial incentives and having advisers of a similar age, although there is mixed evidence on the benefits of age-specific training.
- The evidence highlights four key areas of support that would benefit from enhancement:

– In-work support from personal advisers: this could ensure client retention and advancement, particularly at transitional points in employment (for instance, following the withdrawal of financial incentives).
– Specialist provision: PAs perceive a lack of opportunity (or perhaps resources) to refer clients to specialist providers to address the specific problems faced by older clients (related to the perceptions, age and experiences of clients).
– Work with employers: not enough has been done to tackle age discrimination.
– Careers guidance: older clients need guidance in finding work in a new occupation.

The report identifies ways in which future policies and programmes may be able to build on current provision, to enhance the assistance on offer to older clients. These include:

• a greater focus on the 'inactive' and long-term unemployed;
• reviewing current training provision to ensure that it properly addresses client needs;
• improved awareness of the support available through Jobcentre Plus;
• a review of intervention periods for current programmes;
• greater integration of programmes;
• skills training before moving into a job; and
• short work trials for the long-term jobless, in particular.

CONCLUDING COMMENTS

Older workers currently appear to occupy a rather stronger position in the UK labour market than they have for some considerable time, at least in terms of the attention they have received from policy makers. A new emphasis on extending working lives, coupled with a buoyant economy, has coincided with a halt to the long-term decline in their employment rates, and a reversal, although as shown, the meaning of this is unclear. Their position remains somewhat ambiguous. While this has certainly shifted in their favour, there are areas of public policy where age does appear to continue to count against them. An 'age-free' employment policy has not fully emerged, with arguably, a youth bias remaining.

Perhaps this is inevitable and policymakers are simply being realistic. Added to these limits on public intervention is policy rhetoric on reactivation that sits uneasily with the reality of many older workers' labour market positions. It is questionable whether the levels of support needed to truly maintain their labour market competitiveness could be made available, indeed, whether what help is available is little more than pretence, policy makers fully aware of the daunting task, but not daring to admit it. Even for those with skills, it is a challenging environment. For the long-term unemployed and those claiming disability-related benefits, whose prospects of reemployment are quite poor, there are serious questions as to how far they really can be reintegrated.

Older workers are currently doing this well against a background of long-term economic growth and a tight labour market. A fuller test of their status in the labour market, and the willingness of policy makers to act on their behalf, would be if the British economy went into recession. There is no particular reason to assume that they would not find themselves under the same kinds of pressures they have faced previously. In the long view, it has to be asked whether their present circumstances represent a radical shift or only a familiar pattern. Though campaigners may rightly claim a recent victory with the introduction of legislation outlawing age discrimination, this is merely the foothills in the shadow of the mountain that is securing and maintaining employment opportunities.

This raises further questions: with remunerated work precluded for many, can active ageing be realized and what form might this take, or is it, realistically, the preserve, primarily, of those from higher socioeconomic groups. Constructing a vision of active ageing that that is more inclusive should be an objective of gerontologists and policymakers. In the meantime, the inevitable conclusion should be that, amid the hyperbole of the so-called looming crisis of population ageing, the history of older workers should not be forgotten.

NOTES

1. http://news.bbc.co.uk/1/shared/bsp/hi/pdfs/30_11_05_exec_summ.pdf.
2. The Employer Training Pilots (ETP) were established in September 2002, to test the effectiveness of an offer of free or subsidized training to employees, wage compensation (of various levels) to their employers for giving time off to train plus access to information, advice and guidance.

REFERENCES

Baker, Richard (2004), 'Age discrimination: implementing the directive in the EU', accessed at www.lawzone.thelawyer.com/cgi-bin/item.cgi?id=110183&d= pndpr&h= pnhpr&f=pn.
Blake, D. (2003), 'The United Kingdom pension scheme: key issues', accessed at www.lse.ac.uk/ubs/pdf/dpll.pdf.

Cabinet Office (2001), *Towards Equality and Diversity: Implementing the Employment and Race Directives*, London: HMSO.

Cabinet Office Performance and Innovation Unit (2000), *Winning the Generation Game – Improving Opportunities for People Aged 50–65 in Work and Community Activity*, London: HMSO.

Chartered Institute of Personnel and Development (CIPD) (2005), *Who Trains at Work*, London: CIPD.

Comptroller and Auditor General (2003), *Developing Effective Services for Older People*, HC 518 Session 2002–2003, London: The Stationery Office.

Department for Education and Employment (DfEE) (1998), *Action on Age: Report of the Consultation on Age Discrimination in Employment*, Sudbury (UK): DfEE Publications.

Department for Education and Skills (2001), 'Celebrating older learners', accessed at www.lifelonglearning.co.uk/cols/

Department for Education and Skills (2005), *Skills: Getting On in Business, Getting On at Work*, March, http://www.dfes.gov.uk/publications/skillsgettingon/

Department of Trade and Industry (DTI) (2003), *Equality and Diversity: Age Matters*, London: DTI.

DTI (2004), *Fairness for All: A New Commission for Equality and Human Rights*, London: The Stationery Office.

Department for Work and Pensions (DWP) (2002), *Simplicity, security and choice: working and saving for retirement*, London: The Stationery Office.

Department for Work and Pensions (DWP) (2003), 'Simplicity, Security and Choice: Working and Saving for Retirement. Action on occupational pensions', Government Green Paper, June, London.

DWP (2004), *Building on New Deal: Local Solutions Meeting Individual Needs*, London: The Stationery Office.

DWP (2006), *Older Workers: Statistical Information*, Spring 2006, London: DWP, accessed at www.agepositive.gov.uk/publications/Statistical_Information_Spring_2006.pdf.

Disney, R. and S. Smith (2001), The Labour Supply Effect of the Abolition of the Earnings Rule, Institute of Fiscal Studies: London.

Dixon, S. (2003), 'Implications of population ageing for the labour market', *Labour Market Trends*, February, 67–76.

Education and Employment Committee (2001), *Age Discrimination in Employment*, London: The Stationery Office.

Employers' Forum on Age (EFA) (1999), *Employer Awareness of the Code of Practice on Age Diversity: Report on a Survey of Senior Decision Makers in Small and Medium Enterprises*, London: EFA.

Employment Department (1991), *Training Older Workers*, Sheffield:

Foresight Ageing Population Panel (2000), *The Age Shift – Priorities for Action*, London: Department of Trade and Industry.

Glover, Ian and Mohamed Branine (2001), *Ageism, Work and Employment*, Aldershot, UK: Ashgate.

Goldstone, Carol and Deborah Jones (2001), 'Evaluation of the code of practice on age diversity in employment', in *Age Diversity, Summary of Research Findings*, Nottingham: Department for Education and Employment.

Hayward, Bruce, Sally Taylor, Nick Smith and Glenys Davies (1997), *Evaluation of the Campaign for Older Workers*, London: Department for Education and Employment.

Hirsch, Donald (2003), *Crossroads After 50: Improving Choices in Work and Retirement*, York: Joseph Rowntree Foundation.

HM Government (2005), *Opportunity Age. Meeting the Challenges of Ageing in the 21st Century*, accessed at www.dwp.gov.uk/publications/dwp/2005/opportunity_age/Opportunity-Age-Volume1.pdf.

Hotopp, U. (2005), 'The employment rate of older workers', *Labour Market Trends*, February, 73–88.

Houses of Commons Hansard (2007), accessed at www.publications.parliament. uk/pa/cm200607/cmhansard/cm070726/text/70726w0003.htm.

House of Lords Select Committee on Economic Affairs (2003a), *Aspects of the Economics of an Ageing Population*, vol. 1, Norwich: The Stationery Office.

House of Lords Select Committee on Economic Affairs (2003b), *Aspects of the Economics of an Ageing Population*, vol. 2, Norwich: The Stationery Office.

Itzin, Catherine and Christopher Phillipson (1993), *Age Barriers at Work: Maximizing the Potential of Mature and Older People*, Solihull, UK: Metropolitan Authorities Recruitment Agency.

Loretto, Wendy, Sarah Vickerstaff and Phil White (2005), *Older Workers and Options for Flexible Work*, Manchester: Equal Opportunities Commission.

Lyon, P., J. Hallier and I. Glover (1998), 'Divestment or investment? The contradictions of HRM in relation to older employees', *Human Resource Management Journal*, **8** (1), 56–66.

McNair, S. (2006), 'How different is the older labour market? Attitudes to work and retirement among older people in Britain', *Social Policy and Society*, **5** (4), 485–94.

Metcalf, Hilary and Pamela Meadows (2006), *Survey of Employers' Policies, Practices and Preferences Relating to Age*, Department for Work and Pensions research report no. 325, Leeds: Corporate Document Services.

Moore, Joanne, Barbara Tilson and Gill Whitting (1994), 'An international overview of employment policies and practices towards older workers', Employment Department research series no. 29.

Moss, Nicola and Jessica Arrowsmith (2003), *A Review of What Works for Clients Aged Over 50*, London: Department for Work and Pensions.

Naegele, Gerhard and Alan Walker (2006), *A Guide to Good Practice in Age Management*, Luxembourg: Office for Official Publications of the European Communities.

National Statistics (2005), 'Pension trends – archived December 2006: labour market and retirement highlights', accessed 12 April, 2007 at www.statistics. gov.uk/CCI/nugget.asp?ID=1670&Pos=5&ColRank=2&Rank=896.

Platman, K. (2003), 'The self-designed career in later life: a study of older portfolio workers in the United Kingdom', *Ageing and Society*, **23** (3), 281–302.

Pound, Elspeth, Yekaterina Chzhen, Janet Harvey, Monica Magadi, Juliet Michaelson, Steven Finch, Emily Tanner and Sarah Butt (2007), *Evaluation of the Adult Learning Grant Cohort 2 (Wave 2)*, Coventry: Learning and Skills Council.

Robertson, Ivan T., Peter B. Warr, V. Butcher, M. Callinan and P. Bardzil (2003), *Older People's Experience of Paid Employment: Participation and Quality of Life*, Bristol: The Policy Press.

Sennett, Richard (2006), *The Culture of the New Capitalism*, London: Yale University Press.

Taylor, Philip (2002), 'Improving employment opportunities for older workers: developing a policy framework', report to the European Commission, prepared for The Ninth EU-Japan Symposium Improving Employment Opportunities for Older Workers, Brussels, 21–2 March.

Taylor, Philip (2003), 'A New Deal for older workers? The employment situation for older workers in the United Kingdom', in Tony Maltby, Bert de Vroom, Maria-Luisa Mirabile and Einer Øverbye (eds), *Ageing and the Transition to Retirement. A Comparative Analysis of European Welfare States*, Aldershot, UK: Ashgate.

Taylor, Philip (2006), *Employment Initiatives for an Ageing Workforce in the EU-15*, Luxembourg: Office for Official Publications of the European Communities.

Taylor, P. and P. Urwin (2001), 'Age and participation in vocational education and training', *Work, Employment and Society*, **15** (4), 763–79.

Taylor, Philip and Alan Walker (1996), 'Intergenerational relations in employment', in Walker, Alan (ed.), *The New Generational Contract*, London: UCL Press, pp. 159–86.

Taylor, Philip, Christine Tillsley, Julie Beausoleil and Robert Wilson, with Alan Walker (2000), *Factors Affecting Retirement*, London: Department for Education and Employment.

Trades Union Congress (2003), *Setting New Goals: Disabled People, Work and Poverty*, London: Economic and Social Affairs Department.

Trinder, Christopher (1992), *Present and Future Patterns of Retirement*, London: Public Finance Foundation.

Walker, A. (1985), 'Early retirement: release or refuge from the labour market?', *The Quarterly Journal of Social Affairs*, **1** (3), 211–29.

Walker, Alan (2002), 'Active strategies for older workers in the UK', in European Trade Union Institute (ETUI) (ed.), *Active Strategies for Older Workers*, Brussels: ETUI, 403–35.

Westergaard, John, Iain Noble and Alan Walker (1989), *After Redundancy*, Oxford: Polity Press.

5. Age and work in the United States of America

Sara Rix

The traditional notion of retirement – where one stops working completely and enjoys leisure time with friends and family – is obsolete.

(Reynolds *et al.*, 2005: 1)

If [baby boomers] follow in the footsteps of workers now in their early 60s, perhaps one-third of the men and nearly half of the women will be out of the labor force before their 62nd birthday.

(US Congress, Congressional Budget Office, 2004b: 1)

INTRODUCTION

Like the rest of the industrialized world, the United States is ageing. The number of pensioners is projected to rise dramatically as the baby boomers, born between 1946 and 1964, begin collecting Social Security benefits, which for many could occur as early as 2008. That is when the oldest boomers turn 62 and first become eligible for Social Security retired worker benefits. The ratio of workers to retirees is shrinking, a situation that has long generated concern about the ability and willingness of workers to assume a growing burden of retirement income support.

Yet the demographic situation in the United States is not as dire as it is in many European countries or Japan. The fertility rate is near replacement level; immigration continues to fuel population growth; and the total population is projected to continue increasing. Helping to replenish the labour force will be the nearly 99 million 'echo boomers' who were born between 1976 and 2001 (Sincavage, 2004). Although Social Security's Old-Age and Survivors Insurance programme is under strain, it is not projected to become insolvent until 2041, according to the Social Security and Medicare Boards of Trustees (2007), or until 2052, according to the Congressional Budget Office (US Congress, 2005). Even then, the programme should still be able to pay about three-quarters of promised retirement benefits.

For these reasons, older workers have not commanded the attention of policymakers in the United States that they have in Western Europe and Japan. Although there seems to be growing recognition of the substantial contribution that delayed retirement could make to the economy, the Social Security trust funds, and workers themselves, a sense of urgency about prolonging working lives is lacking. There is nothing along the lines of the European Union's Stockholm and Barcelona targets, which, respectively, aim for an increase to 50 per cent in the labour force participation rate of persons aged 55–64 by 2010 and a five-year increase in the effective retirement age by the same date.[1] If anything, the push to expand older worker employment opportunities in the United States is being driven to a considerable extent by middle-aged and older workers themselves, very high percentages of whom say they expect to work in retirement (AARP, 1998; 2002b; 2003b; 2004a), academics, other researchers, and policy analysts who have written extensively on the benefits of raising the effective retirement age, and some employers who have been experiencing labour and skills shortages. For the most part, however, employers have not yet made much effort to hire and retain older workers, although many contend that they are willing to do so (US General Accounting Office, 2001; US Government Accountability Office, 2005; Walker, 2005).

At present, about 17 per cent of the civilian labour force is at least age 55, a figure that is officially projected to rise to just under 21 per cent by 2014 (Toossi, 2005).[2] Despite the echo boom and the projected growth in the older workforce, US labour force growth is slowing, a development with a potentially adverse impact on economic and federal revenue growth and the federal budget (US Government Accountability Office, 2005).[3] Increasing the labour force participation of older persons beyond that projected is viewed by many economists as one way to mitigate the impact. Goldman Sachs has calculated that if the labour force participation rates for older persons were to rise to the rates exhibited by the preceding five-year cohorts (for instance, if the participation rate for persons 60–4 rose to that for persons 55–9), the US labour force would grow by 17 per cent between 2005 and 2025, rather than by 10 per cent; GDP growth would be substantially greater as well (Lawson, 2005).

OLDER WORKERS IN PROFILE

Participation Rates Do an About Face

Older Americans are more likely to work than their counterparts in many other developed nations. In 2004, the employment rate for persons aged

55–64 in the United States was 59.9 per cent in contrast to only 41 per cent for the European Union as a whole and 42.5 per cent for the 15 pre-accession countries (US Department of Labor, 2005b; European Commission, 2005). The US employment rate for older persons is obviously well above the 2010 Stockholm target; it has also been rising lately. Recent trends in labour force participation at upper ages in the United States represent a shift from the declining participation that characterized most of the twentieth century. Among men aged 65 and older, for example, the labour force participation rate began falling well before the Second World War, reversed slightly during the war, and resumed declining once the war ended and rising wealth promised a reasonably comfortable retirement for growing numbers of Americans. Between 1950 and 1985, men's participation rate fell by 30 percentage points, from 45.8 per cent to 15.8 per cent. The participation rate for women in this age group was low to begin with and fluctuated only modestly over the same period; however, it, too, showed an increase during the war. Still, from 1950 to 1985, the participation rate for aged 65-plus women fell from 9.7 per cent to 7.3 per cent.

The picture has been somewhat different for the 55–64 age group, whose labour force participation rate actually rose somewhat after the war (Figure 5.1). Even though men were increasingly unlikely to remain at work, their

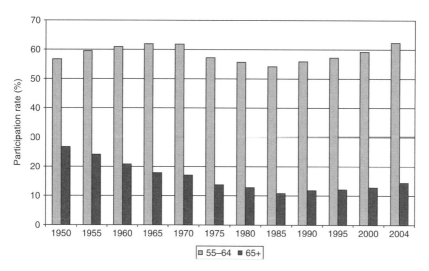

Sources: US Department of Labor, Bureau of Labor Statistics, *Handbook of Labor Statistics* (1985) and *Employment and Earnings* (1986, 1991, 1996, 2001, 2005b).

Figure 5.1   Labour force participation rates of the population aged 55–64 and 65+, United States, selected years, 1950–2004

participation rate declines were modest during the 1950s and 1960s. Women's sharply increasingly participation, however, offset the decline among men, but that did not last, and the participation rate for persons aged 55–64 fell slightly during the 1970s and 1980s. For the 55-plus population as a whole, the participation rate declined for almost four decades after the end of the war.

The watershed year as far as overall labour force participation rates for older persons in the United States are concerned was 1985. It was about then that participation rates, after the decades-long slide, began to rise, a shift that is clearly evident in Figure 5.1, which portrays a 15 per cent increase in participation for the 55–64 age group and a 33 per cent increase for the 65-plus population. The latter group's participation rate remains below that for 1950, but the rate for the former group is now above what it was at mid-century.

Within the 55–64 age group, the participation rate increase has once again been largely the result of the changing behaviour of women, whose attachment to the labour force has increased steadily for at least the past half-century. The rate for men, on the other hand, has remained quite stable since the mid-1980s (Table 5.1).

Participation rate increases for the 65 and over segment have been even greater than for 55–64-year olds, 50 per cent between 1985 and 2004, and although women in this age group are still less likely than men to be in the labour force, the increase in their participation has been more substantial: 52 per cent versus 20 per cent. But where the increase has been especially noteworthy is in what might be referred to as the 'retirement age' population, those aged 65–69.[4] Here the participation rate for both sexes combined has risen by 50 per cent, with the women's rate once again rising more than the men's. For the United States, this may be the age group for which further increases in participation are most promising; however, accomplishing that may require a more concerted focus on retaining workers, especially men, in their late 50s and early 60s. At least for now, it still appears easier for older workers to retain their jobs than to find work.

Just what explains the rising participation rates is a matter of some disagreement. *The Monthly Labor Review* of the US Bureau of Labor Statistics (BLS) states uncategorically that

> one of the most important factors in the increase in the labor force participation rate of older workers has been governmental policies and legislation aimed at eliminating mandatory retirement and outlawing age discrimination in the workplace. In addition, the removal of age restrictions and taxes on the work of older individuals in 2000 further caused the labor force participation rate of this age group to increase. (Toossi, 2005: 37)

Evidence to support this statement is considerably more nuanced. Based on an analysis of the 'limited' research on the impact of both federal and

Table 5.1   Labour force participation rates for older persons in the United
           States, by sex and age group, selected years, 1975–2004 (%)

	1975	1980	1985	1990	1995	2000	2004
Both sexes							
50–4	70.9	72.9	74.2	77.5	78.3	80.3	79.8
55–64	57.4	56.0	54.2	55.9	57.2	59.2	62.3
55–9	65.3	64.4	64.2	67.0	68.1	68.8	71.1
60–4	48.4	46.3	43.8	44.9	45.1	47.1	50.9
65+	13.8	12.6	10.8	11.9	12.1	12.8	14.4
Men							
50–4	90.0	89.1	88.6	88.8	86.4	86.8	85.4
55–64	75.8	72.3	67.9	67.7	66.0	67.3	68.7
55–9	84.4	81.8	79.6	79.8	77.4	77.1	77.6
60–4	65.7	61.0	55.6	55.5	53.2	54.8	57.0
65+	21.7	19.1	15.8	16.4	16.8	17.5	19.0
Women							
50–4	53.3	57.8	60.8	66.9	70.7	74.1	74.5
55–64	41.0	41.5	42.0	45.5	49.2	51.8	56.3
55–9	47.9	48.6	50.3	55.3	59.5	61.2	65.0
60–4	33.3	33.3	33.4	35.5	38.0	40.1	45.4
65+	8.3	8.1	7.3	8.7	8.8	9.4	11.1

Sources: US Department of Labor, Bureau of Labor Statistics, *Employment and Earnings*
(1976, 1981, 1986, 1991, 1996, 2001, 2005b).

state age discrimination laws, Neumark (2001: 35) concludes only that 'a relatively positive assessment of age discrimination legislation in the United States is more warranted than a negative assessment'. Some analyses have found little or no impact of the earnings test on work decisions (Leonesio, 1990; Gruber and Orszag, 2003), at least initially (Song, 2003/2004),[5] while others point to a more sizable impact (Friedberg, 2000; Loughran and Haider, 2005).

Richard Johnson (2002) views the reversal in labour force participation among men as something of a puzzle; his analyses lead to the conclusion that it cannot be attributed to developments such as Social Security reforms,[6] a decline in defined benefit pension coverage, or slower labour force growth, any one of which might have been expected to increase the employment of older men. Perhaps, he suggests, the reversal is due to 'increased predisposition for work', although he has no explanation for why that might have occurred in 1985. He therefore cautions policymakers against assuming that the increase will continue, as the reasons for it are not understood. Most likely, a number of factors – separately and in combination and affecting different workers differently – have contributed to these rising rates. Whatever the reason(s), the increases are good news for those who see greater labour force activity on the part of older persons as a way to alleviate the growing costs of pension and health care expenditures for the aged and alleviate what some anticipate in the way of labour and skills shortages.

If Americans act on their expectations, labour force participation rates for older persons will continue to rise. Over the past decade, public opinion polls have fairly consistently indicated that two-thirds or more of middle-aged and older persons in the United States plan to work in some capacity in retirement. These include:

- 67 per cent of workers aged 53 and older and 69 per cent of boomers aged 45–52 in the 1997 Retirement Confidence Survey (Yakoboski and Dickemper, 1997);
- 80 per cent of boomers in 1998 (AARP, 1998);
- 69 per cent of 45–74 year olds in 2002 (AARP, 2002b);
- 95 per cent of preretirees aged 55–64 who, as of 2002, planned to retire (Taylor, 2002);
- 68 per cent of workers aged 50–70 in 2003 (AARP, 2003b);[7]
- 79 per cent of boomers in 2003 (AARP, 2004a); and
- 65 per cent of workers aged 50–70 in 2005 (Metlife/Civic Ventures 2005).[8]

To be sure, the extent to which these workers will realize their expectations is as yet unknown. Nearly 30 years ago, many workers were indicating a preference for something other than exiting the labour force at an early or the normal retirement age. Just over half of workers surveyed in a 1978 Harris poll said that rather than retire, they would prefer to continue working full or part time as long as they were able or retire and find a job with another employer (Johnson and Higgins, 1979). What these workers ended up actually doing is not known; many of them undoubtedly did retire, often at young ages, as labour force participation rates at upper ages continued to fall for several more years. Some of these workers, however, may have contributed to the rising participation rates evident several years later, perhaps as part of the third to half of all eventual retirees who, according to Quinn (1999), move from career jobs to bridge employment before total and permanent retirement.

Workers offer a variety of reasons why they expect to work in retirement – personal fulfilment, the desire to be productive or make a contribution, and other nonpecuniary reasons are typically mentioned. When probed about the most important factor, needing the money, followed by access to health care, rises to the top (AARP, 2003b). Working retirees continue to work for the same reasons preretirees say they expect to work in retirement: personal fulfilment and related reasons are very important but again, if forced to choose, financial explanations dominate (AARP, 2003b).[9] Over time, financial reasons for expecting to postpone retirement seem to have become more important to boomers, greater numbers of whom reported that they would be working in retirement for such reasons in 2003 than five years earlier (AARP, 2004a), perhaps because as they have gotten closer to retirement age, the consequences of poor savings habits have become clearer.

The recent AARP boomer survey was conducted after the sharp market downturn of 2001. With a growing percentage of pensions in the form of self-directed 401(k) plans with no benefit guarantees, that slump seems to have had an impact on plans for retirement. One survey found that the majority of workers aged 50–70 who had invested in the market had lost money, and about 20 per cent of those were pushing back the date of retirement as a result (AARP, 2002a). In its 2003 Retirement Confidence Survey, the Employee Benefit Research Institute (2003) found that due to financial reasons, one-third of workers aged 45 and over have changed their retirement age. Munnell *et al.* (2003) estimate that participation in defined contribution pension plans adds about one year to working life.

Workers, of course, do not move the stock market. Nor, despite their best efforts, can they count on continued good health. They do, however, have some say over when they will retire[10] and may increasingly opt to delay retirement to compensate for paltry savings and augment eventual retirement income. Earnings are becoming a growing source of income in old age (Social Security Administration, 2005). The Congressional Budget Office reports that the Social Security benefits of workers who postpone collecting them until age 70 would be nearly double the benefits at age 62 (US Congress, 2004a). Information such as this could serve as a powerful inducement, especially for those in good health and with good jobs and flexible schedules, to delay retirement.

Into the Future

The Bureau of Labor Statistics projects continued increases, some of them substantial, in the labour force participation rates of older persons in the United States (Table 5.2). Nonetheless if workers view their mid-to-late 60s and early 70s as the 'retirement years' during which they expect to work, BLS projections do not have two-thirds or more remaining at work.

Two projected changes stand out in Table 5.2. The first is that projected increases are much greater for persons in their mid-to-late 60s and older

Table 5.2   *Labour force participation rates of persons aged 55 and over in*
             the United States, by sex and age, 2004 and projected 2014 (%)

Sex and age	2004	2014	Per cent change
Both Sexes			
55–9	71.1	73.6	3.5
60–4	50.9	55.4	8.8
65–9	27.7	33.2	19.9
70–4	15.3	17.9	17.0
75 and over	6.1	9.6	57.4
Men			
55–9	77.6	76.6	−1.3
60–4	57.0	59.4	4.2
65–9	32.6	37.9	16.3
70–4	19.4	21.5	10.8
75 and over	9.0	13.1	45.6
Women			
55–9	65.0	70.7	8.8
60–4	45.4	51.8	14.1
65–9	23.3	28.7	23.2
70–4	12.0	15.0	25.0
75 and over	4.3	7.2	67.4

Source: US Department of Labor, Bureau of Labor Statistics, *Employment and Earnings*
(2005b, January editions) and projections at ftp://ftp.bls.gov/pub/special.requests/ep/
labor.force.

than for younger persons. The labour force participation rate for persons
aged 75 and over is projected to rise by nearly 60 per cent but that for the
55–9 age group by just 3.5 per cent. Even so, only about one in ten people
75 or older is expected to be working or looking for work in 2014.

The second notable projected change is that for every age group, participation rate increases are far greater for women than men – in fact, among
men aged 55–9, a slight decline is projected. The result of these developments would be a continued narrowing of the gender gap in participation.

Overall, 41 per cent of the 55 plus population may be in the labour force
in 2014, representing a fairly steady increase since 1985. Participation,
however, is still projected to be below what it was in the early post-war years
(for instance, 43 per cent in 1950).

Many factors could help push these participation rates up even further –
the financial considerations discussed above, as well as improved health
status (discussed below), greater educational attainment, and less physically demanding jobs, all of which are associated with longer working lives.

Of critical importance is employer demand. Many observers argue that substantial labour shortages are, or could be, in the offing (US Government Accountability Office, 2005), and that older workers will be tapped to fill available jobs. Mulvey and Nyce (2004) estimate that under conservative productivity growth assumptions, the country could be short the equivalent of 8.9 million full-time workers in 2010 and 18.1 million in 2020.

Official statistics offer little guidance when it comes to labour and skills shortages. The Bureau of Labor Statistics is not in the business of projecting labour shortages, although its projections are often erroneously cited to support predictions of them. Cappelli (2003) is one employment expert who is not convinced that the United States faces substantial labour shortages. Indeed, employers will undoubtedly take numerous steps to forestall or deal with shortages, including encouraging more women to work and to work more hours, seeking further relaxation of immigration restrictions, moving jobs offshore, and investing in labour-minimizing technology. However older workers are also likely to be part of the solution. Some employers, especially in the health and education industries, are already confronting labour shortages and have been introducing programmes and policies specifically aimed at retaining older workers (see, for example, AFSCME, 2001; AARP, 2004b). The Federal Government also stands to lose a sizable portion of its workforce to retirements in the near future and may also find it necessary to devise ways to attract or retain more older workers.

What Are These Workers Doing?

In many respects, America's older workers are not all that different from 'prime-age' workers (that is, those between the ages of 25 and 50 or 55). The large majority of workers aged 55 and over are wage and salary workers. Self-employment, however, rises with age, in part because the self-employed tend to retire later than their wage and salary counterparts (Quinn, 1998) and in part because many workers move to self-employment later in life: nearly one-third of self-employed persons aged 50 and over in the United States became self-employed at or after age of 50 (Karoly and Zissimopoulis, 2004). Small business owners followed by independent self-employed workers are much more likely than wage and salary workers to have flexibility at work. Flexibility does seem to help keep some of the oldest workers in the labour force (Haider and Loughran, 2001), the greater flexibility that business owners and other self-employed workers have 'may well help to explain why workers, 50 or older, are more likely than younger workers to be self-employed or small business owners' (Bond *et al.*, 2005: 10).

Middle-aged and older workers can be found in virtually every industry and occupation, although relatively few are in the more physically demanding industries such as mining and agriculture; nor are many found in technical occupations, although the same can be said of younger workers. Four out of every ten workers aged 55 or older workers are employed in the services industry. Two industries, services and trade, claim about six in ten workers in all age groups older than 20.

Compared with middle-aged and prime-aged workers, workers aged 65 and over are somewhat more likely to be in retail trade, quite likely because of the widespread availability of part-time work and flexible schedules.

With respect to both industry and occupation, gender differences are more apparent than age differences. Service industries employ more than half of middle-aged and older women, for example, but only about one-third of their male counterparts. Women, including those who are middle-aged and older, are about four to five times as likely as older men to have administrative support jobs. Not surprisingly, they are much less likely than men to be in blue-collar occupations.

Older workers express considerable interest in flexible work schedules and scaling back their work hours (US Department of Health and Human Services, 1993; Watson Wyatt Worldwide, 2004; Brown, 2005) and, to the extent possible, they act on that interest. Nearly one in four (23 per cent) workers aged 55 and over, for example work part-time versus one in six (17 per cent) workers under the age of 55 (US Department of Labor, 2005b). Very little part-time employment in the United States, especially among older workers, is involuntary.

Flexibility and part-time and/or part-year schedules are inherent in much contingent work, or work that assumes a relatively short-term attachment to a job, but such work is not that common among older workers. The Bureau of Labor Statistics has articulated three alternative measures of contingent work, none of which employs more than 5 per cent of the older workforce (US Department of Labor, 2005a).[11] While gender differences in contingent employment are nonexistent for the aged 55–64 workforce, women aged 65 and over are somewhat more likely than men in this group to be contingent workers under the most expansive definition (7 per cent versus 4 per cent). Overall, older workers are underrepresented in the contingent population.

Older workers, however, are overrepresented among workers with certain alternative (or non-traditional) work arrangements,[12] specifically independent contract and on-call work. Workers aged 55 and over were, for example, 16 per cent of the employed population in 2004 but 27 per cent of independent contractors (such as consultants) and 18 per cent of on-call workers. These workers are underrepresented in the temporary help agency worker population, which is somewhat surprising, given an effort on the part of some larger temporary agencies to attract older workers. Gender differences in work arrangements are pronounced, with older men more likely than women to be independent contractors; older women are more likely than older men to be on-call, agency and contract workers.

Many self-employed workers are independent contractors, some of whom entered this type of work as a result of job loss and confronting barriers to reemployment. This arrangement may provide the flexibility many older workers say they want, but the work itself cannot always be predicted and may not offer adequate earnings potential to workers who lack marketing or entrepreneurial skills. For older workers with income from other sources, such potential may not be that critical.

Unemployment

In the strictest sense, unemployment is not an older worker problem in the United States. In 2004, the 55 plus labour force had an average unemployment rate of 3.7 per cent, well below the 5.5 per cent level for the labour force as a whole.

For the total labour force, the unemployment rate reached a post-war high in 1982, when it stood at 9.7 per cent (US Department of Labor, 2005b); the rate for the 55–64 workforce peaked at 5.6 per cent the following year. High unemployment rates have long characterized young Americans, and they still do, but the rates for older workers have been relatively low, at least when compared with those for the total population. A booming economy at the end of the 1990s and into 2000 contributed to exceptionally low unemployment rates for all age groups, including middle-aged and older workers. As of 2000, only 2.4 per cent of the labour force aged 55–64 were out of work and looking for a job (Table 5.3). Although the job situation for workers of all ages, especially men, deteriorated with the market downturn of 2001, the unemployment rates for all age groups 50 and over were nonetheless below 4 per cent by 2004.

Unemployment rates for women aged 50 and over, as evident in Table 5.3, have more often than not been lower than the rates for men in the same age group, but with few exceptions, the differences in unemployment by sex have not been great. To the extent that they obscure the problems that job loss poses for older workers, the low unemployment rates for older workers can be misleading. The job search for the workers concerned can be long and discouraging.

Between January 2001 and December 2003, nearly 1.7 million workers aged 55 and older were displaced from their jobs as a result of a plant closing or move, insufficient work, or abolition of their shift/position (US Department of Labor, 2004a). This was a greater number than had been displaced in the previous three-year period, during which 1.2 million older

Table 5.3 Unemployment rates for older persons in the United States, by sex and age group: selected years, 1975–2004 (%)

	1975	1980	1985	1990	1995	2000	2004
Both sexes							
Total, 16+	8.4	7.1	7.2	5.5	5.6	4.0	5.5
50–4	5.2	3.7	4.5	3.2	3.2	2.4	3.7
55–64	4.6	3.3	4.3	3.3	3.6	2.5	3.8
55–9	4.5	3.3	4.5	3.5	3.6	2.4	3.8
60–4	4.7	3.3	4.0	3.1	3.6	2.7	3.8
65+	5.3	3.1	3.2	3.0	4.0	3.1	3.6
Men							
Total, 16+	7.9	6.9	7.0	5.6	5.6	3.9	5.6
50–4	4.9	3.3	4.5	3.3	3.5	2.5	3.7
55–64	4.3	3.4	4.3	3.8	3.6	2.4	3.9
55–9	4.2	3.2	4.4	3.9	3.6	2.3	3.9
60–4	4.4	3.5	4.3	3.1	3.5	2.7	3.9
65+	5.4	3.1	3.1	3.0	4.3	3.4	3.7
Women							
Total, 16+	9.3	7.4	7.4	5.4	5.6	4.1	5.4
50–4	5.8	4.3	4.5	3.2	3.0	2.3	3.6
55–64	5.1	3.3	4.3	2.8	3.6	2.5	3.6
55–9	5.0	3.4	4.7	2.9	3.6	2.5	3.6
60–4	5.2	3.0	3.6	2.5	3.7	2.7	3.7
65+	5.1	3.1	3.3	3.1	3.7	2.8	3.4

Source: US Department of Labor, Bureau of Labor Statistics, *Employment and Earnings* (January 1976, 1981, 1986, 1991, 1996, 2001, 2005b).

workers lost their jobs (US Department of Labor, 2002); displacement rates, however, are typically higher among younger workers (Farber, 2005).

By January 2004, more than half (52 per cent) of aged 55 plus workers displaced between 2001 and 2003 were re-employed. This was an improvement over the previous period tracked by the Bureau of Labor Statistics, when only 49 per cent had found work, but it was well below the re-employment rate for the displaced worker population aged 25–54, 69 per cent of whom were working by January 2004.

The older the displaced worker, the greater the probability that he or she will drop out of the labour force. As of January 2004, one in five displaced workers aged 55–64 and more than three in five aged 65 and older were no longer in the labour force. In addition, for the 65 plus population, the proportion re-employed in January 2004 was lower than it had been for the same age group of displaced workers as of January 2002 (25 per cent versus

*Table 5.4   Duration of unemployment and percentage unemployed 27 or
more weeks, by selected age group, 2004*

Age group	Total (000s)	Mean duration (weeks)	Percentage unemployed 27+ weeks
Total, 16+	8149	19.6	21.8
25–54	4650	21.4	24.5
55–64	682	26.0	31.1
65+	179	25.2	29.6

Source: US Department of Labor, Bureau of Labor Statistics, *Employment and Earnings*
(2005b).

30 per cent) and the proportion out of the labour force was up (55 per cent
to 61 per cent).

It typically takes older unemployed workers longer to find work than it
does their younger counterparts, and many give up the job search in the
process. Duration of unemployment rises with age, with job seekers aged
55 and over spending an average of about 25 weeks looking for work in
2004, compared with about 21 weeks for workers aged 25–54. Jobseekers in
the United States either find work or drop out of the labour force within six
months or so. Only one in three workers aged 55 or over spent 27 or more
weeks on job-search, compared with one in four workers aged 25–54
(Table 5.4). Displaced older workers who do become re-employed are more
likely than their younger counterparts to experience earnings losses on their
new jobs (US Congress, 1993; Couch, 1998; Hipple, 1999).

The extent to which these re-employment differences reflect age discrimination cannot be determined with any confidence. American employers,
mindful of the Age Discrimination in Employment Act (ADEA), are unlikely
to admit to discriminating, and workers may not recognize or want to bother
with dealing with it when it occurs. Employers do, however, harbour reser-
vations about older workers, especially when it comes to technological competence and ability to learn new technology (AARP, 1995, 2000a, 2005).
Higher health care costs are another cause for concern to employers. Older
workers believe that age discrimination is a problem in the workplace. Two-
thirds of employees aged 45–74, for example, report that they have person-
ally experienced or witnessed discrimination on the job due to age, and they
tend to believe that workers start to face discrimination around age 49
(AARP, 2002b). In a study of age discrimination in the labour markets of
two states, Lahey (2005) sent out resumes for similarly qualified 35-year-old
and 62-year-old job applicants and found that the younger job seeker was 40
per cent more likely than the older one to get called in for an interview. Lahey

also reports that 'in states where it is easier to sue [that is, those with local age discrimination laws], older white men work fewer weeks than those in states where it is harder to sue'. Adams and Neumark (2007) in a review of the evidence on age discrimination find ample evidence for it and that age is a factor in evaluation job applicants.

Older job-seekers may be holding out for wages more comparable with those in their previous jobs, which could explain some of the lengthier job-searches, as may a lack of up-to-date skills. Some of the labour force withdrawal may be due to a relatively substantial gap between previous earnings and probable earnings offered for a new job (Farber, 2005). Improving older worker employability by fostering a training 'culture' is a key focus of the Organisation for Economic Co-operation and Development's (OECD) recent synthesis of review of older worker employment policies in 21 countries (OECD, 2005b).

Enhancing the job-finding success of older workers is critical to the continued employment of displaced and other workers, for once older workers leave the labour force, their probability of returning is low and declines over time. Although there is some anecdotal evidence of an increase in retirees returning to work ('More retirees return to work force,' *Wall Street Journal*, 8 December 2005; 'Retirees back at work with flexibility,' *USA Today.com*, 10 June 2005),[13] most older workers who are not in the labour force profess no interest in being there. In recent years, fewer than 3 per cent of the aged 55 plus population not in the labour force have indicated that they would like to be working.[14] An even smaller percentage could officially be labelled 'discouraged', that is, they are available for work but are not seeking employment because they do not believe that work is available, think they lack the necessary schooling or training, fear that employers will think of them as being too old, or anticipate some other type of discrimination. Only 84 000 persons were classified as discouraged by the Bureau of Labor Statistics in 2004 (US Department of Labor, 2005b). Nonetheless given the extensive body of polling and other research on the employment interests of older workers, it seems reasonable to conclude that substantially more older Americans would remain in or return to the workforce if attractive work options and inviting workplaces were more readily available.

THE CURRENT ECONOMIC DEBATE SURROUNDING THE AGEING OF THE POPULATION IN THE UNITED STATES

The economic debate on ageing in the United States, which is really more a discussion at this point, focuses largely on the costs of providing health care to a burgeoning older population. Medicare, America's health care programme for the 65 plus population, is generally regarded as unsustainable; America's comptroller general contends that 'If there is one thing that could bankrupt America, it is health care, and it's out of control' (Walker, 2005; David M. Walker in Kaiser Family Foundation, 2005: 42).[15] Reluctance to make some of the hard choices required to overhaul Medicare, to say nothing of the total US health care system, (which leaves 16 per cent of the population, or nearly 46 million people, uninsured (US Department of Commerce, 2005)),[16] is pervasive.

Social Security's Old-Age and Survivors Insurance programme has long been viewed as the third rail of politics and thus politically untouchable. President George W. Bush nonetheless made Social Security reform, specifically, the introduction of individual accounts to this pay-as-you-go defined benefit system, a cornerstone of his second term; however, he has so far been unable to generate sufficient support for partial privatization, despite an active campaign on his part to garner public support for the accounts. At the time of writing they appeared to be off the table, although they were a hotly debated topic for much of 2005.

Although Social Security's long-term solvency is at issue, the programme is on a sounder fiscal basis than Medicare. However even if full solvency is restored, Social Security alone is not sufficient to provide an adequate post-retirement standard of living for most Americans. This fact, coupled with a population that has shown little predisposition to save much, general stagnation of private pension coverage expansion since the mid-1970s, and the shift from defined benefit pension plans to defined contribution plans, may be what it takes to get boomers, in particular, to remain at work longer if they hope ultimately to achieve financial security in retirement. Yet the availability of Social Security at age 62 may be contributing to a mindset that benefits should be collected at that young age; most workers opt for the reduced benefits available before the full retirement age.

Economists, policy analysts, and other researchers are at present more likely than politicians to be pondering the implications of an ageing society and to proffer solutions to deal with them. America's retirement income system is in need of reform: in addition to Social Security's long-term insolvency, many private pension plans are under-funded, and the agency that insures traditional defined benefit plans is under stress. At the government level, though, there has been relatively little debate or discussion about how extended working lives might help.

American workers may say that they expect and even want to work in retirement, but they by no means support further retirement age increases (see Rix, 1999). Many of the proposals to restore long-term solvency to the Social Security system would increase the age of eligibility for full benefits above that in current law, eliminate a hiatus in current law that provides a pause in the increase from 66 to 67, and/or index the eligibility age of benefits to increases in life expectancy. Senator Charles Grassley (R-IA), former chairman of the Senate Finance Committee who at the time of publication was 74 years old, has proposed a phased in increase to age 69 (Espo, 2005).

Despite its unpopularity, a higher eligibility age for full Social Security benefits is likely to feature prominently in Congressional deliberations on Social Security reform, since increasing the age could make a substantial contribution to shoring up the system. With today's 65-year-olds having a life expectancy that is nearly six years greater than it was when Social Security was introduced (Arias, 2004) and projected to continue rising, 'paying for' some of the additional years by working longer may gain wider acceptance. Among government agencies, fostering longer working lives has been most extensively addressed by the US Government Accountability Office (GAO, formerly known as the General Accounting Office). GAO has produced a number of reports on the ageing workforce and encourages efforts to assist workers who want to remain in the labour force beyond retirement age (Bovbjerg, 2005).[17] It warns of 'the loss of many experienced workers and possible skills gaps in certain occupations [which] could have adverse effects on productivity and economic growth' (Bovbjerg, 2005: 1) and stresses that more years in the workforce may be part of the solution to the pressures that forthcoming retirements will place on Social Security and Medicare.

In 2001, GAO recommended that the Department of Labor establish an interagency taskforce charged with soliciting input from other vested interests such as employers and unions and developing legislative and regulatory proposals for issues raised by an ageing workforce (US General Accounting Office, 2001). A taskforce was established in 2004, but GAO now argues that the challenges the country faces 'warrant a higher priority and a high-visibility campaign involving a wider group of employers as well as employees' (US Government Accountability Office, 2005: 32).

Older workers may not be high on the Congressional agenda, but they are by no means absent. The US Senate Special Committee on Aging (a non-legislative committee) occasionally holds hearings on older worker issues[18] and will likely hold more as the potential consequences of boomer retirement become harder to ignore. In 2000, Congress passed the Senior Citizens' Right to Work Act, which eliminated the benefit loss experienced by working Social Security recipients above the normal retirement age whose earnings exceeded an annually adjusted threshold. In 2005, Senator Herb Kohl (D-WI) introduced the Older Worker Opportunity Act (S.1862), designed to promote employment opportunities for older persons who want to work longer. Among other provisions, this bill would establish a tax credit for phased or flexible work programmes, provide an eldercare tax credit, extend access to COBRA health care coverage[19] for certain workers, define 'older workers' as one of several hard-to-serve populations under the Workforce Investment Act, and improve access to training and employment services for those workers. A force would examine barriers to continued employment, assess the effectiveness of the Older Worker Opportunity Act no later than three years after its establishment, and organize a formal conference on the ageing workforce.

Age discrimination in employment has been illegal in the United States since the passage of the Age Discrimination in Employment Act (ADEA) in 1967.[20] In 1986, mandatory retirement in almost all occupations was eliminated, and in 2005, the US Supreme Court ruled that disparate impact claims were allowed under the ADEA. This means that older workers can seek redress against policies that appear age neutral but that disproportionately harm older workers.

In 1983, Congress passed legislation raising the age of eligibility for full Social Security retired worker benefits; the increase began to be implemented for workers turning age 62 in 2000. Although dealing with the long-term solvency of the system was the reason for the change, it was predicated on the assumption that older persons – at least most of them – could function effectively at the later ages. At the same time, Congress added a work carrot or sweetener to the retirement-age stick: the delayed retirement credit payable to those who delay retirement after the normal retirement age and up to age 70 has been gradually increasing and will be more actuarially fair by 2008. While this means workers who postpone retirement will not suffer lifetime benefit losses, the impact of this increase may be undermined by the provisions of the Senior Citizens' Right to Work Act.

Finally, The Internal Revenue Service has issued proposed regulations to eliminate a number of barriers to formal phased retirement programmes. The Pension Protection Act of 2006 enables workers to collect private pension benefits at age 62 and continue working for the same employer; the inability to do this has been viewed as a major impediment to employers offering phased retirement.

OLDER WORKERS AND ACTIVE AGEING

'Active ageing,' per se, has not received the attention in the United States that it seems to have had in Europe. Today's older Americans, especially the baby boomers, are seen as materially different from the aged of generations past (Johnson, 2005) and are expected to be active later in life than their parents and grandparents.

'Successful ageing' and 'productive ageing' have been addressed in various books and reports (see Bass *et al.*, 1993; Bass, 1995; Rowe and Kahn, 1998; Morrow-Howell *et al.*, 2001), but the terms themselves never seemed to catch on. They do, however, reflect a shift in perceptions of older Americans as ill and disengaged to generally healthy and capable of contributing to society much later in life. General increases in health status at upper ages have been reported (National Research Council and Institute of Medicine, 2004); disability rates among the aged have fallen (Manton and Gu, 2001); self-reports of being in only fair or poor health have declined (National Center for Health Statistics, 2005); and morbidity is believed to have been compressed (Fries, 2005). In addition, jobs in today's economy are less arduous than they were in the past. If there is a sense of 'active ageing' in the United States, it is that the healthier older population is for the most part capable of working longer. Rising labour force participation rates at upper ages would indicate that the assumption is correct, at least for a growing percentage of the population.

Recent headlines have touted '60 [as] the new 55' (Lawson, 2005), or even '60 [as] the new 30' (AARP, 2003a). Whichever is closer to the truth hardly matters; what is significant is that 'old age' in America is being pushed back because older persons are increasingly assumed to be actively ageing.

The Meaning of 'Active Ageing' for Older Workers

The conventional view of retirement in the United States has been one of a one-time total and permanent separation from long-term or even lifelong employment. But while many workers did spend all or most of their working lives with a single employer and 'retire' but once, lifetime employment in the United States has apparently been more myth than reality (Yakoboski, 1998). Moreover, far from abrupt, the retirement of many workers has been gradual, as they have voluntarily or involuntarily 'eased' into retirement via bridge jobs or transitional employment between career jobs and full retirement (Quinn, 1999).

The extent to which bridge employment enables workers to remain active in the workforce beyond what they would have done had they stayed with their longer-term or career employers is not known. It is commonly believed, however, that phased and partial retirement[21] could keep workers active later in life. On the other hand, these options could encourage workers to scale back their work hours sooner than they otherwise would. Recent research by Chen and Scott (2006) finds little evidence for the latter, but they caution that more research on this issue is desirable.

According to Watson Wyatt Worldwide (2004), about two-thirds of 50-to 70-year-olds would like to scale back their work hours or have more flexibility on the job, and about one-third indicated that they would work longer than otherwise planned if they had the opportunity to phase into retirement. Flexibility appears to be important to individuals who remain at work after their 65th birthday (Haider and Loughran, 2001).

Despite the myriad polls that point to plans and wishes to remain active later in life by working in retirement, American workers actually send mixed messages about working. Somewhat less than four out of ten boomers say they never want to retire, but just over four in ten cannot wait to do so (AARP, 2004a). Boomers have also indicated that they would like to stop working for pay altogether at the rather young average age of 59.7 years (AARP, 1998). Moreover, circumstances over which they have little control may alter workers' post-retirement plans and expectations. In 2004, the Congressional Budget Office reported that 4 million boomers had already left the labour force, most commonly because of disability; a high percentage of the disabled were collecting Social Security Disability Insurance (SSDI) benefits (US Congress, 2004b). Stringent eligibility criteria for SSDI have prevented this disability programme from becoming the alternative pathway to early labour force exit that programmes in some other countries appear to be. For many older Americans, active ageing may be an elusive goal.

Active ageing encompasses more than paid work, of course. Millions of older Americans volunteer and plan to go on doing so in retirement. According to Metlife/Civic Ventures (2005), more than half (53 per cent) of persons aged 50–70 reported volunteering for at least one organization in the past 12 months. Persons aged 65 and older are somewhat less likely to volunteer than most younger age groups, but volunteering among this age group has risen since 2002, and if they do volunteer, older persons put in more hours than younger volunteers (US Department of Labor, 2004b).

The contributions older volunteers make to their communities are by no means inconsequential. The estimated value of the formal, informal, and care giving volunteer work of Americans aged 55 and over ranged from $97 billion to $201 billion for 2002, with a best estimate of $162 billion or over $2500 per person (Johnson and Schaner, 2005). Over half of boomers expect to spend more time on community service and volunteering in retirement (AARP, 2004a), which could be a boon for the organizations that depend on volunteers.

Longer work lives could have an adverse impact on volunteer work and caring, if workers need to scale back their non-employment activities as a result. A lack of time is by far the most common reason that employed persons give for not volunteering; as would be expected, part-time workers are less likely than their full-time counterparts to be pressed for time (US Department of Labor, 2004b). Care giving could also suffer for the same reasons, forcing workers with caring responsibilities to choose between them and paid employment. Phased or partial retirement or other flexible work options might make it easier for workers to combine work and nonwork activities like volunteering, care giving and having fun.

Even though the large majority of boomers expect to work in retirement, they see those years largely in terms of spending more time with family, pursuing nonwork interests, and leisure (AARP, 2004a). They are also interested in retirement work that contributes to the greater good, although they are not necessarily sanguine about their chances of finding it (Metlife Foundation/Civic Ventures, 2005).

LOOKING AHEAD

Americans, the banking group HSBC (2005: 6) maintains, are rejecting the old perspective of retirement, just a generation after the United States 'pioneered the idea of leisured retirement', seeking instead a new phase that incorporates both work and leisure periods. Dora Costa (1998: 133), in an examination of the history of retirement in the United States, argues that 'a preference for leisure is the main motivation for the retirement of growing numbers of workers'. Most workers will eventually retire, but it is likely to take more of them longer to do so than in previous generations. Whether retirement is being reshaped or redefined remains to be seen, but rising participation rates at upper ages indicate that working lives have become longer for a sizable minority of some older age groups.

Many experts in the United States believe that extending working life is a good thing and should be encouraged (Burkhauser *et al.*, 1996; Johnson, 2005; Walker, 2005). With more experienced workers on the job, an ageing workforce could actually be a more productive one (Laitner and Stolyarov, 2005). However while some observers advocate raising the early and/or full Social Security eligibility ages, others prefer programmes and policies that result in a voluntary prolongation of working life. More flexible work options, phased retirement, and better part-time jobs are believed to facilitate such an extension.

On the whole, older workers clearly seem prepared to work longer, but they would like it to be on their own terms. Boomers, in particular, are likely to expect to have it all: more and better work options later in life combined with sufficient time to pursue other activities. They will not all get it, however, for despite the shift to a knowledge-based economy, millions of US workers can be found in physically demanding jobs or unsafe or unpleasant work environments that do not lend themselves to prolonged working lives (OECD, 2005a). A not inconsequential percentage of these workers lack the skills and ability to move easily into something new; the OECD recommends a policy focus on low-skilled workers of all ages to promote current and future well-being (OECD, 2005a).

A variety of factors may prevent or discourage many who want to keep working from doing so: poor health, outdated skills, a paucity of flexible work options, unappealing part-time employment opportunities, the availability of Social Security benefits at age 62, defined benefit pension plan rules that penalize workers for postponing retirement, caring responsibilities, spousal retirement decisions, and employers, who have their own questions and concerns about older workers.

Despite the potential for an increasingly active old age, older persons face health issues that may affect their ability to work or their attractiveness to employers. Chronic health conditions increase with age (National Research Council and Institute of Medicine, 2004); over half of the Metlife/Civic Venture (2005) respondents who do not plan to work in retirement gave poor or declining health as the reason, as did over half of the nonworking retirees. The disabled boomers analysed by the Congressional Budget Office will increase in number and, without workforce accommodations, likely leave the labour force. The severity of workplace injuries increases with age, as does recovery time (Rogers and Wiatrowski, 2005).[22] Fatal injuries are more common among older workers. And while certain occupations (for example, transportation) are associated with a high number of injuries involving time away from work, Rogers and Wiatrowski (2005: 28, 30) have found that among workers aged 65 and older, retail sales was one of the occupations with the greatest number of falls on the same level, suggesting, perhaps contrary to expectation, 'that falls are much more prominent among all occupations at this age level, and that the job does not have to be one that is traditionally considered high risk or dangerous to lead to a fall among an older worker (sic).'

Questions about performance and productivity at upper ages may also affect the prospects of older workers to retain or find work (US Congress, 2004b). Although some research concludes that age is a poor predictor of performance (Sterns and McDaniel, 1994), OECD (2005b) finds declining physical and cognitive capacities with age. These declines, OECD contends, do not necessarily affect performance, as workers may compensate for the declines or workplace adjustments may offset them. Nonetheless they may influence employer decisions about the value of older workers. Perceptions that older workers are paid more than they are worth have led to suggestions that wage adjustments (that is, lower wages) might make older workers more attractive to employers (Rebick, 1993; OECD, 2005b). Higher health insurance costs may also discourage employers from hiring or retaining older workers (US Congress, 2004b; Mulvey and Nyce, 2004).

Employer concerns about older worker costs, performance, and technological competence, for example, are likely reflected in the difficulty older workers have in finding work, the dearth of formal phased retirement options and attractive job opportunities, and continued age discrimination, especially in hirings and terminations. Still, employer efforts across a number of industries to reach out to older workers and/or to implement practices that attract and retain older workers (see, for instance, AARP, 2004b) are a sign that some employers are receptive to older workers, at least when the labour market is tight. Nevertheless, research on phased retirement has found few formal programmes but many ad hoc opportunities to ease into retirement (Hutchens, 2003), suggesting that employers want considerable discretion over providing the flexible options that so many older workers say they want. Furthermore, although age discrimination in employment is illegal, employers can and do find ways to divest themselves of workers they no longer need or want. Older workers may be at particular disadvantage in the global economy where corporate restructuring and downsizing result in job dislocation that may or may not involve age discrimination.

There is no evidence that an age-free employment is emerging, or that workers even want one. On the one hand, age discrimination laws imply that work decisions should be age-neutral, but on the other, age neutrality is inconsistent with programmes and policies aimed at hiring and retaining older workers. A concerted effort on the part of agencies and Congress to address older worker issues, if that occurs, may mean that age-free employment is an unrealistic goal. Cappelli (2005), however, notes that there are legal concerns about special or differential treatment of certain workers, which may discourage employers from offering older workers what they want – flexibility, in particular.

Properly designed and implemented, most programmes and policies that stand to expand employment opportunities for older people should benefit workers of all ages. Nevertheless, it is hard to imagine that age will ever not be a factor in employers' personnel decisions. Better monitoring and enforcement of the Age Discrimination in Employment Act could reduce the number of adverse employment decisions based on age. Dissemination of effective older worker employment practices implemented by successful businesses might encourage other employers to reach out to those workers as well.

Predicting the future is fraught with hazards, particularly when a prediction applies to as large and diverse a population as US baby boomers. Boomers have shaped American institutions all their lives, and there is no reason to assume that they will not do so to retirement if they choose. The media certainly expect them to and may be contributing to changing expectations about the retirement years. The frequent references to surveys highlighting how many workers expect to work in retirement may be influencing what people say, especially those who have not given much thought to their retirement years. Nonetheless the statistics on work expectations across surveys are so consistent that they do seem to reveal a real change in expectations for millions of Americans.

More affluent, better educated, and healthier older persons (see Haider and Loughran, 2001) will undoubtedly find it easier to remain in the workforce in the so-called retirement years. The ADEA does make it easier for those workers, many in very good jobs, to remain at work if they desire, and many will do so, although they would apparently like to do so at reduced hours.

Nonetheless many of the new jobs will be in occupations that do not require the skills and attributes that these workers possess. Demand for home health workers, truck drivers and fast-food workers is expected to be great. The appropriateness of the match between supply and demand will affect which and how many older workers actually remain in the labour force. A discrepancy between what workers say they want and feel they deserve and what is available could well temper older workers' enthusiasm for continued employment.

As noted above, the majority of US employers have not yet felt the need to address issues of older worker hiring and retention. For some employers, at least, that day may be close at hand. In addition, in short order, boomers will be reaching those so-called 'retirement years'. What they end up doing and how the rest of society responds should soon be known.

DISCLAIMER

The views expressed in this chapter are those of the author and do not necessarily represent the official policy of AARP.

NOTES

1. The Stockholm target was agreed to in 2001 and the Barcelona target in 2002.
2. Every other year, the Bureau of Labor Statistics (BLS) publishes medium-term labour force projections that extend for ten years. The most recent medium-term projections available as of this writing are for 2014 (Toossi, 2005). In 2002, BLS produced projections through 2050 by projecting labour force participation rates for various categories (for example, age, sex, race) to 2015 and holding the 2015 rates constant thereafter. Participation rate changes after 2015 are thus due to changes in the size of the categories,

whose participation rates can vary (Toossi, 2002). The participation rate for the 65-plus population was projected to rise through 2015–20 and then to fall. However the 2005 projection for 2014 exceeds those rates, underscoring the difficulties inherent in long-term labour force projections.

3. The 2004–14 annual growth rate in the US labor force is put at 1 per cent, in contrast to 1.2 per cent for 1994–2004 and 1.4 per cent for 1984–94 (Toossi, 2005: Table 6).

4. The age of eligibility for full Social Security benefits (the so-called 'normal retirement age') was set at 65 when the Social Security Act was passed in 1935. It is rising gradually to 67.

5. Song (2003/2004) found that higher earners had a significant increase in earnings in response to elimination of the earnings test but the same effect was not found among lower earners. In addition, the test's elimination apparently had no significant effect on employment, at least in the short run.

6. Johnson (2002) analyses several reforms to Social Security and concludes that lowering the financial penalty for working is 'the most plausible cause of lower retirement rates at age 65' (p. 13), but even that explains only about 6 per cent of the change in male labour supply as ages 65 to 69.

7. These were workers who expect to work in retirement or never retire.

8. These were employed or unemployed and looking for work who expect to work in retirement or never retire.

9. Working retirees are far less likely to mention a need for health care, most likely because they are older and more of them are eligible for health care under Medicare; some may also be receiving retiree health benefits.

10. Their say is not absolute, of course. Employers can and do rely on a variety of generally legal means to rid themselves of workers they no longer want, and many of those workers are older. Nonetheless the Age Discrimination in Employment Act offers important protections to workers who wish to remain in the labour force at older ages.

11. See US Department of Labor, 2005a for these definitions, which refer to workers 'who do not have an implicit or explicit contract for ongoing employment'. The three estimates vary according to whether the self-employed and independent contractors are included, how long workers expect their job to last, and how long they have been working at their job.

12. These include independent contractors, on-call workers, temporary help agency workers, and workers provided by contract firms (US Department of Labor, 2005a).

13. At http://www.usatoday.com/money/perfi/retirement/2005-06-08-retiree-main_x.htm.

14. There were 40.5 million in this age group who were not in the labour force in 2004 (US Department of Labor, 2005b). Figures for earlier years can be found in US Department of Labor, Bureau of Labor Statistics, *Employment and Earnings*, January editions from 1999 to 2004.

15. Medicaid, the health care programme for America's poor, is another significant and costly source of health care for the aged as it pays for the long-term care of indigent elderly.

16. These figures are for 2004.

17. See, for example, US General Accounting Office (2001 and 2003); US Government Accountability Office (2005).

18. In 2005, the Committee held a hearing on redefining retirement in the twenty-first century. In 2004, hearings were held on whether mandatory retirement still made sense and on the 'silver ceiling' confronting older workers.

19. Under the Consolidated Omnibus Budget Reconciliation Act (COBRA), workers and their families who lose their employer-provided health care due to, for example, job loss or death of the covered worker may purchase that insurance at group rate for a limited period, generally 18 months.

20. The ADEA originally protected workers ages 40 to 65. Subsequent amendments raised and then eliminated the upper age limit.

21. Although definitions of phased and partial retirement vary, Chen and Scott (2006) have defined phased retirement as reduced hours with the same employment and partial retirement as reduced hours with a different employment.

22. Workers who experienced a nonfatal injury or illness at work spent eight days away from work in 2003, but time away rose to 12 days for workers aged 55–64 and 18 days for those aged 65-plus (Rogers and Wiatrowski, 2005).

REFERENCES

AARP (1995), *American Business and Older Workers: A Road Map to the 21st Century*, Washington, DC: AARP.

AARP (1998), *Boomers Look Toward Retirement*, Washington, DC: AARP.

AARP (2000a), *American Business and Older Employees*, Washington, DC: AARP.

AARP (2000b), *Easing the Transition: Phased and Partial Retirement Programs, Highlights*, Washington, DC: AARP.

AARP (2002a), *Impact of Stock Market Decline on 50-70 Year Old Investors*, Washington, DC: AARP.

AARP (2002b), *Staying Ahead of the Curve: The AARP Work and Career Study*, Washington, DC: AARP.

AARP (2003a), *AARP: The Magazine*, November and December.

AARP (2003b), *Staying Ahead of the Curve 2003: The AARP Working in Retirement Study*, Washington, DC: AARP.

AARP (2004a), *Baby Boomers Envision Retirement II: Survey of Boomers' Expectations for Retirement*, Washington, DC: AARP.

AARP (2004b), *Staying Ahead of the Curve 2004: Employer Best Practices for Mature Workers*, Washington, DC: AARP.

AARP (2005), *American Business and Older Employees: A Focus on Midwest Employers*, Washington, DC: AARP.

Adams, Scott and David Neumark (2007), *Age Discrimination in US Labor Markets: A Review of the Evidence*, San Francisco, CA: Public Policy Institute of California.

American Federation of State, County and Municipal Employees (AFSCME) (2001), 'To drop or not to drop,' *Collective Bargaining Reporter*, revised edn, accessed at www.afscme.org/wrkplace/cbr 399_3.htm.

Arias, Elizabeth (2004), 'United States Life Tables, 2004', *National Vital Statistics Reports*, **53** (6), published by the National Center for Health Statistics.

Bass, Scott A. (ed.) (1995), *Older and Active*, New Haven, CT and London: Yale University Press.

Bass, Scott A., Francis G. Caro and Yung-Ping Chen (eds) (1993), *Achieving a Productive Aging Society*, Westport, CT: Auburn House.

Bond, James T., Ellen M. Galinsky, Marcie Pitt-Catsouphes and Michael A. Smyer (2005), 'Context matters: insights about older workers from the National Study of the Changing Workforce', *Research Highlights*, **1**, published by the Center on Aging and Work.

Bovbjerg, Barbara D. (2005), 'Redefining retirement: options for older Americans,' testimony before the Special Committee on Aging, US Senate, GAO-05-620T, Washington, DC, 27 April.

Brown, Kathi (2005), *Attitudes of Individuals 50 and Older Toward Phased Retirement*, Washington, DC: AARP.

Burkhauser, Richard V., Kenneth A. Couch and John W. Phillips (1996), 'Who takes early social security benefits? The economic and health characteristics of early beneficiaries', *Gerontologist*, **36** (6), 789–99.

Cappelli, Peter (2003), 'Will there really be a labor shortage?', *Organizational Dynamics*, **32** (3), 221–33.

Cappelli, Peter (2005), 'Don't fool yourself: this won't be easy for employers,' in *Commentary on the Metlife Foundation/Civic Ventures New Face of Work Survey*, accessed 12 April 2007 at www.civicventures.org/publications/surveys/new_face_of_work/nfw_commentaries.pdf.

Chen, Yung-Ping and John C. Scott (2006), *Phased Retirement: Who Opts for It and Toward What End?*, Washington, DC: AARP Public Policy Institute.

Civic Ventures (2002), *The New Face of Retirement: An Ongoing Survey of American Attitudes on Aging*, Oakland, CA: Civic Ventures.

Costa, Dora L. (1998), *The Evolution of Retirement*, Chicago, IL: University of Chicago Press.

Couch, Kenneth (1998), 'Late life job displacement', *Gerontologist*, **38** (1), 7–17.

Economic Policy Foundation (EPF) (2001), 'Future labor and skill shortages jeopardize American prosperity,' *Employment Forecast*, 23 October, accessed at www.epf.org/pubs/newsletters/2001/ef20011025.pdf.

Employee Benefit Research Institute (2003), 'Retirement in America,' 2003 Retirement Confidence Survey, accessed 12 April 2007 at www.ebri.org/pdf/surveys/rcs/2003/03fsamer.pdf.

Espo, David (2005), 'Proposal to raise retirement age,' *CBS News*, 15 June, accessed at www.cbsnews.com/stories/2005/06/15/politics/printable701921.shtm.

European Commission (2005), accessed 13 November 2005 at epp.eurostat.cec.eu. int/portal/page?_pageid=1996,39139751&_dad=portal&_schema=PORTAL& screen=welcomeref&open=/strind/emploi&language=en&product=EU_key_ indicators&root=EU_key_indicators&scrollto=188.

Farber, Henry (2005), 'What do we know about job loss in the United States? Evidence from the Displaced Workers Survey, 1984–2002,' *Economic Perspectives*, **29** (2), 13–28, accessed 12 April, 2007 at http://64.233.161.104/search?q= cache: kFXk0aMOF_8J:www.chicagofed.org/publications/economicperspectives/ep_2qt r2005_part2_farber.pdf+Farber+%22job+displacement%22+2005& hl=en.

Friedberg, Leora (2000), 'The labor supply effects of the Social Security earnings test', *Review of Economics and Statistics*, **82** (1), 48–63.

Fries, James M. (2005), 'Compression of morbidity: in retrospect and in prospect', *International Longevity Center Issue Brief*, 2 (2).

Gruber, Jonathan and Peter Orszag (2003), 'Does the Social Security earnings test affect labor supply and benefits receipt?', *National Tax Journal*, **56** (4), 755–73.

Haider, Steven and David Loughran (2001), 'Elderly labor supply: work or play?', unpublished paper prepared for the Third Annual Conference of the Retirement Research Consortium, Washington, DC, 17–18 May.

Hipple, Steven (1999), 'Worker displacement in the mid-1990s', *Monthly Labor Review*, **122** (7), 15–32.

HSBC (2005), *The Future of Retirement in a World of Rising Life Expectancies*, London: HSBC Group Head Office, accessed at www.hsbc.com/futureof retirement.

Hutchens, Robert (2003), *The Cornell Study of Employer Phased Retirement Policies: A Report on Key Findings*, Ithaca, NY: Cornell University School of Industrial and Labor Relations.

Johnson, Richard (2002), 'The puzzle of later male retirement', *Economic Review*, (3), 5–26.

Johnson, Richard W. (2005), *Working Longer to Enhance Retirement Security*, Older Americans' Economic Security series brief no. 1, Washington, DC: Urban Institute.

Johnson, Richard W. and Simone G. Schaner (2005), *Value of Unpaid Activities by Older Americans Tops $160 Billion per Year*, Perspectives on Productive Aging series brief no. 4, Washington, DC: Urban Institute.

Johnson and Higgins (1979), *1979 Study of American Attitudes toward Pensions and Retirement*, New York: Johnson and Higgins.

Kaiser Family Foundation (2005), transcript to 2005 White House Conference on Aging, Day One Opening Plenary, 12 December, accessed 12 April 2007 at www.kaisernetwork.org/health_cast/uploaded_files/121205_whcoa_open_transcript.pdf.

Karoly, Lynn and Julie Zissimopoulis (2004), *Self-Employment and the 50+ Population*, Washington, DC: AARP Public Policy Institute.

Knowledge@Wharton (2004), 'Redefining retirement in the 21st century', 16 June, accessed 12 April 2007 at http://knowledge.wharton.upenn.edu/index.cfm?fa=viewfeature&id=996.

Lahey, Joanna N. (2005), 'Do older workers face discrimination?', Boston College Center for Retirement Research issue brief no. 33, Chestnut Hill, MA.

Laitner, John P. and Dmitriy Stolyarov (2005), 'Technological progress and worker productivity at different ages', University of Michigan Retirement Research Center working paper 2005-107, Ann Arbor, MI.

Lawson, Sandra (2005), '60 Is the new 55: how the G6 can mitigate the burden of aging', presentation at Idea Exchange, AARP Global Aging Program, Washington, DC, 30 November.

Leonesio, Michael V. (1990), 'The effects of the Social Security Earnings Test on labor-market activity of older Americans: a review of the evidence', *Social Security Bulletin*, **53** (5), 2–21.

Loughran, David and Steven Haider (2005), 'Do the elderly respond to taxes on earnings? Evidence from the Social Security Earnings Test', RAND Labor and Population working paper WR-223, Santa Monica, CA, accessed at www.rand.org/pubs/working_papers/2005/RAND_WR223.pdf.

Manton, Kenneth G. and XiLiang Gu (2001), 'Changes in the prevalence of disability in the United States black and nonblack population above age 65 from 1982 to 1999', *Proceedings of the National Academy of Sciences*, **98** (11), 6354–9.

Metlife Foundation/Civic Ventures (2005), *New Face of Work Survey*, San Francisco, CA: Civic Ventures.

Morrow-Howell, Nancy, James Hin and Michael Sherraden (eds) (2001), *Productive Aging: Concepts and Challenges*, Baltimore, MD: Johns Hopkins University Press.

Mulvey, Janemarie and Steven Nyce (2004), *Strategies to Retain Older Workers*, University of Pennsylvania, The Wharton School, Pension Research Council working paper PRC WP 2004-13, Philadelphia.

Munnell, Alicia H., Kevin E. Cahill and Natalia A. Jivan (2003), 'How has the shift to 401(k)s affected the retirement age?', Boston College Center for Retirement Research issues in brief IB #13, Chestnut Hill, MA.

National Center for Health Statistics (2005), *Health, United States, 2005*, Hyattsville, MD: National Center for Health Statistics.

National Research Council and Institute of Medicine (2004), *Health and Safety Needs of Older Workers*, Washington, DC: National Academies Press.

Neumark, David (2001), 'Age discrimination legislation in the United States', National Bureau of Economic Research working paper 8152, Cambridge, MA.

Organisation for Economic Co-operation and Development (OECD) (2005a), *Ageing and Employment Policies: United States*, Paris: OECD.

OECD (2005b), *Live Longer, Work Longer*, Paris: OECD.

Quinn, Joseph F. (1998), 'New paths to retirement,' paper presented at the Pension Research Council Conference Forecasting Retirement Needs and Retirement Wealth, Wharton School, University of Pennsylvania, Philadelphia, 27–28 April.

Quinn, Joseph F. (1999), 'Retirement patterns and bridge jobs in the 1990s,' Employee Benefit Research Institute issue brief no. 206, Washington, DC.

Rebick, Marcus (1993), 'The Japanese approach to finding jobs for older people,' in Olivia S. Mitchell (ed.), *As the Workforce Ages*, Ithaca, NY: ILR Press.

Reynolds, Scott, Neil Ridley and Carl E. Van Horn (2005), *A Work-Filled Retirement: Workers' Changing Views on Employment and Leisure*, Newark, NJ: Rutgers University John J. Heldrich Center for Workforce Development.

Rix, Sara E. (1999), 'Social Security reform: rethinking retirement-age policy (A look at raising Social Security's retirement age)', AARP Public Policy Institute issue brief no. 40, Washington, DC.

Rogers, Elizabeth and William J. Wiatrowski (2005), 'Injuries, illnesses, and fatalities among older workers', *Monthly Labor Review*, **128** (10), 24–30.

Rowe, John W. and Robert Kahn (1998), *Successful Aging*, Baltimore, MD: Johns Hopkins University Press.

Sass, Steven A. (2003), 'Reforming the US retirement income system: the growing role of work', Boston College Center for Retirement Research global brief no. 1, Chestnut Hill, MA.

Sincavage, Jessica R. (2004), 'The labor force and unemployment: three generations of change,' *Monthly Labor Review*, **127** (10), 34–41.

Social Security Administration (2005), *Income of the Population 55 or Older, 2002*, Washington, DC: Social Security Administration.

Social Security and Medicare Boards of Trustees (2007), *Status of the Social Security and Medicare Programs: A Summary of the 2007 Annual Reports*, accessed at www.socialsecurity.gov/OACT/TRSUM/trsummary.html.

Song, Jae G. (2003/2004), 'Evaluating the initial impact of eliminating the social security earnings test,' *Social Security Bulletin*, **56** (1), 1–15.

Sterns, Harvey L. and Michael A. McDaniel (1994), 'Job performance and the older worker', in Sara E. Rix (ed.), *Older Workers: How Do They Measure Up?*, Washington, DC: AARP.

Taylor, Humphrey (2002), *The New Vision of Retirement is Very Different Than the Traditional Image of Retirement*, Rochester, NY: The Harris Poll.

Toossi, Mitra (2002), 'A century of change: the US labor force, 1950–2050', *Monthly Labor Review*, **125** (5), 15–28.

Toossi, Mitra (2004), 'Labor force projections to 2012: the graying of the US workforce', *Monthly Labor Review*, **127** (2), 37–57.

Toossi, Mitra (2005), 'Labor force projections to 2014: retiring boomers', *Monthly Labor Review*, **128** (11), 25–44.

US Congress, Congressional Budget Office (1993), *Displaced Workers: Trends in the 1980s and Implications for the Future*, Washington, DC: Congressional Budget Office.

US Congress, Congressional Budget Office (2004a), *Retirement Age and the Need for Saving*, Washington, DC: Congressional Budget Office.

US Congress, Congressional Budget Office (2004b), *Disability and Retirement: The Exit of Baby Boomers from the Labor Force*, Washington, DC: Congressional Budget Office.

US Congress, Congressional Budget Office (2005), 'Updated long-term projections for Social Security', accessed 12 April 2007 at www.cbo.gov/showdoc.cfm?index=6064&sequence=0.

US Department of Commerce, Bureau of the Census, Housing and Household Economic Statistics Division (2005), 'Health insurance coverage: 2004 – highlights', accessed 12 April 2007 at www.census.gov/hhes/www/hlthins/hlthin04/hlth04asc.html.

US Department of Health and Human Services, National Institute on Aging (1993), 'Health and Retirement Study', press release, 17 June, Washington, DC.

US Department of Labor, Bureau of Labor Statistics (1976), *Employment and Earnings*, **22** (1), Washington, DC: US Government Printing Office.

US Department of Labor, Bureau of Labor Statistics (1981), *Employment and Earnings*, **28** (1), Washington, DC: US Government Printing Office.

US Department of Labor, Bureau of Labor Statistics (1985), *Handbook of Labor Statistics*, Washington, DC: US Government Printing Office.

US Department of Labor, Bureau of Labor Statistics (1986), *Employment and Earnings*, **33** (1), Washington, DC: US Government Printing Office.

US Department of Labor, Bureau of Labor Statistics (1991), *Employment and Earnings*, **38** (1), Washington, DC: US Government Printing Office.

US Department of Labor, Bureau of Labor Statistics (1996), *Employment and Earnings*, **43** (1), Washington, DC: US Government Printing Office.

US Department of Labor, Bureau of Labor Statistics (2001), *Employment and Earnings*, **48** (1), Washington, DC: US Government Printing Office.

US Department of Labor, Bureau of Labor Statistics (2002), 'Worker displacement, 1999–2001', news release, USDL 02-483.

US Department of Labor, Bureau of Labor Statistics (2004a), 'Worker displacement, 2001–03', news release, USDL 04-1381.

US Department of Labor, Bureau of Labor Statistics (2004b), 'Volunteering in the United States, 2004', news release, USDL 04-2503.

US Department of Labor, Bureau of Labor Statistics (2005a), 'Contingent and alternative employment arrangements, February 2005', news release, USDL 05-1433.

US Department of Labor, Bureau of Labor Statistics (2005b), *Employment and Earnings*, **52** (1), Washington, DC: US Government Printing Office.

US General Accounting Office (2001), *Older Workers: Demographic Trends Pose Challenges for Employers and Workers*, GAO-02-85, Washington, DC: US General Accounting Office.

US General Accounting Office (2003), *Older Workers: Employment Assistance Focuses on Subsidized Jobs and Job Search, but Revised Performance Measures Could Improve Access to Other Services*, GAO-03-350, Washington, DC: US General Accounting Office.

US Government Accountability Office (2005), *Older Workers: Labor Can Help Employers and Employees Plan Better for the Future*, GAO-06-80, Washington, DC: US Government Accountability Office.

Walker, David M. (2005), 'A look at our future: when baby boomers retire,' remarks presented before the 2005 White House Conference on Aging, Washington, DC,

12 December, accessed 12 April 2007 at www.gao.gov/cghome/whitehouse walker 1205/index.html.

Watson Wyatt Worldwide (1999), *Phased Retirement: Reshaping the End of Work*, Washington, DC: Watson Wyatt Worldwide.

Watson Wyatt Worldwide (2004), *Phased Retirement: Aligning Employer Programs with Worker Preferences*, Washington, DC: Watson Wyatt Worldwide, accessed 12 April 2007 at www.watsonwyatt.com/research/printable.asp?id=w-731.

Yakoboski, Paul (1998), 'Debunking the retirement policy myth: lifetime jobs never existed for most workers', Employee Benefit Research Institute issue brief no. 197, Washington, DC.

Yakoboski, Paul and Jennifer Dickemper (1997), 'Increased saving but little planning: results of the 1997 Retirement Confidence Survey', Employee Benefit Research Institute issue brief no. 191, Washington, DC.

6.   Labour market policies regarding older workers in the Netherlands

Kène Henkens and Joop Schippers

INTRODUCTION

In their capacity as macro-level actors, the Dutch Government and social partners are aware of the need to raise the labour force participation of older workers (see, among others, SER, 1999). That is why at the Lisbon summit in 2000 the Government enthusiastically endorsed the so-called Lisbon targets to promote the labour force participation of older workers. Even though participation of older workers has increased during the last few years it is still below the target level of 50 per cent. Von Nordheim-Nielsen (2005) states that without the active support and commitment from employers, trade unions and older workers themselves, employment rates are unlikely to improve sufficiently. Recent research demonstrates that workers in Europe increasingly anticipate working longer than is currently the case (Velladics et al., 2006). However at the same time it also shows that the vast majority of older workers themselves still like and expect to retire years before the official retirement age (for instance, Van Dalen and Henkens, 2002, 2005; Heyma, 2001). Dutch government policy during the last decade has primarily been aimed at discouraging the use of different routes to exit the labour market by increasing the 'exit-penalty' in terms of replacement rates. Much less attention has been given to employer behaviour, the focus of this chapter. Most decisions on how to deal with the ageing of the workforce will have to be taken by individual organizations, or will, at least, be implemented within these organizations. Earlier research among employers carried out in the USA and several European countries shows that many employers tend to be biased towards older workers and there is often a lack of corporate focus on older employees, reflecting an absence of programmes to retain and retrain them (Barth et al., 1993; Chui et al., 2001; Guillemard et al., 1996; Henkens, 2005; Taylor and Walker, 1998). Particularly when economic prospects are poor, older workers find themselves in a vulnerable position, since early retirement is often seen as a less painful way to prune the workforce than large-scale layoffs.

POLICY BACKGROUND

Intertwining Demographic and Labour Market Developments

The decline in participation rates among older workers cannot be seen in isolation from structural developments in the Dutch labour market. From the beginning of the 1970s, large cohorts of the so-called baby boom generation entered the labour market. In the same period, women's labour market behaviour started to change dramatically due to industrial modernization. Women's employment in the Netherlands has been characterized by a radical and rapid change over recent decades (Hartog and Theeuwes, 1985; Henkens *et al.*, 2002; Vlasblom and Schippers, 2004). Figure 6.1 shows the dramatic change in the age and sex composition of the Dutch labour force.

The large baby boom cohorts and the structural increase in female labour participation provided an abundant supply of labour throughout the last quarter of the twentieth century. The more or less permanent situation of excess supply in the labour market allowed employers to deal with workers relatively 'carelessly'; a little 'scratch' or 'scar' was enough to discard a worker, as enough replacements were readily available. This careless dismissal policy on the part of employers put pressure on the government to provide obsolete workers, the formally unemployed, disabled or early retired, with sufficient income. Especially when macroeconomic policy was still governed by Keynesian ideas, the purchasing power argument contributed heavily to the plea for high replacement rates.

Also, developments on the demand side of the labour market contributed to the tendency to replace older cohorts of workers with younger cohorts. Increased global interconnectedness has led to the need for flexibilization and rationalization of production processes. As a result of technological developments, there has been increasing demand for workers able to apply new knowledge and a reduced demand for unskilled workers. While workers with up-to-date knowledge were found primarily among people who had recently left education, unskilled workers were overrepresented among older and mid-career workers. They needed to adapt to new developments or risk being put out on the street together with the obsolete vintages of capital goods. In recent studies, it has been argued that globalization creates more labour market insecurity for vulnerable groups like youth and ethnic minorities (Blossfeld *et al.*, 2006). A similar effect may be operating for the old, not only because they are more likely to be unskilled, but also because if they are skilled, they may be less able to adjust to new technologies.

The confrontation of changes in labour supply and labour demand is reflected in a sharp increase in unemployment from 1975 which lasted until

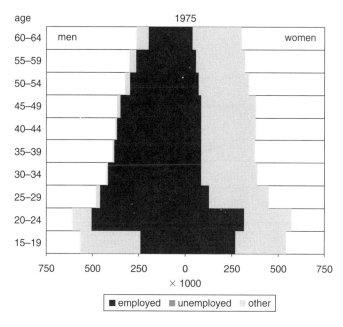

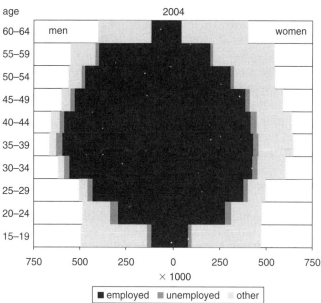

Figure 6.1   Age and sex composition of the working age population and working population, 1975, upper panel, and 2004, lower panel

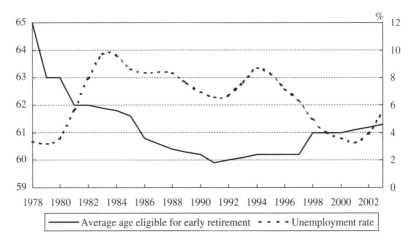

Figure 6.2   Unemployment rate and average age at which older workers are eligible for early retirement, 1978–2002

the mid-1980s (see Figure 6.2). The introduction and extension of early retirement regulations as a response to the rapid increase of unemployment at the beginning of the 1980s, part of the so-called 1982 Wassenaar Agreement between employers' organizations, trade unions and the Government (Remery *et al.*, 2002), is visible in the decrease of the average age at which workers were eligible for early retirement.

More so than in other European countries, government policies in the Netherlands were specifically aimed at increasing employment opportunities for newcomers to the labour market. Efforts to decrease youth unemployment, another part of the Wassenaar Agreement, went hand in hand with indications that many older workers had difficulties coping. Many had been employed since the Second World War in demanding jobs. The dominant exit culture was and is reinforced by strong seniority based salary systems. As a result, employers are not inclined to hire or train older workers. Participation in training decreases quickly after age 40 (Ester *et al.*, 2003) and prospects of re-entering employment after a spell of unemployment are small. The mobility of older workers is dominated by exit mobility (retirement).

So, the intertwining of demographic and labour market developments in the Netherlands resulted in an early exit culture, which was realized through a complex system of early exit pathways. Government financially supported early retirement experiments because of the expected social consequences: positive effects on youth employment and greater freedom of choice for older workers. From the employers' viewpoint, however, the job opportunity argument in favour of early retirement was of secondary importance.

Employers regarded early retirement an effective means of gradually disposing of relatively expensive, less productive employees leading to a reduction or rejuvenation of the staff group.

Pathways Out of the Labour Market

The three most important pathways out of the labour market have been (and still are) early retirement, disability and unemployment. The first early retirement schemes were introduced in 1976, providing employees with the opportunity to terminate their jobs voluntarily before reaching the pensionable age of 65. Initial experiments were aimed at the education and construction sectors. Other branches of industry soon followed. Such schemes were based on collective agreements between trade unions and employers both at sector and firm levels. Workers and employers shared the costs through a pay-as-you-go system.

Employers who wanted to get rid of (particularly older) workers for whom no early retirement scheme was available often used two welfare pathways to non-employment: disability and unemployment schemes. The disability route, in particular, was frequently used to lay off older workers. The use of this scheme not only for medical but also for labour market reasons was 'legitimized' by the social partners and government (de Vroom, 2004).

Growth in the number of workers participating in one of the disability schemes to almost one million at the beginning of the 1990s in combination with the need to cut back welfare state expenditure resulted in a first attempt to close off one of the popular pathways out of the labour market. During several steps, and not without considerable industrial unrest, disability benefits have been reduced, the criteria to enter a disability scheme have become more stringent and several penalties have been introduced into the system to discourage employers to 'dump' workers (Klosse, 2003). Altogether these measures have been rather successful. The inflow of workers into disability arrangements had fallen dramatically by the turn of the century and has further declined since then.

Earlier research, however, had already pointed out that the three pathways out of the labour market are not independent: restrictions in one irrevocably result in an increase in another (Van Imhoff and Henkens, 1998). So, closing the disability gateway out of the labour market resulted in more pressure on arrangements in the areas of unemployment and early retirement, respectively. That is why, in recent years, the Government in its attempts to increase older workers' labour force participation has directed its arrows at these other arrangements (de Vries, 2005). Tax law changes have brought a halt to public financial support for pay-as-you-go based early retirement schemes. Currently, most branches of industry can still utilize early retirement, but based on an actuarial system which, put briefly, means that the earlier workers want to retire the higher price they have to pay in terms of lower benefits. The shift from pay-as-you-go based early retirement schemes to actuarial schemes has been supported by Dutch unions, partly in response to decreasing intergenerational solidarity. With growing attention to the problems of dejuvenation and ageing, younger cohorts of workers have become more aware of the risk that they, aged in their 50s or 60s, may no longer benefit from the fruits of early retirement arrangements. This has resulted in growing opposition to pay-as-you-go based early retirement schemes.

So, after blocking this second road into early retirement the Government could concentrate on the third and final one: that of unemployment schemes. Blocking this route has been one of the main goals of the conservative cabinet that was in office in the Netherlands between 2002 and 2007. Once again, one sees a picture of more stringent rules and lower benefits. Added to this is a requirement that older workers (aged 57.5 plus) seek work after they become unemployed.

Looking at the development of participation rates of older men and women over the years (see Figure 6.3) one might conclude that Dutch policies regarding active ageing, in the sense of working longer and retiring later, have been rather successful. The trend towards ever lower participation rates for older workers has been reversed. Particularly during the second half of the 1990s there was a sharp increase among older men and women.

In order not to overstate the impact of policy measures one should keep in mind, however, that this same period has witnessed one of the biggest booms of the post-war Dutch economy, with many industries facing severe staff shortages (Remery *et al.*, 2003, Henkens *et al.*, 2005) and abundant job opportunities for almost all workers. Even so, despite the buoyant economy, research shows that older workers were still at the end of the job queue (Remery *et al.*, 2003). Moreover, after economic decline set in around 2003 many older workers found that they were first in line to be laid off and that employers were disinclined to hire them. Older workers continue to be confronted with employment discrimination. The number of unemployed persons aged 55–65 tripled between 2002 and 2006. And since all pathways out of the labour market have been 'sobered down' (as it is often called in policy documents) they now offer less protection against poverty than they used to. As a result, being laid off, becoming (partly) disabled or using an early retirement scheme much more often results in older workers dropping below the poverty line than was the case one or two decades ago.

So, it is time to shift focus and try to understand how employers deal with changing social security regulations and the ageing of their workforces. This is the key to developing successful and sustainable activating policies in the

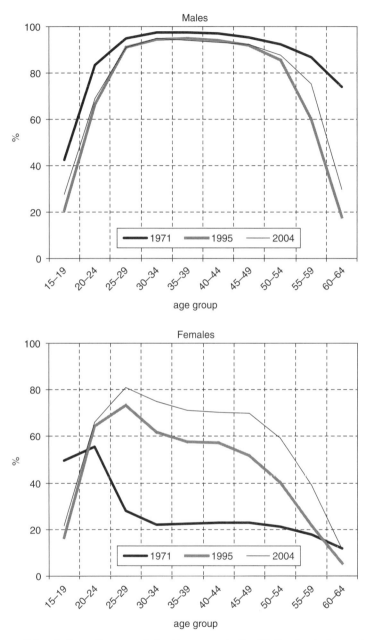

Figure 6.3   Labour force participation rates in the Netherlands for males, upper panel, and females, lower panel for 1971, 1995 and 2004

long run. In the second part of this contribution we present results of two surveys that were carried out in 2000 among 1000 organizations and in 2005 among 600 organizations (for details see Remery *et al.*, 2003; van Dacen *et al.*, 2006). These surveys offer the opportunity to consider employer behaviour towards older workers in the Netherlands between 2000 and 2005. In 2000 the Dutch labour market was characterized by increasing labour shortages and the lowest level of unemployment in more than two decades. By 2005 the situation had changed drastically with rates returning to levels not seen since the early 1990s.

THE IMPLICATIONS OF AGEING

In 2000 and 2005 an overwhelming majority of respondents (about 75 per cent) tended to associate an increase in the average age of their workforce with higher labour costs. The bottom line of Table 6.1 shows that a far smaller percentage of employers expected an increase in productivity: a mere 7 per cent said they found this (very) likely. Employers also tended to look upon older staff as employees with a high level of absenteeism and a resistance to change (more than 50 per cent in both years). Half the respondents also felt that the way in which work was organized would have to be reviewed, that working conditions would have to be improved and that ageing would have negative consequences for adaptation to new technology.

A small group of employers felt that an ageing workforce would have a negative effect on the company's image. More than half the respondents,

Table 6.1   Expected consequences of an ageing workforce 2000 and 2005 (%)

Consequences	2000	2005
Increase in labour costs	73	77
Greater resistance to change	57	56
Increase in absenteeism	56	53
Increase in know-how and experience	55	61
Review of the way in which work is organized	52	46
Need to improve working conditions	50	46
Less enthusiasm for new technology	50	44
Fewer conflicts within the organization	15	13
Negative effect on organization's image	15	16
Increase in productivity	7	7

Source: Employers survey, 2000 and 2005.

however, expected that an increase in the average age of their workforce would result in an increase in know-how and experience. About fifteen per cent believed that an ageing workforce would result in less conflict.

An important conclusion we can draw from Table 6.1 is that, despite changing labour market conditions and increasing participation rates of older people, employers' views are very stable. Differences in perceived consequences of ageing prove to be very small over the years, and also the ranking of consequences is almost the same. These results suggest that stereotypical views regarding older workers are relatively stable and do not easily change in response to changing economic conditions or the composition of the workforce (see Henkens, 2005).

MEASURES FOR OLDER WORKERS

One of the aims of both surveys was to study the degree to which employers were taking steps to improve the employability of older workers. Respondents were presented with a list of measures and asked to indicate whether their organization was implementing these measures, or was considering doing so. The list was based on an earlier study into age-conscious personnel policies (Schaeps and Klaassen, 1999). Table 6.2 presents the results for 2000 and 2005.

Comparing the results for the years 2000 and 2005 suggests that employers cut back on their policies towards older workers. They may have done so for business reasons. This reversal, however, might also be the result of the introduction of a law banning all forms of age discrimination in the labour market in 2004. Strict court rulings have resulted in the abolition of a whole series of benefits for and protective measures designed for older workers. In 2005 the number of organizations that provided flexible working hours and training programmes decreased. Moreover accommodating measures such as ergonomic improvements and initiatives geared towards the reduction of workload were reduced. In both years the most widely implemented measures were found to be measures aimed at accommodating older staff. Ergonomic measures were implemented by a majority of employers. Additional leave/increased holiday entitlement for older staff was also common, as were measures such as part-time early retirement or part-time pre-pension and flexible working hours. Measures such as introducing age limits for irregular work/shift work, exemptions from working overtime for older workers, and reducing the workload for older staff were slightly less common, but were nevertheless implemented by between one third and two-fifths of employers. Moving older workers to posts at a lower level with an accompanying loss of salary, commonly

Table 6.2 *Degree to which employers implemented measures, or were considering implementing measures, aimed at older staff in 2000 and 2005 (%)*

Measures	2000		2005	
	Is being implemented	Is being or will be considered	Is being implemented	Is being or will be considered
Part-time early retirement/part-time pre-pension	51	27	47	29
Additional leave/ increased holiday entitlement	62	21	57	27
Prolonged career interruptions	12	34	10	34
Age limits for irregular work	35	22	31	26
Exemption from working overtime for older workers	34	32	29	33
Flexible working hours	47	32	21	23
Training programmes for older workers	21	46	13	47
Reducing workload for older workers	41	44	33	52
Reducing older workers to a lower rank and a loss of salary (demotion)	7	38	6	41
Ergonomic measures	65	22	50	38

Source: Employer survey, 2000 and 2005.

known as demotion, was found among less than one in ten organizations. While 8 per cent of respondents did not implement any of these age conscious policy measures in 2000, the percentage was 17 per cent in 2005. As for the measures that employers said they were considering, or said they might consider implementing in the near future, training programmes topped the list in both years, followed by workload reduction for older workers. These relatively high percentages indicate that many employers anticipate that their ageing workforces, or the prospect of an ageing workforce, may necessitate adjustments of personnel policies. Demotion may also become a more popular option, with almost two-fifths of respondents stating they were considering this possibility. Having said that, it should be noted that demotion was also a measure that a majority of employers said they did not intend implementing.

Note that the measures presented to the respondents were not all geared specifically to the situation of older staff. Some of the measures were of a more general nature. The possibility of interrupting one's career for a prolonged period of time, and more flexible working hours, could, for example, be implemented to support people who want to combine a job with childcare. In practice, it is mainly women who wish or need to do so. Research has shown that measures such as prolonged career interruptions and flexible working hours are more common in organizations that employ relatively large numbers of women (den Dulk, 2001).

The general picture that emerges from the table is that of a relatively large number of employers already implementing elements of an age-conscious personnel policy. This observation needs to be qualified, however. First of all, we must not forget that popular measures such as part-time early retirement, age limits for irregular work and flexible working hours tend to be part and parcel of collective labour agreements (CLAs) in the Netherlands. Recent research has shown, for example, that 87 per cent of CLAs offer employees one or more opportunities to retire early (that is, before the mandatory retirement age of 65) and 68 per cent include a provision under which older workers may be exempted from working irregular hours (Schaeps and Klaassen, 1999). Although the details of CLAs were not addressed in the survey, the results show that companies that had negotiated collective agreements were more apt to implement the measures mentioned than companies that had not committed themselves to a collective agreement. Note also that the most widely implemented measures tend to be those that 'spare' older workers (fewer obligations and more privileges) such as additional leave, increased holiday entitlement, a workload reduction, age limits for irregular work, or an exemption from working overtime. These measures are often costly and reduce the employability of older staff. Employees who make use of schemes enabling them to take part-time early retirement partially withdraw from the labour force, whereas most of them would have remained full-time employed otherwise (see Ghent *et al.*, 2002). This tends to incur additional costs for employers without providing anything in return. A measure that does generate returns is the option of offering older staff training. This measure tends to improve employability and keep older workers on the staff, whether part-time or full-time, whilst at the same time generating income for the employer. Only one-fifth of the companies studied had adopted this measure, however. Almost half the employers said they were considering implementing this measure or expected they would in the future, but approximately one-third were not enthusiastic, and said they would not consider this possibility. As said, the 2004 law against age discrimination has resulted in a lot of uncertainty with respect to the question of what measures still can and what measures primarily regarding older workers can not be utilized any longer.

The foregoing sections have shown that while employers are increasingly confronted with ageing workforces, measures designed specifically at retaining older staff have been given relatively little attention, at least for the time-being. A common assumption is that growing labour shortages are the best assurance that the participation of older people in the labour force will be stimulated, even though more pessimistic prophets warn that the transfer of many jobs to Asian countries like India and China might reduce labour demand and future labour shortages will not become a reality. In a tight labour market, the urge to lay off large numbers of older staff tends to decrease. Does this however also mean that employers are increasingly targeting older workers when recruiting new staff? Or do they perhaps prefer to recruit other categories of employees? These questions will be addressed in the following section.

OLDER WORKERS IN THE JOB QUEUE

The Dutch labour market changed from a 'sellers' market' in 2000 to a 'buyers' market' by 2005. Table 6.3 shows that in 2000 employers used a wide range of measures to attract potential employees.

The answer given most frequently in 2000 was recruiting more women (51 per cent). Measures such as improving the employability of staff (44 per cent) and reintegrating the partially disabled (38 per cent) were also widely implemented. This latter option was, moreover, being considered by another 42 per cent of employers. Among measures being considered by employers, offering employees higher pay and/or better employment conditions scored highest, followed closely by encouraging staff to continue working until the age of 65. This latter measure was being implemented by no more than 12 per cent of employers. Offering higher wages to retain or recruit personnel was being implemented by one-third (34 per cent) of employers. Moving production abroad was not seen as an option for most employers and recruiting personnel abroad to alleviate staff shortages was not being considered by almost three-quarters of employers. Replacing employees by labour-saving technology was not considered a viable option by most respondents: one quarter had done so already, one third were considering doing so, but almost half did not place much faith in this solution. This result is surprising given recent wage trends. It appears that the majority of

Table 6.3 *Measures taken by organizations in response to current or near-term staff shortages in 2000 and 2005 (%)*

Measures	2000		2005	
	Is being implemented	Is being or will be considered	Is being implemented	Is being or will be considered
Increasing the employability of workers	44	40	41	49
Substituting technology for labour	21	29	18	34
Encouraging workers to continue working until the age of 65	12	44	12	52
Relocating production capacity abroad	4	5	3	7
Reintegrating the disabled	38	42	26	42
Recruiting more women workers	51	18	21	23
Offering higher wages	34	48	9	43
Recruiting more older workers	19	39	8	39
Recruiting staff from abroad	10	17	6	17
Calling back retired employees or staff who have taken early retirement	10	21	3	13

Source: Employers survey, 2000 and 2005.

those surveyed did not see the pay rises agreed in various collective wage agreements and the labour shortages in the market as an incentive to go in search of new labour-saving and productivity-enhancing technologies. Here we should add, however, that for a large group of our respondents, possibilities for introducing new technology are rather limited (for instance, for municipalities, employers in the care sector). The same holds for moving production abroad.

Surprisingly, even in the tight Dutch labour market of 2000 very few employers saw older staff as a potential pool of labour. No more than 12 per cent of all organizations encouraged their employees to continue working until they were 65, although a substantial number (46 per cent) said they were considering, or would consider doing so. Although no more than one in five employers were found to be actively recruiting older workers, over two-fifths saw this as a possible option aimed at preventing staff shortages. Having said that, an equally large percentage said they would not be prepared to recruit older workers if they actually suffered staff shortages. Calling back retired employees or staff who had taken early retirement appears to be even less of an option. A mere 10 per cent of employers were already doing so, and less than a quarter said they would consider doing so.

If we compare the results of 2005 with 2000 we see a strong decrease in the percentages of employers wanting to recruit more female workers and disabled workers. One should realize, however, that female participation rates have increased so much during the last decade (especially among younger cohorts of women) that this pool of additional labour supply is quickly running dry. The share of employers opting for the recruitment of older workers fell from 19 per cent in 2000 to only 8 per cent in 2005. The ranking of workers from the non-standard categories remained the same, with the position of older workers almost at the bottom end. Also interesting to note is the marked fall in the percentage of employers offering higher wages: from 34 per cent in 2000 to 9 per cent in 2005.

CONCLUSIONS

Active ageing, in the sense of working longer and retiring later, is a core Government policy priority in the Netherlands. Over the last decade a large number of reforms of exit pathways have been implemented and new reforms are planned (Reday-Mulvey and Velladics, 2005). Together with an upswing of the Dutch economy, which resulted in a reduction of lay-offs of older workers, participation rates increased substantially. Moreover, younger cohorts of female workers no longer leave the labour market after childbearing, but remain employed, also at a more advanced age. As such, Dutch policies proved to be successful in reversing the exit trend, although European targets to delay the average exit age by five years in the near future will not be met. One of the impediments is the gap between the macro-level rationality to raise older workers' participation rates and the micro-level rationality of individual workers and individual employers who often still support the exit culture. This chapter has shown that, while active ageing is an issue prominent on the Government's agenda, it is seldom a priority within organizations.

The results of surveys carried out in 2000 and 2005 show that employers view the ageing process of their workforce with concern about increasing labour costs without increasing productivity. Few personnel policies are targeted at the delay of retirement age and recruitment preferences and behaviours are biased against older workers. Older people are at the end of the job queue, after other categories of employees. Many employers are only inclined to recruit older workers where no other candidates are available. This brings us to the flipside of the coin of increasing participation rates in the Netherlands. Workers may be better off in terms of protection against forced early exit from the labour force on the one hand. However those workers that fall out of employment despite restrictions to exit may be less well off, not only in terms of financial benefits, but also in terms of prospects to re-enter the labour force.

Active ageing, in terms of stimulating people to remain active in some way after retirement from the labour market, is not an issue of Dutch government policy at all. From a policy perspective the so-called *pensionados* have only a twofold role: they receive their monthly state pension and they consume services from the health sector. In its Life Course Policy Report from 2002 (SZW, 2002) the Government recognized that the gap between the mandatory retirement age of 65 and the average age up to which people remain relatively healthy is growing and that a lot of talent and capabilities remain unused. Only recently some scientists, NGOs and one of the Government's advisory councils have raised the question whether modern society can and should afford to leave this resource unused and, if not, how to organize older people's contribution to society. This first round of discussions has resulted in so much opposition already that it remains to be seen whether the Netherlands shall ever see the first concrete measure on active ageing after retirement.

REFERENCES

Barth, Michael C., William McNaught and Philip Rizzi (1993), 'Corporations and the aging workforce', in Philip H. Mirvis (ed.), *Building the Competitive Workforce: Investing in Human Capital for Corporate Success*, New York: John Wiley and Sons, pp. 156–200.

Blossfeld, H.P., S. Buchholz and D. Hofäcker (eds) (2006), *Globalization, Uncertainty and Late Careers in Society*, London: Routledge.

Chiu, W.C.K., A.W. Chan, E. Snape and T. Redman (2001), 'Age stereotypes and discriminatory attitudes towards older workers: an East-West comparison', *Human Relations*, **54** (5), 629–61.

Dalen, H.P. van and K. Henkens (2002), 'Early retirement reform. Can it and will it work?' *Ageing and Society*, **22** (2), 209–31.

Dalen, H.P. van and K. Henkens (2005), 'The double standard in retirement and work – the case of the Netherlands', *Geneva Papers of Risk and Insurance, Issues and Practice*, **30**, 693–710.

Dulk, L. den (2001), *Work-family Arrangements in Organisations. A Cross-national Study in the Netherlands, Italy, the United Kingdom and Sweden*, Rotterdam: Rozenberg Publishers.

Ester, P., R. Muffels and J. Schippers (eds) (2003), *De organisatie en de oudere werknemer*, Bussum: Coutinho.

Ghent, L.S., S.G. Allen and R.L. Clark (2001), 'The impact of a new phased retirement option on faculty retirement decision', *Research on Aging*, **23** (4), 671–93.

Guillemard, A., P. Taylor and A. Walker (1996), 'Managing an ageing workforce in Britain and France', *Geneva Papers on Risk and Insurance*, **21** (4), 478–501.

Hartog, J. and J. Theeuwes (1985), 'The emergence of the working wife in Holland', *Journal of Labour Economics*, **3** (1 Pt 2), 235–55.

Henkens, K. (2005), 'Stereotyping older workers and retirement: the managers' point of view', *Canadian Journal on Aging*, **24** (4), 35–48.

Henkens, K., Y. van der Grift and J. Siegers (2002), 'Changes in female labour supply in the Netherlands 1989–1998: the case of married and cohabiting women', *European Journal of Population*, **18** (1), 39–57.

Heyma, Arjan (2001), *Dynamic Models of Labour Force Retirement. An Empirical Analysis of Early Exit in the Netherlands*, Amsterdam: Tinbergen Institute and University of Amsterdam.

Imhoff, E. van and K. Henkens (1998), 'The budgetary dilemmas of an aging workforce: a scenario analysis for the public sector in the Netherlands', *European Journal of Population*, **14** (1), 39–59.

Klosse, Saskia (2003), *Moderne sociale zekerheid: efficiency met behoud van fundamentele waarden*, Maastricht: Oratie Maastricht University.

Reday-Mulvey, G. and K. Velladics (2005), 'Employment of older workers in the Netherlands: recent reforms', *European Papers on the New Welfare*, **1** (May), 110–16.

Remery, C., K. Henkens, J.J. Schippers and P. Ekamper (2003), 'Managing an aging workforce and a tight labour market: views held by Dutch employers', *Population Research and Policy Review*, **22** (1), 21–40.

Remery, C., A. van Doorne-Huiskes and J.J. Schippers (2002), 'Labour market flexibility in the Netherlands: looking for winners and losers', *Work, Employment and Society*, **16** (3), 477–96.

Schaeps, M.J.M. and C. Klaassen (1999), *Ouderenbeleid. Een Onderzoek naar Maatregelen in Ondernemingen en Afspraken tussen Sociale Partners met Betrekking tot de Arbeidsparticipatie van Oudere Werknemers*, The Hague: SZW/Arbeidinspectie.

Sociaal Economische Raad (SER) (1999), *Bevordering arbeidsdeelname ouderen*, Den Haag: SER.

Ministerie van Sociale Zaken en Werkgelegenheid (SZW) (2002), *Verkenning Levensloop*, Den Haag: SZW.

Taylor, P. and A. Walker (1998), 'Employers and older workers: attitudes and employment practices', *Ageing and Society*, **18** (6), 641–58.

Velladics, K., K. Henkens and H.P. van Dalen (2006), 'Do different welfare states produce different individual policy preferences? Opinions on pension reforms in Eastern and Western Europe', *Ageing and Society*, **26** (3), 475–95.

Vlasblom, J.D. and J.J. Schippers (2004), 'Increases in female labour force participation in Europe. Similarities and differences', *European Journal of Population*, **20** (4), 375–92.

Von Nordheim-Nielsen, F. (2005), 'Active ageing: a core policy priority for the European Union', *European Papers on the New Welfare*, **1** (May), 66–78.
Vries, B. de (2005), *Overmoed en onbehagen*, Amsterdam: Uitgeverij Bert Bakker.
Vroom, B. de (2004), 'The shift from early to late exit: changing institutional conditions and individual preferences: the case of the Netherlands', in Tony Maltby, Bert de Vroom, Maria-Luisa Mirabile and Einer Øverbye (eds), *Ageing and the Transition to Retirement: a Comparative Analysis of European Welfare States*, Aldershot, UK: Ashgate, pp. 120–54.

7. Pulling up the early retirement anchor in France

Anne-Marie Guillemard and Annie Jolivet
(translated from French by Noal Mellott)

OLDER WORKERS IN PROFILE

Below 30 per cent prior to the year 2000, the employment rate of 55–64 year-olds has increased since then: from 30 per cent in 2000 to 37.8 per cent in 2005.[1] Nonetheless it is premature to draw the conclusion that the situation of ageing workers has changed significantly over the past few years. The increase in the employment rate is, to a large degree, mechanical (Conseil d'Orientation des Retraites, 2004), masking, as it does, differences between men and women. Men are still leaving the world of work early, but this trend is counterbalanced by the advancing age of the larger number of working women and by persons from the baby boom generation reaching the age of 50, and thus swelling the ranks of the older age groups with those from the group with highest economic activity and employment rates (see Figure 7.1). Women still often take retirement later than men, since they have not contributed long enough to qualify for a full pension from the National Old Age Fund (CNAV) at the age of 60. For instance, three out of ten women start receiving benefits from this fund at 65, compared with one in ten men.

Early withdrawal from the labour force has been curbed considerably in recent years. Restrictions on budgeted full-time early exit through a special National Employment Fund allowance (allocation spéciale du Fonds national de l'emploi, ASFNE) have been tightened. In 2002, an end was put to the job substitution allowance (allocation de remplacement pour l'emploi, ARPE). Created in October 1995 by the UNEDIC unemployment insurance fund, it enabled workers with at least 40 years of retirement pension contributions behind them to retire before 60, on the condition that their employer took on a new worker to replace them. Recent early exit schemes have a narrow focus: CAATA (cessation anticipée d'activité des travailleurs de l'amiante, created in 1999) allows workers having been exposed to asbestos to leave the labour force from age 50; and CATS

158

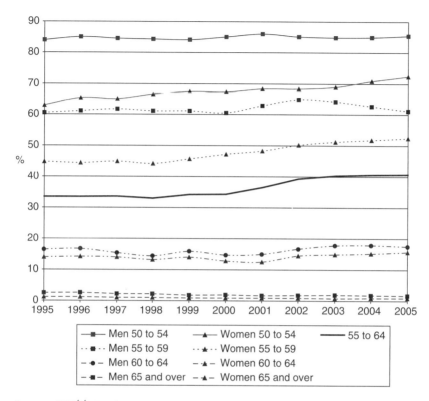

Source: INSÉÉ, *Employment survey* (yearly data prior to 2002, continuous thereafter)

Figure 7.1 Employment rates by age and gender, 1995–2005 (%)

(cessation d'activité de certains travailleurs salariés, created in 2000) allows for partial or total exit from age 55 for workers who have experienced hard working conditions, such as night- or shift-work or assembly line jobs, for a long time, or who are disabled. CATS is transitory: firms may use it for five years at most, provided that an industry-wide agreement has been reached. Several such agreements have been signed.

As public schemes for early withdrawal from the labour force have shrunk however, a growing proportion of this is shifting to unemployment (see Figure 7.2). Ageing wage-earners are more highly exposed to the risk of their jobs being cut. In 2002, persons aged 50 and over made up more than a quarter of dismissals for redundancy and more than a fifth of dismissals for 'personal' reasons (Lerais and Marioni, 2004). From 1998 to 2003, the number of waivers of the Unemployment Fund's requirement to look for work (dispense de recherche d'emploi, DRE) shot up by 40 per

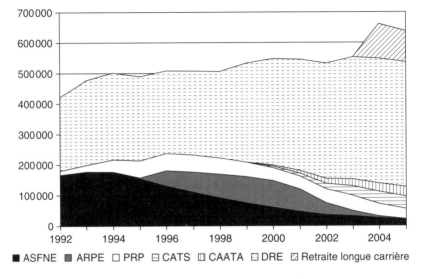

■ ASFNE ■ ARPE □ PRP ⊟ CATS ⊞ CAATA ⊡ DRE ▨ Retraite longue carrière

Sources: DARES (Ministry of Labour), UNEDIC and FCAATA.

Figure 7.2   Early exits, 1992–2005 (numbers end of December)

cent: from 280 000 to 400 000 persons. At the end of 2003, seven out of ten 'pre-retirees' were enrolled on the unemployment register but exempted from the requirement to seek work.

This fast and deep change in the institutional handling of early labour market withdrawal has increased the probability of using pathways out of the labour force that are still open. For example, the new restrictions laid down by the August 2003 Pension Reform Act, which has narrowly focused CATS on working conditions, increased the contributions to be made by a firm for its pre-retirees and raised to 65 the age when an employer can force an employee to retire, have paralleled the development of industry-wide collective agreements providing for retirement before 65, a possibility left open by the reform. Other evidence of this is an increase in long-term illness leave (especially among 55–9 year olds) and in admissions under the asbestos scheme (CAATA). The number of dismissals of 'other sorts' is also high among older wage-earners.

Although 50–64 year-olds are less affected by unemployment, thanks largely to early exit arrangements, those who are unemployed have more difficulty finding work. In 2002, persons aged over 50 represented somewhat less than 6 per cent of the new hires made by establishments employing at least ten wage-earners, even though this age group accounted for nearly 23 per cent of the economically active population (Lerais and Marioni, 2004).

Table 7.1   Long-term unemployment by age and gender (%)

Age group	Men				Women			
Year	2002	2003	2004	2005	2002	2003	2004	2005
15–29	26.0	28.2	28.1	29.5	26.5	28.4	27.4	29.3
30–49	43.9	47.1	44.9	44.6	45.7	46.5	45.6	47.1
50+	63.9	64.5	63.1	63.2	61.8	60.0	60.7	60.9
All	40.6	43.0	41.5	41.8	42.0	42.8	41.8	43.2

Source: INSÉÉ, Employment survey.

According to the ESSA survey, only one out of four establishments in 2000 hired at least one person aged over 50. Only one-third of 50-year-olds on the unemployment register find work, in contrast to half of those who are younger (Anglaret and Bernard, 2003). The older the person, the lower the prospects of leaving unemployment. Ageing wage-earners figure more often among the long-term unemployed (Table 7.1). In 2003, 62 per cent of the unemployed between the ages of 50 and 65 had been jobless for at least one year (compared with 44 per cent of the unemployed in the 25–49 age group); and 20 per cent, for at least two years. When the economy is recovering, the decrease in joblessness among older persons lags behind because of the labour market's 'selectivity'. While the number of job-seekers started tapering off in late 1997, the number of the older unemployed did not start decreasing until the second semester of 1999 (Anglaret and Bernard, 2003).

Finally, a gender-related difference must be noted in the frequency of finding work after a period of joblessness. According to UNEDIC's survey on exit from employment, women aged 50 and over have a higher rate of return to the world of work than men in the same age-group: 44 per cent versus 36 per cent in 2003. However women hold part-time jobs more frequently than men: 18 per cent versus 9 per cent (Anglaret and Bernard, 2003). Finding a job is probably more necessary for women, who are more likely than men to need to complete their pension contributions periods. For example, of the 272 200 people who had taken 'long-career' early retirement from 2004 to the first semester of 2006, 83 per cent were men. Besides this, recruitment of older workers is concentrated in sectors such as health and personal services and is often subsidized through employment policy.

This lack of momentum in the labour market for persons aged over 50 is not a new phenomenon. In 1991, their proportion among recent job hires was 5 per cent, and they represented 18 per cent of the actively employed (6 per cent and 24.3 per cent in 2004 respectively). Nonetheless the number of older people hired grew strongly and steadily from 135 000 in 1996 to

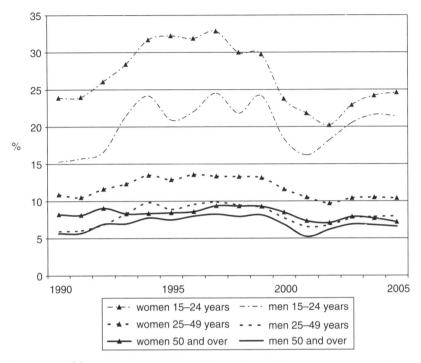

Source: INSÉÉ, *Employment survey* (annual data prior to 2002, continuous thereafter)

Figure 7.3   Average unemployment rates by age and gender (%)

248 000 in 2002. This coincides with the ageing of the economically active population.

For ageing wage-earners as for others categories of labour, overall trends in the labour market have had an impact on the sorts of jobs found. Although still less frequent than for persons aged under 30, job hires under fixed-term contracts are, since 1998, more prevalent among persons aged 50 and over than among those aged in their 30s or 40s (Lerais and Marioni, 2004). In addition 50- to 59-year-olds more often hold part-time or occasional jobs than do the middle-aged (Lainé, 2003); and more persons aged over 50 are working through temporary work agencies: 5.8 per cent in 2002 compared with 3.9 per cent in 1995.

A final point: some jobs found by the older unemployed are subsidized. Since the 1994 Act on Work, Employment and Occupational Training, unemployed people aged 50 and over are one of the target groups for labour market policy. Subsidized contracts especially benefit the older unemployed in the non-profit sector (Employment-Solidarity and Consolidated

Employment contracts, respectively, CES and CEC), but also in the for-profit sector (Initiative Employment contracts, CIE).[2] The proportion of older citizens hired under such contracts has nearly doubled since 1996. In all, 107 230 were hired or had their contracts renewed in 2002. Older women, in particular, have been swept up in this trend. One out of five jobs found by them is subsidized, three times more than for men of the same age and twice as many as for younger women (Anglaret and Bernard, 2003). This again is largely explained by the sectors recruiting older female workers.

The private sector had the same proportion of wage-earners over 50 as the public sector until the end of the 1970s. Afterwards this proportion declined owing to early exit schemes and unemployment. It has been increasing since the mid-1990s, but the difference with the public sector is still widening. In 2002, 24 per cent of employees of the state and local authorities were at least 50 years old, compared with 18 per cent in the private sector (Minni and Topiol, 2004).

The percentage of older persons among non-wage-earners is increasing: nearly 37 per cent of them were aged over 50 in 2002. This can be put down to a delayed entry in the labour market (owing to a longer period of education and the need to accumulate start-up capital), shifting back the end of the career and to the decline of certain professions (in particular, farmers). The self-employed often continue working beyond 60.

THE CURRENT ECONOMIC DEBATE ABOUT THE AGEING POPULATION

The subject of demographic ageing emerged during discussions concerning how to pay for pensions. In recent years, several studies have helped us understand better the issues raised by the ageing of the labour force. The Pension Steering Committee (Conseil d'Orientation des Retraites) set up in June 2000 had an impact on pension system reform. One of its three task forces was devoted to 'Age and Work'. Its first report to the Prime Minister in December 2001 advocated an active, comprehensive policy for employing older workers to be implemented under the leadership of the state, labour unions and employer associations.

In October 2001, the Quintreau Report to the Economic and Social Council (Conseil Économique et Social) also recommended, given predicted population changes, making increased employment among older workers a priority. It also pointed to the differential impact of demographic ageing according to regional area, linked to economic performance. In December 2002, a report by the Commissariat Général du Plan (with input from labour and management) analysed the effects of demographic ageing on future jobs and qualifications. According to the most recent figures available, the number of people taking retirement was set to increase from 480 000 per year between 2000 and 2005 and to 600 000 between 2005 and 2015. Although not all parts of the economy will be affected alike, these two reports highlighted some negative consequences: the difficulty of filling jobs in certain geographical areas or economic sectors with strong growth, competition between sectors and the risk of employment being geographically polarized.

From the foreseeable and predicted, demographic ageing is becoming visible. As of 2006, the large cohorts born between 1946 and 1973 (on average, 840 000 persons per year) are gradually reaching 60, the minimum age for drawing a full pension. They are flanked by the much smaller cohorts born before or during the Second World War and after 1973 (approximately 750 000 per year). Following a period of rejuvenation and a sharp increase in the active population during the 1960s, the advancing age of persons born during the baby boom has, since 1996, pushed the proportion of persons over 50 up from 16 per cent of the active population in 1996 to 20 per cent in 2002 (Minni and Topiol, 2004). This is no temporary situation, since these large cohorts span a 27-year period. The shock wave will last, given the size and duration of the baby-boom cohorts. The economically active population is, therefore, going to decrease by 2006–10, as the baby-boomers taking retirement outnumber persons entering the labour market. According to projections for 2003–50 made in 2001 (using the 1999 census), the working-age population (from 20 to 59 years old) started tapering off in 2006. Regardless of the hypotheses used, this decrease will continue until 2035. It will be less pronounced if immigration increases, but more pronounced if the fertility rate declines to 1.5 children per woman (compared with an average of 1.8 between 1977 and 1998 and 1.9 between 2000 and 2004). Under the baseline scenario, which assumes the continuance of previous rates of fertility, mortality and migration, the population aged from 20 to 59 years will fall by nearly three million between 2000 and 2035, down from nearly 33 million to less than 30 million. The predictions do not differ much for the 20–64 age group, except that the drop takes place five years later.

The impact of the 2003 Pension Reform Act on behaviour patterns and on older persons' employment rates is considered a strategic issue. As Table 7.2 shows, raising the employment rate of older wage-earners is, by far, the major means of increasing the size of the economically active population. Changing behaviour will also delay the date when the working-age population starts declining. In July 2006, INSÉÉ published new projections for the working-age population and the economically active population, based on revised hypotheses and taking into account the 2003 pension

Table 7.2 *Impact of various scenarios on the evolution of the labour force (000s)*

	2002	2007	2012	2020	2030	2050
Trend scenario	26,636	26,979	26,844	26,336	25,570	24,364

Gaps between the trend scenario and variant scenarios (number of additional economically active persons)

	2002	2007	2012	2020	2030	2050
Low fertility				−37	−481	−2,393
High fertility				8	275	2 103
Net migration 0		−181	−335	−629	−954	−1,572
Net migration 100 000		131	284	544	861	1,385
Low unemployment		77	129	138	138	139
High participation of women		15	55	149	282	427
Increase of the effective age of exit		266	1,065	2,724	3,533	3,429

Source: INSÉÉ and DARES, *Labour forces projections 2003–2050.*

reform. The working-age population (from 20 to 59 years old) will still peak in 2006 but will stand still afterwards. Regarding the economically active population, there will also be a stabilization following a faster increase until 2015. However the employment rate of older people is sensitive to the labour market: the lower the global unemployment rate, the higher the employment rate of 55–64-year-olds might turn out to be (Conseil d'Orientation des Retraites, 2006).

Little attention has been paid to the consequences for lifestyles of making careers longer or of putting off the decision to retire. Retirees and preretirees are said to play a major role in non-profit organizations, but no in-depth study has been made. The difficulty of providing support to ageing parents has been a topic of discussion, especially since the heatwave in 2003. Ten days of exceptionally high temperatures in the first half of August 2003 led to 15,000 deaths in France. However managing work and elder care roles has not been considered.

OLDER WORKERS AND ACTIVE AGEING

The first proposals[3] for reform advocated prolonging the duration of contributions to pension funds. During discussions preceding the 2003 Pension Reform Act, the employment of older people was taken to be a major variable in funding the pension system. The Pension Steering Committee reached a consensus about the objective of, above all, keeping people working until the age of retirement with a full pension. Bolstering employment beyond this age was not a priority, either for public authorities, or for labour unions or employers. The term 'active ageing' has not been used in public debate; little interest has been shown in it, and, when mentioned, it has not been clearly defined.

The institutional setting has evolved significantly since the year 2000. For one thing, labour and management have modified the rules of unemployment compensation. As public early exit schemes shrink, unemployment has come to typify older workers. To force firms to stop using unemployment insurance for early exit, a December 2002 agreement reduced, for the first time, the period of coverage for the older unemployed: for 50- to 55-year-olds from 45 to 23 months or, under specific conditions, 36 months. The age for receiving unemployment compensation until retirement without any phased-in reduction of benefits has risen from 55 to 57.

To transpose the 2000 European directive on equal treatment in employment, an act of 16 November 2001 recognized age discrimination. Only a few clauses in the Labour Code straightforwardly mentioned age, and there was no across the board rule against age-based discrimination. Although age did not figure in the first draft of the 2001 act on combating discrimination, it was included by the Senate, but against the Government's opinion. The prohibition on age discrimination is toned down by the phrase: 'differences of treatment are not discriminatory when they are objectively and reasonably justified by a legitimate purpose, in particular for labour market policy, and when the means used to realize it are appropriate and necessary'. Two examples of non-discriminatory behaviour are cited: prohibiting access to jobs or implementing working conditions in order to protect young and older employees; and fixing a maximum age for recruitment because of the training or on-the-job experience necessary for a job or because of the time remaining until retirement. The second example mainly concerns the civil service, where the minimum duration of contributions to the civil service's old age fund is 15 years. An executive order of 2 August 2005 has put an end to age limits in civil service entry examinations of all kinds. The discrimination act seems to have had a limited effect. However some firms and one branch of the economy ('trade mainly for food') have committed themselves to combat age-based discrimination.

The Pension Reform Act of 21 August 2003 includes provisions for keeping older people in employment: the CATS programme was restricted, as explained earlier;[4] company early retirement schemes were taxed; and the age at which an employer could force an employee to retire was raised to 65 (even though the earliest age for filing a claim for a full pension is still 60). This act also created the possibility, strongly demanded by labour unions, for persons at least 56 years old with long careers to be able to retire early, but the eligibility conditions are tight. It also gave a boost to collective bargaining at the national, industry and company levels, and set deadlines for negotiations on certain topics. Company level talks about the employment of older workers and job training for them are mandatory every three years. An employer may retire an employee between the ages of 60 and 65 if the latter is eligible for a full pension and on condition that an industry-wide collective agreement regarding employment and job training is reached before 1 January 2008. Between 2004 and 2005, around 70 agreements were signed that left open the possibility of retirement before age 65. Most of them provide for new hires under various types of contract: full-time jobs under open-ended contracts, apprenticeship and various subsidized contracts related to in-house training (contrats de qualification and contrats de professionnalisation). Some agreements target older workers for training. The Pension Reform Act has also raised the duration of retirement contributions for civil servants, and opened more possibilities for choosing the moment to retire. The eligibility requirements for gradual retirement and for combining work with retirement were loosened.

On 20 September 2003, all employer organizations and labour unions, for the first time since 1994, signed a national agreement on lifelong occupational training. This agreement contains several arrangements, most of them already in place, but facilitates using them. It makes access to training easier for older wage-earners. Employees with more than 20 years' experience, and all workers aged 45 and over, with at least one year of seniority, now have the right to a 'skills audit', to be conducted outside work hours, and have priority for obtaining equivalences based on work-related experiences (validation des acquis de l'expérience, VAE). Additionally, a new scheme, partly transferable from one firm to another, has been set up. This 'individual's right to training' (droit individuel à la formation, DIF) is intended to help employees advance in their jobs at the firm where they are employed. This new individual right to training has been reasserted by an act of 4 May 2004. All employees with more than one year of seniority can obtain a credit for 20 hours of training per year (pro rata for part-timers). This credit can be accumulated during a six-year period. Training might take place during or outside work time, depending on the industry-wide or company-level agreement. Training during working hours does not entail a loss of wages, and any training outside work is paid at 50 per cent of net wages. Employees may decide when they want to use this training credit, but the decision must be formally agreed to by the employer. An innovative element of the scheme is a 'training passport'. Wage-earners can apply for it and record there the knowledge and skills acquired through formal education, occupational training and on-the-job experience.

In line with the 2003 Pension Reform Act, employer and labour organizations have opened general negotiations on working conditions and the employment of older wage-earners.[5] Negotiations about the prevention of and compensation for hard working conditions have turned out to be very complicated. Talks are stuck on defining the conditions that would justify early retirement and on coordinating industry-wide negotiations. On the other hand, negotiations about the employment of older wage-earners, which started in early 2005, ended in an agreement on 13 October 2005 for improving the prospects of keeping these persons in the workforce or helping them return to the labour market.

The agreement sets the objective of a 50 per cent employment rate for 55–64 year olds by 2010 and even sets the target of a 2 per cent increase per year. While some areas have been left to further negotiation (working conditions and unemployment insurance) or public authorities (the national action plan), this agreement addresses four major issues. In order to change perceptions, it calls on business and local authorities to try to make executives, wage-earners and their representatives aware of the employment problems encountered by older persons. These efforts are to be part of a national action plan. Career paths are to be made more secure by anticipating the conditions for retaining wage-earners aged 45 or older, and developing their careers. Under the national training agreement of 5 December 2003, wage-earners are entitled to a 'careers guidance interview' during the 'later phase' of their careers: every five years after the age of 45. A third topic is to help bring the older unemployed back into the labour market. A special fixed-term contract has been designed for persons aged over 57 who, registered as job-seekers for more than three months, have signed a 'personal reclassification' agreement. This contract lasts 18 months, but can be renewed once, thus stretching it out to 36 months in comparison with the normal maximum length of fixed-term contracts, renewals included, of 18 months. Other provisions call for sharing an employee's work time between several employers (within a specific group), giving priority to 'professionalization contracts' for persons aged over 45 and prohibiting age-based criteria in hiring. Finally, improving working conditions and adapting employment conditions (in particular, work schedules and the time spent working) should ensure the best possible fit between job requirements and each worker's changing capacities. Offices of occupational medicine as well as workplace health and safety committees are to be involved. As an exemption to the agreement of 5 December 2003, workers at least 50 years old are entitled to an 'individual training entitlement' (DIF). More funds have been earmarked for the skills audits and validation of work-acquired experience of employees over 45; and administrative procedures have been speeded up. These wage-earners will be the first in line for access to the 'professionalization period' scheme (période de professionnalisation).

In early June 2006, the Government presented a joint national action plan drafted by a three party task force. Covering the period 2006–10, this sets three objectives with regard to older wage-earners: support for keeping them in the labour force, increasing the prospects of the jobless returning to employment, and reducing the likelihood of an abrupt departure at the end of career. The 'Delalande contribution', which penalizes firms that dismiss wage-earners over 50 (but with many exemptions),[6] will be phased out by 2010. The possibility of undertaking sector specific negotiations which aim to bring the retirement age down to below 65 years of age will be eliminated. Existing agreements are scheduled to end in December 2009. As a counterpart, a fund for improving working conditions is to be reoriented towards age management and to receive increased resources for this purpose; and arrangements for guidance counselling are to be extended to firms with fewer than 500 wage earners. A national campaign was launched in September 2006 with the aim of changing social perceptions of older workers. Besides the fixed-term contract for the older jobless, the plan stipulates that public unemployment services are to propose targeted benefits and that certain subsidized employment contracts are to be reserved for persons at least 50 years old. No mention is made of reforming the conditions for waiving the requirement to look for work. Finally, gradual retirement is to be opened in 2008 to wage-earners who have contributed for 150 quarters to the Old Age Fund and, therefore, are not entitled to a full pension. Furthermore, the possibilities for combining work with retirement are to be broadened in 2007; the 'premium' (*surcote*) for retiring later than the age of entitlement to a full pension is to increase as a function of the time spent working longer. Tripartite actors (State, trade unions and employer organizations) are to be involved in the follow-up to this plan.

It is not easy to judge the coherence of the actions undertaken or imagined. First, the various factors underlying the employment of older people have been tackled separately; negotiations have spread out over time and been carried out without any overall view. Second, certain proposals will probably have little impact or are not priorities. The new fixed-term employment contract is supposed to improve employment prospects for older unemployed but is not so different from already existing fixed-term contracts. Moreover it does not take into account the age of access to a full pension. The aforementioned premium might be either not attractive enough or have a windfall effect. The broader possibilities for combining work and retirement are too recent to be perceived as a real means of modifying behaviours. Third, some measures can be seen either as a step backwards or a means to ease transition. In the 2007 Social Security Finance Act, provisions of the national plan of action regarding agreements bringing retirement age down to under 65 years of age have been adopted. However unexpectedly, firms covered by existing agreements have been given the possibility, between 2010 and 2014, of offering voluntary retirement to employees aged at least 60 and eligible for a full pension. This is evidence of how difficult it will be to shift the actual social and institutional orientation away from early exit.

Reports released since the Pension Reform Act tend to concentrate on reforming the existing institutional framework. They focus on the means of regulating the passage from economic activity to retirement. Their recommendations refer mainly to reforms of the pension system and to needed changes to the arrangements (disability and unemployment insurance, exemption from job-search) that keep people from prolonging economic activity or are disincentives for staying in the labour force. For example, the report (d'Autume *et al.*, 2006) for the Economic Advisory Council (Conseil d'Analyse Économique) considers that upholding the principle of retirement at 60, still the benchmark for public opinion, is one of the major factors accounting for France's poor position in employing older workers. Given the short career prospects for persons aged in their 50s, firms have no incentive to invest in them; and these persons lack any ambition or motivation for working longer. Likewise, Cahuc's report (2005: 2) argues that the 'low employment rate of older people comes from problems in the supply and demand of labour that interact with each other and, to a large degree, take their origin in public measures that provide incentives to ageing wage-earners to withdraw from the labour force early'. The 2004 annual report by the Inspection Générale des Affaires Sociales (2004) on age management and employment policy is alone in mentioning a wide range of reasons why training and employment policies should be viewed as strategic.

Given rising joblessness in the mid-1970s and in an effort to create openings, France chose to offer generous compensation for early exit. A consensus thus formed among public authorities, employers, labour unions and wage-earners about using age to ration jobs so as to adjust to fluctuations in the labour market. This choice for 'sharing' work on an age basis and for 'social management' of unemployment did not have the hoped-for impact on the labour market. In particular, it did not free jobs for young people. However it has deeply marked mentalities and spawned deviant effects, thus creating the situation in which the country is still bogged down. Above all, expectations for early exit have pervaded the mentalities and behaviours of all parties.

Owing to the foregoing choice, a rationale of age-based segmentation has spread into the design of public programmes and the practices of firms. Young people are proposed measures for 'insertion in employment' or 'youth jobs', whereas older wage-earners are offered support for early exit. As a consequence, age-based discrimination in the world of work has thrived with, as an inevitable result, a reinforcement of age-based stereotypes and a widespread devaluation of older citizens in the labour market. Since age has become a legal criterion for waiving the requirement to look for work, older persons are deemed unemployable.

Public policies, still based on institutional measures, pay little heed to the driving forces that shape behaviour patterns. Some incentives have been provided to employers, while others directly target older wage-earners (for instance, shortening the period of unemployment compensation or opening prospects through VAE equivalences). Financial incentives prevail.

Public policies waver between choosing a curative or preventive approach. Only a cure can remedy the current situation, but prevention is indispensable in order to organize flexible, but secure, career trajectories and to create working conditions acceptable for persons of any age. The agreement on the employment of older people as well as the law and agreement on lifelong training contain measures open as of the age of 45, this being evidence of the continuation of an age-based segmentation. This holds even more so for the key measure contained in the agreement on the employment of older persons: the fixed-term contract (18 months renewable once) for the jobless aged over 57.

A final point: public authorities as well as employer and labour organizations are hesitating about how to encourage the older unemployed to return to the labour market, while, of course, unemployment agencies pay more attention to jobless young people. Modifying the current institutional setting, changing the pension system's parameters and putting an end to pre-retirement cannot undo the solidly anchored early exit mentality. By failing to focus on collective representations of age and on the cognitive basis of underlying actions, motivations, justifications and referents that shape behaviours, reforms risk being unworkable.

For employers, the issues are now more clearly identified. There is a growing proportion of ageing wage-earners among the workforces of quite a few establishments. Sooner or later, others that have a high proportion of the middle-aged in their workforces, will be in the same situation. Firms are faced directly with the need to keep older employees working until retirement and with the difficulty of doing so. Some companies (and branches) seized the opportunities opened by the agreement on the employment of senior citizens, or even anticipated them. Nonetheless, firms still have not fully realized the implications of having ageing workforces. There is little awareness of the issues related to working conditions. On the contrary, working conditions that are spreading are harder to bear as age advances and, therefore, are not compatible with the growing number of older wage-earners who are working. In parallel, the possibilities for sheltering older employees are becoming slimmer (the externalization of certain tasks, the 'hardening' of 'soft' working conditions, reduced chances for mobility) or are far from sufficient given the numbers involved.

Prolonging the time spent working at the end of careers or maintaining employees in their jobs until retirement age depends not only on firms but also on the decisions made by individual wage-earners. Studies of the conditions for maintaining people in employment until retirement or prolonging careers have shown how important the work actually performed is in the ability and desire to continue working. Difficult working conditions and meaningless jobs, which are monotonous or lack opportunities to learn or obtain recognition, strongly motivate early exit (Volkoff and Bardot, 2004). The hardest point to assess about the pension reform act is, for sure, its impact on the decision to delay retirement.

NOTES

1. Eurostat, Labour Force survey. From Employment Survey, INSÉÉ estimated this age-group's rate to be 40.7 per cent in 2005. The two institutions do not use the same definition – age at the start of the year for Eurostat, age reached during the year for INSÉÉ – whence the difference, since economic activity rates are quite different depending on age.
2. These various subsidized contracts are not specific to older wage-earners.
3. In particular, the Charpin and Teulade reports in 1999 and 2000, respectively.
4. Originally, the conclusion of a sectoral agreement on CATS made companies exempt from their share of social security contributions on the allowances paid to the workers concerned, whether or not they strictly met the criteria about working conditions.
5. The August 2003 pension reform provided for general negotiations about how to define and take into account hard working conditions; but with regard to the employment of ageing wage-earners, it provided for negotiations only at the industry and company levels.
6. Under the Delalande Amendment, passed by the National Assembly in 1992, companies have to make extra payments to the Unemployment Compensation Fund when dismissing older workers for redundancy. Prior to this, a company had to pay an amount equal to three months of wages in order to dismiss anyone 55 years old or older. Under the amendment, this amount has been considerably increased, and the age has been set at 50.

REFERENCES

Anglaret, D. and S. Bernard (2003), 'Chômage et retour à l'emploi après cinquante ans: une moindre exposition au chômage, des difficultés pour retourner en emploi', *Premières synthèses*, **45** (1), 1–4.
D'Autume, A., J.-P. Betbèze and J.-O. Hairault (2006), *Les seniors et l'emploi en France*, report to the Conseil d'Analyse Économique, 58, Paris: Documentation Française.

Cahuc, P. (2005), 'Le difficile retour en emploi des seniors', *Document de travail du Centre d'Observation Économique*, **69**.

Commissariat Général du Plan (2002), *2005: le choc démographique, défi pour les professions, les branches et les territoires*, report by the task force Qualifications et Prospective, Paris: Documentation Française.

Conseil d'Orientation des Retraites (2004), *Retraites: les réformes en France et à l'étranger; le droit à l'information – Deuxième rapport*, Paris: Documentation Française.

Conseil d'Orientation des Retraites (2006), *Troisième rapport du Conseil d'orientation des retraites – Retraites: perspectives 2020 et 2050*, Paris: Documentation Française.

Inspection Générale des Affaires Sociales (2004), *Rapport annuel 2004 – Gestion des âges et politiques de l'emploi*, Paris: Documentation Française.

Guillemard, A.-M. (2003), *L'âge de l'emploi – Les sociétés à l'épreuve du vieillissement*, Collection U, Paris: Armand Colin.

Lainé, F. (2003), 'La mobilité professionnelle et salariale des salariés âgés à travers les DADS', *Document d'études DARES*, **66**.

Lerais, F. and P. Marioni (eds) (2004), 'Dossier Âge et emploi. Synthèse des principales données sur l'emploi des seniors', *Document d'études DARES*, **82**.

Minni, C. and A. Topiol (2004), 'Les entreprises face au vieillissement de leurs effectifs', *Économie et Statistique*, **368**, 43–63.

Organisation for Economic Co-operation and Development (OECD) (2005), *Vieillissement et politiques de l'emploi – France*, Paris: OECD.

Quintreau, B. (2001), *Ages et emploi à l'horizon 2010*, report to the Conseil Économique et Social, Paris: Journaux Officiels.

Volkoff, S. and F. Bardot (2004), 'Départs en retraite, précoces ou tardifs: à quoi tiennent les projets des salariés quinquagénaires?', *Gérontologie et Société*, **111**, 71–94.

8. Active ageing in employment – prospects and policy approaches in Germany

Frerich Frerichs and Gerhard Naegele

INTRODUCTION

The pronounced ageing and shrinking of the German population has led to concerns about rising social security costs and future labour shortages, resulting in recent public policy changes affecting older workers. Labour market initiatives have aimed at increasing labour force participation among this group, while enterprise level active age management strategies have aimed at improving conditions for older workers' employment. Prolonging working life is increasingly viewed as a key component of 'active ageing'.

This stands in stark contrast to the widespread practice of early retirement in the 1980s and 1990s, supported by a strong consensus between enterprises, trade unions, the state and workers themselves. The result has been prevailing low economic activity rates for workers from age 55. Furthermore, the risk of older workers becoming unemployed is far above average.

Against the background of a pronounced trend towards early exit, the question arises as to whether, so far, enough has been done to achieve active ageing in Germany, or if this concept really only provides a convenient rhetoric for policy makers intent on reducing the cost of social welfare. Therefore, in this chapter current labour market initiatives for older workers will be reviewed and assessed. The focus here is on public policies, but the views of the social partners will also be considered, as will what has been developed at company level. To put all this in context, the current status of older workers in the labour market and projections regarding the age profile of the labour force will be described.

DEMOGRAPHIC CHANGE AND LABOUR FORCE PARTICIPATION

According to demographic forecasts, the population of Germany will decline substantially over the next few decades, the average age of the population will increase, and the age structure of the population will change (Statistisches Bundesamt, 2003). Decreasing birth rates and increasing life expectancy are the main reasons for this development. It is estimated that between the years 2001 and 2020, the population size will remain stable, but by 2050 it will have declined by approximately seven million people.

It should be noted that the population in the working age group (age 20 to 64) will decline substantially only after 2020. From a mid-term perspective, this is quite important for active labour market policy. It means that population developments will not lead automatically to a decline or shortage of labour until 2020, and if unemployment remains relatively high as it is predicted to (see below), older workers will remain a vulnerable group (Bellmann *et al.*, 2003; Frerichs and Naegele, 2001).

Also in the background, it should be noted that the ageing of the workforce in Germany will take place much earlier, mainly between 2005 and 2020. In this mid-term perspective, the share of older workers aged 50 to 64 will increase from 24.0 per cent to 34.0 per cent, whereas the share of workers aged 30 to 49 will decline from 54 per cent to 45 per cent (see Figure 8.1).

The influence of demographic change on the prospects of older employees from different industry sectors in general and individual firms in particular is not easy to predict. On the one hand, if the current situation in the labour market were to ease, the ageing of the labour force would prompt companies to increase recruitment of older workers and to improve their employability. Firms will need to learn how to function and to remain innovative with a workforce whose average age is increasing. On the other hand, if unemployment continues to run high, there will be a persisting risk that older workers will remain one of the 'problem groups' in the labour market, as ageing does not affect all branches in the economy homogeneously and certain companies, particularly, innovative and expanding ones will still be able to recruit disproportionately high numbers of younger workers.

LABOUR FORCE PARTICIPATION

One of the most striking changes in the German labour market in recent years has been a sharp drop in labour force participation among older workers, particularly men. Although the trend towards early retirement had begun in the early 1970s, it became more pronounced in the 1980s and early

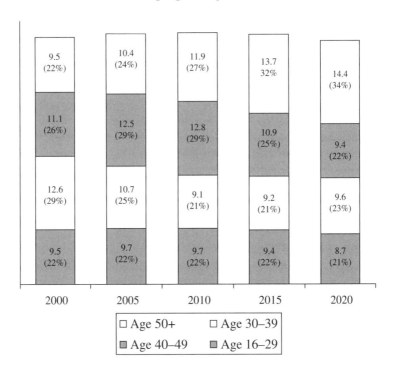

Source: Prognos, 2002: 62.

Figure 8.1   Labour force potential in million persons (%)

1990s. It was the result of overall low employment growth and, after the reunion of East and West Germany, early retirement was the most popular tool for adapting the labour market as the economy transformed.

For men, the decline in labour force participation begins as early as age 55. Among the 55–9 age group, labour force participation declined from 85.7 per cent to 78.7 per cent between 1975 and 2000 (see Table 8.1). Between 1990 and 1995, this development was reinforced due to the process of German reunification. However the most pronounced decline in labour force participation of men took place in the 60 to 64 age group. Between 1975 and 2005, participation rates almost halved, from 58.3 per cent to 31.4 per cent.

For women, the situation is quite different. Due to cohort effects, over time, rates have increased among older age groups (up to those aged 55 and 59 years) (Sing, 2003), from 38.4 per cent to 58.1 per cent in the 55 to 59 age group between 1975 and 2000 (see Table 8.1). However labour force participation has declined somewhat in the 60 to 64 age group, from 16.4 per cent to 13.2 per cent over the same period.

Table 8.1   *Labour force participation rates by age group, Germany (1975–2004)* [a] *(%)*

Age group	1975	1980	1985	1990	1995	2000	2002	2003	2004
Men									
50–4	93.1	93.3	93.3	93.2	92.6	91.7	91.5	91.8	91.6
55–9	85.7	82.3	79.1	81.1	75.8	78.7	80.4	81.6	82.2
60–4	58.3	44.2	33.0	35.0	29.5	31.4	35.1	36.6	38.9
65 and over		7.4	5.1	5.3	4.1	4.4	4.4	4.5	4.4
Women									
50–4	47.4	47.1	50.2	57.8	69	72.6	74.9	76.4	77.3
55–9	38.4	38.7	37.8	43.8	49.7	58.1	60.1	61.5	63.3
60–4	16.4	13	10.9	12.5	10.9	13.2	16.9	18.1	20.4
65 and over		3	2.1	2	1.5	1.5	1.8	1.8	1.8

Notes: [a] 1975–90 for West Germany, 1995–2000 for Germany.

Source: Micro-census.

In recent years, an increase in labour force participation rates among older workers can be observed. For example, between 2000 and 2004 the participation rate for men aged 55 to 59 rose by 3.5 percentage points, and in the age group 60 to 64, an even stronger increase of 7.5 percentage points occurred, although from a very low level (see Table 8.1). For women in this age group, a similar effect can be seen. This may be viewed as a first indication that raising the statutory retirement age and reform of early retirement pathways (see below) are affecting retirement behaviour (Büttner, 2005a). Furthermore labour market participation in this period has been favoured by the fact that cohorts of older workers were rather small (Kistler, 2004).

However much of this increased labour market participation is caused by a growing number of so-called 'minor', that is low paid and part-time jobs, taken by older women (Büttner, 2005b). Even more critical, the increase in labour force participation goes hand in hand with an increase in unemployment rates among workers aged 60 to 61. Between 1999 and 2003, an increase of 4.2 per cent for 60 year old workers and 3.5 percentage points for those aged 61 could be observed (Büttner, 2005b).

Therefore it is doubtful whether all older workers will have the opportunity to stay in employment until the statutory retirement age of 65. If unemployment stays high they may face a prolonged period of unemployment before retiring. The introduction of a higher (early) retirement age, without consideration of the differences within various groups of older workers and without increasing their work opportunities and improving working conditions, may worsen the already precarious labour market situation of many of them, rather than securing their employment (Frerichs and Naegele, 2001; OECD, 2005). In particular, those who are forced to leave the labour force due to redundancy or ill health could face a prolonged period of unemployment and increasing poverty.

If working conditions do not change significantly the numbers of workers who need to take up a disability pension may increase. Another already visible result of recent pension reforms is the high share of new retirees (42.6 per cent) receiving a reduced old age pension (Kaldybajewa, 2005). Under both scenarios, income levels will be significantly lower than they have been in the past.

Against the background of recent pension reforms, the proportion of older workers who plan to leave the labour market at age 60 dropped from 50 per cent to 35 per cent between 1996 and 2002 (Engstler, 2006). However, uncertainty about when to leave gainful employment has risen accordingly. The proportion of older workers who could not state at what age they expected to retire has risen from 18 per cent to 32 per cent over the same period (Engstler, 2006; see also Rothkirch and Partner, WSI and Zenit, 2005).

UNEMPLOYMENT AMONG OLDER WORKERS

A major challenge for German policy makers concerning active ageing is that labour force participation needs to be increased at a time of very high overall employment and the exceptionally high risk of unemployment that older employees are subject to. In 2003, the unemployment rate for the 55 to 60 age group was 16.7 per cent, compared with 12.1 per cent for the 35 to 40 age group (see Table 8.2). There is a particularly sharp increase in the unemployment ratio at the age of 50. Older women are even more prone to unemployment than older men.

In recent years, the most worrying development has been an increase in unemployment among the 45 to 55 age group, which cannot utilize early retirement and faces a long spell of joblessness. In the past ten years, the number of unemployed in this age group has risen from approximately 750 000 to almost 1.1 million. By contrast, the number of those aged 55 and over registered as unemployed has dropped significantly, from approximately 800 000 to 480 000. However this cannot be seen as an improvement in the labour market situation of older workers. It is mainly due to the fact that older jobless people aged 58 and over who receive unemployment benefits are not required to be registered unemployed if they agree to retire

Table 8.2   Ratio of unemployed by age group, Germany 2003 (%)

Age group	Men and women	Men	Women
20–5	14.4	17.0	11.7
25–30	13.4	15.0	11.6
30–5	11.5	11.2	11.8
35–40	12.1	11.3	13.2
40–5	13.3	12.9	13.8
45–50	14.0	14.0	14.1
50–5	16.6	15.9	17.3
55–60	16.7	15.8	17.9
60–5	9.3	8.9	10.3
All	13.3	13.3	13.5

Source: Federal Employment Agency.

as early as possible without pension cuts. Older workers have increasingly made use of this option. Between 2000 and 2003, the number of individuals using this scheme almost doubled: from about 190 000 to 360 000.

Furthermore, unemployment for older workers in Germany is characterized less by the risk of becoming unemployed than by the problem of remaining so. In 2003, and according to the statistics of the Federal Employment Agency, 55.1 per cent of all unemployed people aged 55 to 60 faced a duration of unemployment longer than one year, while in the 60 to 65 age group this ratio was 53.9 per cent. This was far above the ratio of long-term unemployment among those aged 20 to 25, at 8.9 per cent, while in the 25 to 30 age group it stood at 22.2 per cent.

FUTURE PROSPECTS FOR THE OLDER UNEMPLOYED

The latest forecasts show that, despite a significant decline in the size of the German population in the long-term (up to 2050), unemployment will probably stay at a high level for the next two decades (see Prognos, 2002). For 2010, the Prognos-Institute estimates an unemployment rate of 8.2 per cent. In other words, about 3.5 million people are expected to be unemployed at this time. By 2020, it is estimated that the unemployment rate will still be rather high at 6.2 per cent (that is, 2.7 million people). Forecasts made by the so-called Rürup-Commission (BMGS, 2003) are similar: 8.8 per cent by 2010, and 7 per cent by 2020. These are the two most optimistic forecasts. Others predict an even higher unemployment rate (for a comparative overview see Kistler, 2004). It is expected that only after the year 2020, will unemployment fall to a moderate level of 4 or 5 per cent.

Older jobless individuals and in particular, the long-term unemployed, have the poorest prospects of being re-employed of any group. It cannot be expected that their situation will improve significantly over the next two decades if there is no substantial economic growth.

PUBLIC POLICY RESPONSES

The decline in labour force participation rates and high unemployment among older workers not only reflects the strategic personnel policy measures of German enterprises, but is also the result of a long-lasting broad 'social consensus' of various societal groups: employers, workers, trade unions, work councils, and local labour market agencies concerning the value of early retirement (Naegele, 2002).

Currently, there is a strong tendency in public policy towards cancelling this consensus. Respective initiatives to end early retirement, first launched at the beginning of the 1990s, have been reinforced since. The pressure on public sector funding of old age pensions and predicted labour and skill shortages in the long-term, that is after 2020 when unemployment is expected to fall, can be seen as the main driving forces behind this. Thus, with pension reforms in 1992, 1996 and 1999, the German Government decided to raise both the general pension age and the age limit for specific types of pensions. As of the year 2005, only the customary age limit of 65 is valid. Employees who still wish to retire earlier will have to accept a 3.6 per cent reduction in their pension for each year they retire early. A further recent development in this context is the decision of the Federal Government from February 2006 to raise the age limit for pensions from 65 to 67 between 2012 and 2029.

Despite the early start of these pension reforms, it was only at the beginning of the new millennium that the 'greying of the labour market' in terms of active labour market policy for older workers was acknowledged as being an important policy issue. In March 2001, the partners of the so-called 'Alliance for Jobs, Training and Competitiveness', which included representatives of government, trade unions and employers' associations, and which operates at the federal level, agreed on a special programme for promoting the employment of older workers. In so doing, a paradigm shift concerning public policies for older workers occurred. For the first time, government and the social partners turned away jointly from an early retirement policy. They focused explicitly on preventing older workers from becoming unemployed and promoting their reintegration. Their joint declaration included the following proposals (Gemeinsame Erklärung, 2001):

- raising awareness among business and workers of the benefits of life-long learning;
- promoting vocational training for older workers, based on both voluntary in-company actions as well as on collective bargaining;
- implementing financial incentives for vocational training of older workers aged 50 and over in small and medium-sized companies; and
- lowering the qualifying age for wage subsidies from 55 to 50 years.

Elements of these proposals were incorporated in the Job-Aqtiv-Law (JOB – A = activate, Q = quality, T = train, I = invest, V = mediate) which came into force in January 2002. The law aims to transform current employment policy, which mainly concentrates on those who are already unemployed, into one which is preventive. Its basic approach is to promote employment while increasing requirements for the unemployed (that is, a carrot and stick approach). For example, employment offices are now obliged to work out a job profile for every unemployed person, based on their skills and work experience. Furthermore, a 're-integration contract', which records the necessary steps to be undertaken both by the unemployed person and the employment agency to achieve reintegration into the labour market, is required. By doing this, the Government intends to create the basis for a more 'active' strategy. With respect to older workers, a specific measure to promote vocational training has been introduced. Since 2002, employment agencies are able to fund vocational training for workers aged 50 and over if they are employed in a company with fewer than 100 employees and if the company pays their salary while they participate.

In further advancing this approach, in autumn 2002, a commission called 'Modern Services on the Labour Market' (also known as the 'Hartz-Commission')[1] was established by the Federal Government. It proposed a comprehensive reform of labour market policies in Germany (Hartz *et al.*, 2002: 19):

> Employment promotion policy will be reshaped into an activating labour market policy with particular emphasis on a personal contribution towards economic integration on the part of the unemployed, a concept which will be both supported and secured by a host of relevant services and support programmes.

The proposals made were multidimensional, consisting of 13 components, ranging from radical reform of public employment services to rather vague notions concerning the participation of the nation's elite. Up to the summer of 2004, these proposals were translated into statutory provisions by the Federal Government. Altogether, four 'Laws concerning modern services for the labour market' have been implemented (referred to as Hartz I, II, III and IV).

Hartz I, in particular, contained a number of elements which aimed to improve older workers' labour market prospects. These included:

- Unemployed persons aged 50 and over or employees threatened by unemployment would, for a limited period of time, receive a monthly subsidy amounting to 50 per cent of the difference with their last net remuneration.
- Employers would be exempted from contributing to unemployment insurance (3.25 per cent of the gross wage of the employee) if they hired an unemployed person aged 55 or older.
- From 2003 onwards, the age limit for fixed-term employment was lowered from 58 to 52 years, whereby contracts could be terminated without giving reasons for termination and without time limits, in order to improve older workers' prospects of reintegration.

The original intention of the Hartz-Reforms was to strengthen labour market services and to facilitate job-placement activities. Even more important was a shift in general orientation. Although the Job-Aqtiv-Law stressed that unemployed workers were obliged to take a job, in the wake of the Hartz-Reforms a workfare approach became more dominant. The main focus lay in combating 'welfare dependency' and focusing on recipients' obligations to try to become self-sufficient. The obligation of society towards the 'excluded' (that is, towards the unemployed who were not able to be placed into employment within a short time frame) became less important. This was reinforced in March 2003 when the German Chancellor launched a labour market package and social welfare reforms titled 'Agenda 2010'.

The 'passive' side of labour market policy has been reformed as well, to contribute to the overall activating approach. Two major reforms are of particular importance to older unemployed workers. One is the merging of unemployment assistance and social assistance and the creation of the so-called unemployment benefit II.[2] This new benefit, granted since the beginning of 2005 is a tax-funded, means-tested type of benefit to secure the income of unemployed workers once unemployment benefit I is no longer paid or if the qualifying conditions are not fulfilled. The duration of this benefit is unlimited. However in contrast to the former unemployment assistance, which on average guaranteed an income level of 50 per cent of the last net income (53 per cent for a married person), payment here is reduced to the level of social assistance. Furthermore, from 2006 onwards, receipt of unemployment benefit for older workers will be limited to 18 months (the current duration is 32 months).

The most recent development in labour market policies concerning older workers can be seen in the so-called 'Coalition Agreement' which the governing conservative and social-democratic parties in Germany signed in November 2005 (Press and Information Office, 2005). Here it is stated that together with industry, the social partners, the Länder and the regions, measures need to be put in place to maintain and improve the employability of older unemployed people and to reintegrate them into the workforce. Following the decision to raise the statutory retirement age to 67, the Ministry for Work and Social Affairs furthermore announced that it would pursue the policy measure called '50 Plus Initiative' which started in 2005 to improve the employment prospects of the over 50s (see below).

ACTIVE LABOUR MARKET MEASURES IN GERMANY

Measures in the Realm of the Social Security Code III

The merits of the kinds of policy initiatives referred to in the previous section can only be assessed if their concrete outcomes concerning the labour market integration and employability of older workers are properly evaluated. In Germany, the Social Security Code III widely regulates labour market measures mentioned above and for the unemployed in general. There is a broad spectrum of active labour market policies, most of which are being financed by the Federal Employment Agency budget. The law stresses the need to assess the competences and deficits of each unemployed individual and to derive necessary measures from these. In some cases older unemployed people are considered a specific target group. The Social Security Code requires that the needs of older people, severely disabled people, the long-term unemployed, and people who want to return to their job after a period of absence have to be considered. Furthermore employment agencies are required to keep a record of usage of these measures by the target groups. The so-called 'integration records' explicitly refer to workers aged 50 and over.

Concerning job placement, the role of employment agencies in assisting older workers is more important than for the unemployed in general. In 2003, 390 000 out of 2.45 million unemployed people (that is, 15.7 per cent) who found a job did so with help from the Federal Employment Agencies (BA, 2004). The respective ratio for workers aged 50 or over was 17.8 per cent. Nevertheless, the actual integration of older unemployed in job-placement activities is still rather low. Workers aged 50 and over only constituted 12.1 per cent of all job placements of the Federal Employment Agencies in 2003, whereas they constituted 24.5 per cent of all unemployed people. This lack of integration is partly due to the fact that the ratio of job-placement agents to clients is too low. On average, one job agent deals with 400 unemployed persons. Although the Government aims to reduce this gap to one job agent per 75 unemployed persons, this will not be achievable in the near future. Even officials from the federal employment agency, meanwhile, doubt that a better ratio than one for 150 will be realizable. Job-placement, therefore, can be judged as severely understaffed and, in consequence, older job-seekers are often forced to give up the status of being registered unemployed (Frerichs and Taylor, 2005).

The newly established specific measures for older workers mentioned earlier have only recently been evaluated and their effects are only limited so far:

- Promotion of vocational training for workers aged 50 and over: In 2003, only a few hundred and in 2004 only 1400 older employees were funded by this measure (Expert Commission, 2005). Reasons for low take-up include that small and medium-sized companies often lack knowledge about this measure, with promotional measures judged inadequate, and employment agencies not able to be active enough to provide counselling for employers on how to use it.
- Wage insurance for older workers and exemptions for employers from contributing to unemployment insurance: In 2003 and 2004 approximately 11 000 older employees were funded by the first measure and 7500 by the second. However take-up of the first measure accounts for only 1 per cent of all newly established employment contracts for workers aged 60 to 64 in the given period and take-up of the second measure accounts for only 3 per cent of all newly established employment contracts for workers aged 55 to 64 (Brussig *et al.*, 2006; see also Eichhorst and Sproß, 2005). Labour market experts explain this low adoption rate as being due to administrative deficits in implementation by the federal employment agencies and the fact that incentives are too low for employees and employers (Brussig *et al.*, 2006).
- Reduced age limits for fixed-term employment for older workers: In 2003, the age threshold above which temporary contracts can be drawn up without time limits or justification was lowered to 52. According to a recent evaluation of the Federal Government, this has not raised the employment level of older workers and no increase in temporary contracts for this group could be seen (Bundesregierung,

2006). However what is more important is that this measure was deemed to be age-discriminative by the European High Court in 2005 because employment conditions for all newly recruited older workers could be worsened. The Federal Government thus has to modify the law.

Specific measures for the older unemployed are only part of the whole array of labour market measures which are in force to enhance labour market prospects for all target groups. In the following paragraphs a short overview of the main active labour market measures and their effects on older workers is provided:

- Further vocational training: Further vocational training measures in Germany encompass a broad range of short-, mid- and long-term training schemes through which individuals can obtain occupational knowledge and skills. They can also offer opportunities for career advancement or job change and provide vocational qualifications. Preconditions for funding are that the employment service regards these measures as 'necessary' for job-placement and that a substantial number of participants can expect job-placement afterwards. Recent labour market reforms (Hartz I and II), however, have curtailed the length and amount of funding for individual training measures. This has resulted in a substantial reduction of entries into training measures, which have disproportionately affected older workers (Winkel, 2003). This is due, in part, to the fact that the only training measures that are funded are those that are able to integrate at least 70 per cent of participants into the labour market and that employment agencies do not actively pursue the integration of older unemployed people into public training programmes, particularly when high unemployment rates among this group suggest a lack of job prospects.
- Testing and short-term training measures: Since 1998, so-called 'testing and short-term training measures' have been part of the employment promotion law. These training measures are meant to test the ability and willingness of job-seekers to work and allow for short-term training and probation periods. They are funded for a period of up to eight weeks. All registered unemployed people are eligible, even if they do not receive unemployment benefits.
- Wage subsidies: Both general wage subsidies and age-dependent ones exist. Age dependent subsidies are paid as 'integration' subsidies (Eingliederungszuschüsse) to companies that recruit job-seekers aged 55 or older. As a temporary measure, this age limit was lowered

to 50, in effect until 2006. As a rule, subsidies are paid for a period of 24 months and amount to 50 per cent of all wages paid. Until 2003, subsidies could be increased to 70 per cent if seen as necessary for job placement by the job agent and the payment period could be extended to 60 months. After two years the payment had to be reduced by 10 per cent. From 2004, this subsidy was limited to 36 months.

- Promotion of self-employment: Until recently the only funding available for unemployed people intending to become self-employed was a so-called 'bridging allowance', implemented in 1986. It is an allowance paid voluntarily by the Federal Employment Agency and is equivalent to unemployment benefit rates, which could be obtained instead. Since January 2004, there is a legal right to this kind of funding, although it does not cover any investments costs. It is paid for six months during the establishment period of a business and requires an approved business plan on behalf of the beneficiary. A new instrument for promoting self-employment was created in 2003, known as the 'me-incorporated' provisions. This subsidy funds the cost of living but not capital investment.
- Job creation measures: Job creation measures are a special kind of wage subsidy programme, since a subsidy is seldom paid to private enterprises, but rather to public agencies and non-profit organizations. Projects that are promoted by the Federal Employment Agency must be in the public interest and could not be carried out without this type of support. The aim of job creation measures is to provide temporary employment for unemployed people, in particular long-term unemployed persons, for up to one year. The subsidy pays up to 80 per cent of the normal wage.

The effects of these measures are rather mixed. Table 8.3 provides an overview of the extent to which older unemployed participate. To summarize:

- The most important programme, which funds long-term training, is that in which older unemployed people participate the least. Participation rates have recently dropped from an already low level of around 8 per cent to around 5 per cent.
- Short-term training measures also show low and declining participation rates of older unemployed people: from 14 per cent in 2001 to around 11 per cent in 2003.
- Job creation measures in contrast show increasing participation rates of older unemployed people and they are over-represented in these measures.

Table 8.3   Selected active labour market programmes and participation rates of older workers

Programme	Average number of participants per year, 2001	Ratio of older unemployed, 50 and over		Average number of participants per year, 2002	Ratio of older unemployed, 50 and over		Average number of participants per year, 2003	Ratio of older unemployed, 50 and over
	All age groups	50 and over (%)		All age groups	50 and over (%)		All age groups	50 and over (%)
Training (long)	345 000	8.0		332 000	8.0		259 200	5.3
Job creation	166 500	36.6		125 000	40.6		92 400	39.9
Wage subsidies	109 400	43.9		120 800	49.9		145 900	49.9
Training (short)	51 300	14.0		62 000	13.0		92 700	11.2
Self employment	43 150	11.1		54 300	11.0		72 100	11.4
Independent measures	66 500	12.0		62 900	11.0		48 700	7.5

Source: BA (2002, 2003, 2004).

- Wage subsidies also show increasing participation rates of older unemployed people, and rank second with participation rates of nearly 50 per cent in 2003.
- Promotion of self-employment is characterized by low participation rates among older unemployed people.

Concerning individual measures, the older unemployed are still severely under-represented in short- and long-term training measures and are often actively excluded from them. While representation is above average with respect to wage subsidies and job creation measures, these measures are often associated with significant deadweight effects or lack mechanisms to facilitate integration into the primary labour market (Frerichs and Taylor, 2005). Promotion of self-employment for older workers, with participation rates as low as 11.4 per cent in 2003 is limited, even though integration ratios of older unemployed workers are not much lower than for the unemployed in general and would thus justify higher participation rates (BA, 2004).

50 Plus Initiative

In 2005 the so-called '50 plus initiative' was launched, financed by tax revenues. Over the course of this initiative, 62 regions in Germany will receive assistance for innovative projects, in particular for training and promoting self-employment to improve the employment situation of older workers. Up to 250 million euros were made available for this purpose between 2005 and 2007. At the same time, further regions will be incorporated in a dense and sustainable network to assist older workers, and a cross-regional exchange and learning process ensured.

Due to the recent commencement of this initiative no judgement can be made concerning outcome and effects. However a regional approach which reflects a range of different labour market conditions in the areas of the federal employment agencies can be viewed as a promising start.

Partial Retirement

In the current discussions on labour market and pension policy, part-time work for older employees is regarded as an alternative to early retirement and as an instrument for encouraging more to remain in employment. Thus, the official aim of the partial retirement law (*Altersteilzeitgesetz, ATG*), enacted in 1996, was to ease the transition from work to retirement and provide the opportunity to reduce working time for a certain period. Furthermore, its objective was to promote compensatory recruitment, particularly of unemployed workers or trainees, and thus replace older workers with both younger and unemployed workers. The main features of this partial retirement law are as follows:

- Working time reduction from full-time to half-time employment is possible from the age of 55 onwards for a period of up to ten years.
- Working time can be reduced on a daily, weekly, monthly or yearly basis if an average work time of no less than 18 hours per week is ensured.
- The reduction in employee income, due to part-time work, is compensated out of unemployment insurance funds for a period of up to six years.
- To ensure at least 70 per cent of the last net salary and 90 per cent of pension insurance contributions, subsidies are provided by the Federal Labour Office.
- Preconditions for this compensation are that available part-time jobs must then be filled with unemployed persons or trainees.
- Partial retirement agreements at firm level or among the social partners must last more than three years.

Take-up has risen significantly in the past few years. In the five-year period from 1998 to 2003, the number of yearly funded cases rose from about 13 000 to more than 75 000. However the number of funded cases does not represent the actual adoption of partial retirement in Germany. Since no state subsidies are given in the first 2.5 years of the so-called block model, which does not require older employees to switch to part-time jobs but instead to work full-time for 2.5 years and then leave for a pre-retirement sabbatical of another 2.5 years, these cases are not fully registered in the statistics and need to be estimated. Additionally, companies use partial retirement without claiming state subsidies when they do not want to replace older part-time workers with an unemployed worker or trainee. This also contributes to the fact that take-up of partial retirement is underestimated in the data of the federal employment agency. Data available from the social security agencies show that at the end of 2003, approximately 235 000 older workers aged 55 to 65 were using partial retirement when these non-funded forms were included.

Judging by these figures, it seems that the partial retirement law has been a success so far. However this does not mean that a gradual transition from work to retirement for a substantial number of older workers has been accomplished, nor that their integration into the labour market has been achieved. The 'block model', in combination with pension insurance opportunities, which offer workers the chance to retire at age 60 if they adopt a partial retirement measure, could perhaps be more accurately described as a modified instrument for early retirement than a step towards gradual exit. Federal statistical data show that the block model is the dominant measure adopted by employers and employees. In 2002, only 11 per cent of all new entries for funded partial retirement cases were for non-block models. Thus, in general, the partial retirement law is not actually used to enhance part-time work options for older workers.

COMBATING AGE DISCRIMINATION AND AGE-AWARENESS CAMPAIGNS

Despite the existence of EU actions regarding the prohibition of discrimination in the labour market on grounds of age, Germany only came up with a draft version of a law against discrimination in autumn 2004. This belated development is partly due to the fact that the term 'age discrimination' has not found much recognition amongst politicians or scientists working in the field of old age policy (Frerichs and Naegele, 1997). Furthermore it may also be the result of strong opposition from employers' associations to statutory measures, which are viewed as bureaucratic and ineffective and at the same time limit an employer's freedom of choice. By contrast, trade unions favour enacting legislation against discrimination in the labour market, although views on this are split because early retirement is still seen by many as a socially acceptable means of facilitating exit from the labour market. Finally, however, in 2006 an age discrimination law was enacted, prohibiting direct and indirect discrimination in job-recruitment and training on grounds of age.

Besides age discrimination legislation, some federal initiatives exist which explicitly draw attention to the competences and potential of the ageing workforce and thus try to counteract discriminative behaviours and prejudices based on beliefs that older workers are less productive:

- Demographic Change – Public Relations and Marketing Strategy: Following the completion of a research phase on 'Demography and Employment', the Federal Ministry for Education and Science launched this transfer project between 1999 and 2003 with the aim of heightening awareness of the impact of demographic change on employment, to distribute knowledge about how to achieve balanced age structures and sustain companies' innovative abilities, achieve age-appropriate work and personnel policy, and sustain employment and create new occupational fields for older employees. The main target groups were companies, employers', trade unions, employment services and regional development agencies (Buck and Dworschak, 2003).

- Fifth Commission for Reporting on the Situation of the Elderly: In 2003, the Federal Ministry for Family and Senior Affairs established this expert commission which focuses on the subject of 'promoting the potential of older people in the economy and in society'. The commission submitted its report in 2005 (Expert Commission, 2005) and in 2006, the Federal Ministry for Senior Affairs published it with recommendations for how to retain, promote and use the potential of older people, particularly in the labour market and for training.
- New Quality of Work: In 2002, the national initiative: 'New Quality of Work' (*Neue Qualität der Arbeit* (INQA)) was launched. INQA is a joint initiative of the Federal Government, the Länder, the social partners, the social insurance partners, the Bertelsmann Foundation and businesses. With this initiative the INQA partners intend to bring together people's interest in working conditions that improve the health and employability of workers on the one hand and the need for competitive jobs on the other, and to prompt a broad societal debate on the future of work. With its memorandum 'Demographic Change and Employment. A Call for New Corporate Strategies' (INQA, 2004a) and the campaign '30, 40, 50 plus – healthy work into old age' (INQA, 2004b) INQA intends to encourage business to develop a more constructive and realistic picture of the skills and abilities of older people and, at the same time, that corporate health policy should aim to safeguard the work ability of the younger member of the workforce in the long-term. INQA provides services to companies to help them to recognize and resolve problems posed by demographic change such as a toolbox for HRM development (www.demowerkzeuge.de), a database of good practice (www.inqa.de) and supporting a company network to further develop expertise in this field.

INITIATIVES AND POLICY APPROACHES OF THE SOCIAL PARTNERS

Employers and Employers' Associations

The present official proposals of the Federal Employers' Association (BDA) unmistakably refer to prolonging working life. In so doing, there is a distinct focus on both the financial consequences of demographic change and the currently predicted skill shortage. The financial arguments refer to the prevailing structures of organizing social security in Germany (the

Bismarckian model of social security) which, in the wake of demographic change, would automatically increase labour costs. Consequently, proposals made to increase labour force participation rates of older workers are embedded in a framework which aims to remove one of the most significant 'disadvantages' of employing them: the intensely high (direct and indirect) labour costs. It is assumed that due to seniority-based remuneration systems and age-specific employee protection (for example, against dismissal), the employment of older workers is often more expensive and less attractive to employers. Therefore, reducing age-related labour costs will automatically improve their employment prospects in both internal and external labour markets.

The respective proposals of the Federal Employers' Association (BDA) refer primarily to tariff policy, industrial law, job promotion, and pension and retirement policy. It has demanded (see also BDA, 2002):

- deregulation of collective bargaining protection against the dismissal of older workers;
- reduction of existing age-specific privileges within the unemployment benefit scheme;
- reduction of age-specific privileges in public wage subsidy and job creation schemes;
- deregulation of collective bargaining protecting salaries of older workers;
- reduction of seniority regulations within wages;
- creation of 'true' part-time work for older workers;
- formation of temporary jobs for older job-seekers;
- raising the legal retirement ages gradually after 2010; and
- implementation of financial incentives for work after retirement.

In a recent study (resulting from a project called: 'ProAge–Facing the Challenge of Demographic Change', which was carried out in cooperation with the Federal Employers' Association), the Bertelsmann Foundation and employers' organizations from Denmark, the Netherlands and Ireland undertook empirical investigations and transnational benchmarking seminars to try to reinforce some of the above-mentioned proposals (Bertelsmann Stiftung and BDA, 2003).

Furthermore, in 2002, the BDA published guidelines for employers in which they develop arguments and proposals for the better integration of older workers into employment (BDA, 2002). In particular, they try to raise awareness of some of the benefits of hiring them, such as experience, motivation and reliability. They also try to offer guidance to human resource managers, referring to measures such as flexible working time arrangements, training, health promotion, team-work of both younger and older workers and job-rotation. They stress that employers should apply a performance-related and not an age-related criterion for recruiting and retaining older workers. In addition to these recommendations, they feature public promotion programmes for older workers, taken from the Social Security Code III.

However in many cases it seems that federal and sectoral employers' associations' concern to reduce the incidence of early exit is not shared by representatives of companies, and large ones in particular. Early retirement still plays a strategic role among their personnel policy options in order to adapt to structural changes in the economy. This is mirrored by the overwhelming misuse of the Act on Part Time Work in Old Age, in order to perpetuate early exit (see above). This is especially important for many companies and businesses with current or already foreseeable requirements for reductions in personnel (for example, banking, insurance and telecommunication business, as well as industrial sectors). These companies demand the option of both maintaining early exit options and reducing or shifting respective costs. Another popular argument in companies for promoting early exit concerns older workers with severe health problems or reduced vocational capacities.

Furthermore, employers seem to avoid investing in training and health promotion for the ageing workforce. Initiatives remain mainly at the rhetorical level, with claims that lifelong learning is a joint task for both employees and employers and stating that accumulated working time credits should be used for training measures (Frerichs and Taylor, 2005).

Specific company measures for older workers, which are an indication of age-integrative policies, have not been much developed. Findings from the latest representative company survey conducted by the Federal Institute on Labour Market research (Bellmann *et al.*, 2003) revealed that of all companies who employ older workers, only 11 per cent in East Germany and 12 per cent in West Germany offer integrative measures such as age-specific/age-neutral training, teamwork for mixed-age groups, workplace adaptation to the specific needs of older workers, or phased retirement. This is despite best practice examples demonstrating the feasibility and effectiveness of integrative measures and career management (Bertelsmann Stiftung and BDA, 2003a).

Trade Unions

Trade unions have only recently accepted the shift in labour market policies for older workers (see above). Strong German unions like IG-Metall, which represents the steel and iron industry, and Ver.di, which represents the Public Sector, continued to explicitly demand the maintenance of early exit options under financially and socially acceptable conditions. This was particularly true of IG-Metall, which claimed a 'pension at the age of 60' (*Rente mit 60*) until March 2001. In this context, two primary points can be emphasized:

- labour market principles in accordance with the concept of 'intergenerational solidarity'; and
- early exit as a tool for 'humanizing' the labour world for older workers.

The reasoning behind the latter point is that large groups of ageing workers in certain occupations and sectors (for example, metal working and the professional caring sector) often suffer from severe health problems. Therefore, these workers need to be able to retire earlier under socially acceptable conditions, if they wish to do so. This might also be true for those being threatened by substantial technological and organizational changes, especially if there is little prospect of anticipating and preparing for them in advance. Furthermore socially acceptable pathways into early exit must be preserved for both those imminently threatened by job loss and those unemployed long-term. For most workers, retiring earlier means a distinct improvement in their present life situation.

Trade unions have recently become more focused on policies to keep older workers employed and to improve their employability. This approach has been accepted partly because of the ambivalences and inconsistencies of early exit. Early exit might negatively affect the working conditions of future cohorts of workers (that is, it increases the workload for younger workers), which could lead to a vicious circle. Furthermore, the understanding of trade unions concerning population and workforce ageing and persistent high unemployment of older workers has grown. They realize that there is a need to strengthen age-integrative policies and to focus on flexible working arrangements, health promotion and lifelong learning (Adamy, 2003).

Trade unions still have different views, including those who favour the reintegration of older workers and those who do not. Until recently, there were no official guidelines for a 'trade-unionist older worker policy' in Germany. However with strategic reorientation taking place on this topic, the Federal Trade Union Congress has published the following brochures which deal with the issue of older workers:

- guidelines for older unemployed and older workers to increase their employability (DGB, 2004a);
- guidelines for employers and personal managers to deal with ageing workforces (DGB, 2004b); and

- a strategic paper on major issues concerning the integration of older workers into the labour market (DGB, 2004c).

Older workers are increasingly viewed as a target group by several other trade unions as well, for developing both policy concepts for fighting unemployment and for improving working conditions. The following measures for older workers are examples of subjects which can be found in employment agreements and collective bargaining (Adamy, 2003; DGB, 2004c):

- promoting part-time work, which also includes fighting discrimination in part-time work;
- reducing and/or adjusting working time according to the needs of older workers (for example, older shift-workers);
- developing further vocational training, which is explicitly aimed at so-called 'disadvantaged' groups;
- supporting health promotion and development of in-company health management, supported by statutory measures, regulations, and financial incentives; and
- promoting group work for older workers.

It is safe to conclude that trade unions favour an integrative approach which should not only cover reversal of exit routes but also measures that substantially increase the employability of older workers. Furthermore, socially acceptable ways of exiting early are still seen as necessary for those older workers who are not able to work until the statutory pension age.

Company Approaches

All in all, German companies are not very aware that their staff will be ageing in the near future and that substantial age-related personnel problems might emerge. However some companies are re-thinking older worker issues, the result of significant labour and skills shortages. In the context of the recent project 'Employment Initiatives for an Ageing Workforce', funded by the European Foundation for the Improvement of Living and Working Conditions, such examples of good practice in age management could be identified (Naegele and Walker, 2006).

In the area of recruitment, in 2000 Fahrion Engineering GmbH & Co KG began to focus on older, highly qualified engineers. This recruitment strategy became necessary because it was hard to find suitable staff, partly because of the company's very specific qualification requirements and partly because of competition for labour in the greater regional area. The company posted a job advertisement explicitly appealing to older engineers, foremen and technicians, reading: 'Too old at 45 – superfluous at 55?' In response, the company received over 700 applications. Nineteen engineers (mostly unemployed) were hired for an unlimited period, 15 of whom were older than 50 years. Even today, the company receives applications in response to that advertisement.

Work for the innovation-oriented company MicroTec, a manufacturer in the field of batch production of micro components and micro systems, requires permanent learning due to differing and changing customer requirements. By dint of mixing teams, for instance, by age and gender, management hope to achieve a complementary use of employees' abilities and competences, to promote knowledge transfer between employees and to break down prejudices. This continuous, joint and reciprocal learning while working is realized through a so-called 'benefit partnership'. This means that the concrete exchange of experience must always take place in both directions if it is to succeed and if both the knowledge giver and the knowledge-receiver are to profit from the knowledge exchange. Not only do older employees learn from their younger colleagues, but the latter also learn from the former, for example, the need for perseverance during difficult phases of a project.

Concerning health promotion and workplace design Verkehrs Aktiengesellschaft Nuremberg (VAG), a public transport company, has for some time, addressed the question of how the employability of its older workers can be promoted. In the project 'Improvement of the Work Situation of Drivers of Public Transport' disease occurrences as well as cases concerning fitness for driving were analysed. Following this project, a number of measures were developed by the company, of which the 'special driver group' proved to be the most effective. A driver group is a group of drivers that has been scheduled on the same shifts. In this case a reduction in working hours for drivers over the age of 57, irrespective of their state of health, is available. Older drivers are released from one shift per week (short morning shift) without pay being affected.

However although there is some knowledge about good practice of this kind in Germany (see also INQA, 2004a/2004b; Clemens, 2003; Morschhäuser, 2003; Naegele and Krämer, 2001), activity aimed at transferring this know-how into action on behalf of companies is low. Most German companies, particularly small- and medium-sized ones have not so far exploited this knowledge. Currently, 93 per cent of companies with fewer than five and 83 per cent of those with five to 19 employees, offer no specific workplace measures targeted at their older employees (Bellmann *et al.*, 2003; see also OECD, 2005). In addition only one in two companies would be willing to employ older job applicants without special conditions, while 15 per cent would not hire an older worker as a matter of principle (Bellmann *et al.*, 2003).

This is partly due to the fact that age-related problems have not been widespread due to early retirement schemes and that the most common practice still is to layoff or retire older workers early in the course of restructuring (Bertelsmann Stiftung and BDA, 2003). Furthermore a direct transfer of models of good practice is rarely possible. Rather, they must be adapted to the special needs of a client company, and thus might serve as a starting point for tailor-made age management strategies appropriate to that enterprise (see Naegele and Krämer, 2001).

CONCLUDING COMMENTS

A strengthening of policies towards the reintegration of older workers and a reversal of early retirement has taken place in Germany. This is embedded in a general trend of fostering active and activating strategies which emerges against a background of labour force ageing and concerns about the future funding of pension systems, and is partly influenced by the 'moral pressure' of the open method of coordination at the EU level. In Germany, with the Job-Aqtiv-Law and Hartz-Reforms, profiling measures for the unemployed in general and specific support for older unemployed people has been implemented. In the wake of implementing the principle of 'support and demand', requirements for the unemployed to be active in job-search and for job acceptance have been intensified.

The preceding descriptions and analysis of labour market policies for older unemployed people in Germany show, however, that neither the 'active' side nor the 'passive-activating' side of labour market policy can be seen as 'future proof'. Concerning active policies is can be argued that:

- First, labour market policies for this target group are not advanced enough to cover the need to reintegrate older claimants and, in particular, older long-term unemployed people and those on disability and sickness related benefits. While compared with the situation at the end of the 1990s, a clear shift towards strategies and measures for older unemployed people has taken place, they remain under-represented in general labour market measures such as the promotion of vocational training, self-employment and job-placement activities. In particular, strategies and concrete measures for improving lifelong learning and providing training for all age groups are underdeveloped.
- Second, even if measures are taken, they tend to benefit more advantaged and easier to place older unemployed people. Risk groups such

as the low-skilled or disabled are not strongly represented. Even though profiling measures have been implemented to assess needs, creaming and deadweight effects are widespread.

Exclusion of older workers and women still tends to characterize their relationship with the labour market. In the past, this has been cushioned by early retirement and employment insurance and in consequence poverty among the elderly is largely absent. However the restriction of the formerly generous early retirement options and severe curtailments in respect of unemployment benefit and unemployment assistance have taken away some of the most important adjustment mechanisms to respond to worsening economic conditions and has therefore created a more pressurized situation. In the policy debate, the emphasis on social security has weakened. Substantial pressure has been put on employment protection for older workers as well.

Whether in future, active employment programmes will be a suitable replacement is questionable. In Germany, the process of rethinking the hitherto prevailing 'youth-centred' policies of the social partners and public labour market agencies only began as recently as 2001. Retrenchment of early exit has not accordingly led to an adequate expansion of the funding of active labour market measures. On the contrary, older unemployed people are increasingly at risk of being neglected in training programmes, and targeted programmes for this group and general improvements in job-placement structure have yet to prove whether they really do work. Critical voices emphasize that the true target of the anti-pre-retirement policy in Germany is lowering pension costs and not promoting employment opportunities for older workers.

A prolongation of working life requires that older people have a real prospect of working longer. Both incentives and provisions for individuals to work for a greater number of years and employers to recruit and retain older workers must be improved and backed by legislative measures. However, at the same time, socially acceptable pathways into early exit need to be preserved for certain 'at risk' groups of older workers whose prospects of remaining in or re-entering employment are low: for instance, workers with severe health problems and disabled workers as well as those in workplaces where work pressure is high.

Added to this, even if labour force participation rates among older workers increase, this does not necessarily mean that the quality of working conditions for this age group will be as good as for younger workers. 'Active ageing' that is manifested as periods of precarious employment in a narrow range of jobs with low wages, or even worse, a long period of fruitless job-search, may be worse than early exit. Therefore, employment targets for older workers should be amended by additional targets that guarantee a productive and sustainable integration of older workers in employment, or at least monitor how employment conditions for older workers develop in a qualitative way. Furthermore welfare-to-work policies may increase poverty risks for those older unemployed who cannot easily find a job and at the same time cannot take refuge in early retirement measures. This group will also be lost to community involvement and volunteering, a sound income base being the prerequisite for this.

What is necessary in this respect is a change in paradigm from a reactive 'elderly employee policy' to a preventive policy of employment promotion and protection which is 'age neutral' in this sense of ageing workforces. It goes without saying that this does not mean that we can do without age specific solution models in the future, for example, for the older unemployed. The catalogue of appropriate instruments for active promotion measures is well known and partially tried and tested. It encompasses inter alia updating vocational qualifications, including lifelong learning; adaptation of working hours; health protection and promotion and change of work and profession, including so-called 'second and third careers' (Naegele, 2002).

The realization of this demands not only the cooperation of all groups concerned (government, employers, unions, work councils and, of course, older workers themselves). Coordinated and integrated initiatives which have a preventive character are also essential on different levels (for instance, working time and educational policy; health protection and ergonomics). The following conclusions and recommendations, drawn from a recent research project and scientific conferences, might serve as points of orientation for a strategic change in older worker policy and for a better, future-orientated age management approach (Naegele, 1999; Rothkirch, 2000; Frerichs and Taylor, 2005; Naegele and Walker, 2006):

- Promotion and employment for, and the employability of, an ageing workforce demands action throughout the whole working life (concept of 'age neutrality').
- Active policy approaches should be preventive by combating typical risks of older workers in earlier phases of working life. A dual approach should be adopted, maintaining employability over all of working life but also addressing specific risks or problems for some older workers.
- Multidisciplinary and coordinated approaches are necessary: education, health, training, leisure and family duties, social protection and equal opportunities. This demands attention to work organization and the work environment, and not least to the capabilities of the ageing workforce.

- Systematic coordination of measures (for example, training and working time adjustment, preventive health protection and career planning) is required at both enterprise and public policy level. A close coordination of public and workplace policies is warranted.
- However in-company approaches are the core of an 'active' and future-orientated age management policy. Whether older workers might be able to stay in working life longer or not, is primarily determined within enterprises. In this context the arrangement of adequate workplaces which meet the needs of older workers is of importance (for example, in terms of workload, working time, work environment and job design).
- Although the overall goal is to support older workers to remain in the active workforce and to avoid involuntary early exit, socially acceptable pathways into early exit must be preserved for special ('risk') groups of older workers (for example, the long-term unemployed, workers with severe health problems, and disabled workers).

It can be argued that Germany has still to develop such a comprehensive strategy for active ageing to ensure that people stay in work for longer, particularly after the age of 60, and increase access to training for older workers in the context of lifelong learning.

NOTES

1. Named after Peter Hartz, Human Resource Manager and Member of the Board of Volkswagen AG, who was chairman of this commission.
2. This benefit is also called 'Grundsicherung für Arbeitslose' (Basic Security for Job Seekers).

REFERENCES

Adamy, Wilhem (2003), 'Herausforderungen einer älter werdenden Erwerbsbevölkerung. Oder: Wem nutzt eine alternsgerechte Gestaltung der Arbeitswelt?', in U. Engelen-Kefer and K. Wiesehügel (eds), *Sozialstaat – Solidarisch, Effizient, Zukunftssicher*, Hamburg: VSA, pp. 86–103.
BA (Bundesanstalt für Arbeit) (2002), *Eingliederungsbilanz 2001. Bundesergebnisse*, Nürnberg: BA.
BA (Bundesanstalt für Arbeit) (2003), *Eingliederungsbilanz 2002. Bundesergebnisse*, Nürnberg: BA.
BA (Bundesanstalt für Arbeit) (2004), *Eingliederungsbilanz 2003. Bundesergebnisse*, Nürnberg: BA.
BDA (Bundesvereinigung der deutschen Arbeitgeberverbände) (2002), *Ältere Mitarbeiter im Betrieb. Ein Leitfaden für Unternehmer*, Berlin: BDA.

Bellmann, Lutz, Markus Hilpert, Ernst Kistler and Jürgen Wahse (2003), 'Herausforderungen des demographischen Wandels für den Arbeitsmarkt und die Betriebe', *Mitteilungen aus der Arbeitsmarkt- und Berufsforschung*, **2**, 133–49.

Bertelsmann Stiftung and BDA (Bundesvereinigung der Deutschen Arbeitgeberverbände) (Hrsg.) (2003), *Beschäftigungschancen für ältere Arbeitnehmer. Internationaler Vergleich und Handlungsempfehlungen*, Gütersloh: Bertelsmann.

BMGS (Bundesministerium für Gesundheit und Soziale Sicherheit) (2003), *Nachhaltigkeit in der Finanzierung der sozialen Sicherungssysteme*, Bericht der Kommission (Rürup-Kommission), Berlin: BMGS.

Brussig, Martin, Mathias Knuth and Oliver Schweer (2006), *Arbeitsmarktpolitik für ältere Arbeitslose. Erfahrungen mit 'Entgeltsicherung' und 'Beitragsbonus'*, IAT Report 2006-02, Gelsenkirchen: Institut Arbeit und Technik.

Buck, Hartmut and Bernd Dworschak (eds) (2003), *Ageing and Work in Europe. Strategies at Company Level and Public Policies in Selected European Countries*, Stuttgart: IAO.

Bundesregierung (2006), *Die Wirksamkeit moderner Dienstleistungen am Arbeitsmarkt. Bericht 2005 der Bundesregierung zur Wirkung der Umsetzung der Vorschläge der Kommission 'Moderne Dienstleistungen am Arbeitsmarkt'*, Berlin: Informations- und Presseamt der Bundesregierung.

Büttner, Renate (2005a), *Zunehmende Erwerbsbeteiligung von Älteren*, Altersübergangsreport 2005-04, Düsseldorf and Gelsenkirchen: Hans-Böckler-Stiftung, Institut Arbeit und Technik.

Büttner, Renate (2005b), *Höhere Erwerbsbeteiligung in Westdeutschland – Mehr Arbeitslosigkeit und Frühverrentungen in Ostdeutschland*, Altersübergangsreport 2005-05, Düsseldorf, Gelsenkirchen: Hans-Böckler-Stiftung, Institut Arbeit und Technik.

Clemens, Wolfgang (2003), 'Modelle und Maßnahmen betrieblicher Anpassung älterer Arbeitnehmer', in Mathias Herfuth, Martin Kohli and Klaus Zimmermann (eds), *Arbeiten in einer alternden Gesellschaft. Problembereiche und Entwicklungstendenzen der Erwerbssituation Älterer*, Opladen: Leske + Budrich, pp. 93–119.

DGB (Deutscher Gewerkschaftsbund) (2004a), *50plus – was nun? Wege in den Job. Ein Ratgeber für Arbeitnehmer/innen ab 50*, Berlin: DGB.

DGB (Deutscher Gewerkschaftsbund) (2004b), *Umdenken erforderlich. Vorbeugung sichert Beschäftigung bis zum Rentenalter*, Berlin: DGB.

DGB (Deutscher Gewerkschaftsbund) (2004c), *Demografischer Wandel. Schritte zu einer altersgerechten Arbeit*, Berlin: DGB.

Eichhorst, Werner and Cornelia Sproß (2005), *Arbeitsmarktpolitik für Ältere. Die Weichen führen noch nicht in die gewünschte Richtung*, IAB-Kurzbericht 16, Nürnberg: IAB.

Engstler, Heribert (2006), 'Erwerbsbeteiligung in der zweiten Lebenshälfte und der Übergang in den Ruhestand', in Clemens Tesch-Römer, Heribert Engstler and Susanne Wurm (eds), *Altwerden in Deutschland. Sozialer Wandel und individuelle Entwicklung in der zweiten Lebenshälfte*, Wiesbaden: Verlag für Sozialwissenschaften, pp. 85–154.

Expert Commission (2005), 'Potenziale des Alters in Wirtschaft und Gesellschaft. Der Beitrag älterer Menschen zum Zusammenhalt der Generationen', Fünfter Bericht zur Lage der älteren Generation in der Bundesrepublik Deutschland, manuscript, Bericht der Sachverständigenkommission.

Frerichs, Frerich and Gerhard Naegele (1997), 'Discrimination of older workers in Germany: obstacles and options for the integration into employment', *Journal of Ageing and Social Policy*, **9** (1), 89–101.

Frerichs, Frerich and Gerhard Naegele (2001), 'Anhebung der Altersgrenzen und Herausforderungen an die Arbeitsmarktpolitik', in Corinna Barkholdt (ed.), *Prekärer Übergang in den Ruhestand. Handlungsbedarfe aus Arbeitsmarktpolitischer, Rentenrechtlicher und Betrieblicher Perspektive*, Opladen: Westdeutscher Verlag, pp. 73–102.

Frerichs, Frerich and Philip Taylor (2005), *Labour Market Policies for Older Workers and Demographic Change. A Comparative Analysis of Policy Approaches in Germany and the United Kingdom*, London: Anglo-German Foundation.

Gemeinsame Erklärung (2001), 'Gemeinsame Erklärung des Bündnisses für Arbeit, Ausbildung und Wettbewerbsfähigkeit zu den Ergebnissen des 7. Spitzengespräches am 4. März 2001', Berlin, manuscript.

Hartz, Peter, N. Bensel, J. Fiedler, H. Fischer, P. Gasse, W. Jann, P. Kraijic, I. Kunkel-Weber, K. Luft, H. Schartau, W. Schickler, H.-E. Schleyer, G. Schmid, W. Tiefensee and E. Voscherau (2002), *Moderne Dienstleistungen am Arbeitsmarkt: Vorschläge zum Abbau der Arbeitslosigkeit und zur Umstrukturierung der Bundesanstalt für Arbeit*, Berlin: Kommission Moderne Dienstleistungen am Arbeitsmarkt.

INQA (ed.) (2004a), *Demographic Change and Employment. A Call for New Corporate Strategies*, Dortmund: INQA.

INQA (ed.) (2004b), *30-40-50plus: Gesund arbeiten bis ins Alter. Mit Erfahrung die Zukunft meistern. Altern und Ältere in der Arbeitswelt*, Dortmund: INQA.

Kaldybajewa, Kalamkas (2005), 'Rentenzugang der BfA 2004: Arbeitslosigkeit als wesentlicher Grund für den Rentenzugang bei Frauen und Männern', *Die Angestelltenversicherung*, **52**, 213–21.

Kistler, E. (2004), 'Demografischer Wandel und Arbeitsmarkt – die Debatte muss ehrlicher werden', WSI-Mitteilungen, **2** (5), 71–7.

Morschhäuser, Martina (2003), *Erfolgreich mit älteren Arbeitnehmern. Strategien und Beispiele für die betriebliche Praxis*, Gütersloh: Bertelsmann.

Naegele, Gerhard (1999), *Active strategies for an Ageing Workforce*, conference report to the European Foundation for the Improvement of Living Conditions, Dublin.

Naegele, Gerhard (2002), 'Active strategies for older workers in Germany', in European Trade Union Institute (ETUI) (ed.), *Active Strategies for Older Workers*, Brussels: ETUI, pp. 207–45.

Naegele, Gerhard and Katrin Krämer (2001), 'Recent developments in the employment and retirement of older workers in Germany', *Journal of Aging and Social Policy*, **13** (1), 69–90.

Naegele, Gerhard and Alan Walker (2002), *Ageing and Social Policy: Britain and Germany Compared*, London: Anglo-German-Foundation.

Naegele, Gerhard and Alan Walker (2006), *A Guide to Good Practice in Age Management*, Luxembourg: Office for Official Publications on the European Communities.

OECD (Organisation for Economic Co-operation and Development) (2005), *Ageing and Employment Policies, Germany*, Paris: OECD.

Press and Information Office of the Federal Government (2005), *Coalition Agreement between the CDU, CSU and SPD*, Berlin: Press and Information Office.

Prognos (2002), *Deutschland Report 2002 – 2020*, Basel: Prognos.

Rothkirch, Christoph von (2000), *Altern und Arbeit*, Berlin: Edition Sigma.

Rothkirch and Partner, WSI and ZENIT (2005), *Einstellungen älterer Arbeitnehmer zum Renteneintritt. Eine empirische Untersuchung in nordrhein-westfälischen Betrieben*, Düsseldorf.

Sing, Dorit (2003), *Gesellschaftliche Exklusionsprozesse beim Übergang in den Ruhestand*, Frankfurt am Main: Peter Lang.

Statistisches Bundesamt (2003), Bevölkerung Deutschlands bis 2050, 10 Koordinierte Bevölkerungsvorausberechnung, Wiesbaden.

Winkel, Rainer (2003), 'Verheerende Halbjahresbilanz bei beruflicher Weiterbildung', *Soziale Sicherheit*, **7**, 226–9.

9. Conclusions: the prospects for ageing labour forces

Philip Taylor

TOWARDS ACTIVE AGEING?

Older workers have borne the brunt of industrialized nations' efforts to grapple with the effects of economic restructuring and population ageing. Although a trend towards early retirement has been a common feature of all the industrialized nations as industry restructured at the end of the twentieth century, the extent of this has varied markedly. This volume contains examples of where the participation of older workers declined, but not markedly so (Japan and the USA), and extreme examples of early exit (France, Germany and the Netherlands). But quickly, early retirement has been abandoned as its costs escalated, deficiencies were identified and new priorities associated with population ageing emerged. It is an unpalatable truth that many European governments in particular have been forced to accept that ageing populations and large scale early retirement are incompatible. Although early retirement is a tool that, it seems, industry defaults to, and while a period of almost a quarter of a century out of the workplace is attractive to many individuals, current thinking is that this is not tenable if industrialized economies are to remain competitive (European Commission, 2005a). The European Commission (2003) has estimated that an increase in the effective age of retirement of one year would reduce the expected increase in expenditure on public pensions by between 0.6 and 1 percentage points of GDP. The economic gains alone resulting from 'active ageing' could be enormous. However, there is some pessimism among authors in this volume, particularly those from countries where early exit went deepest, that active ageing is realizable, at least in the near future, and without the risk of hardship for older workers.

At present, at least in the minds of most policy makers and many commentators then, the continued participation of older workers presents an obvious, if not necessarily easy to implement, solution to anticipated shortfalls in social welfare provision and labour shortages associated with ageing populations. At the same time, a business case seeks to align the social objective of working later with the management objective of securing labour supply and remaining competitive. Some sections of industry are indeed turning to older workers as other labour pools dry up, or identifying qualities that make them attractive employment options.

Working later, therefore, seems, at first glance, like an attractive prospect, particularly if one adds benefits for older workers such as income and social participation. It is known from surveys that older workers find this idea attractive. Surely, this has to be better than the past when older age was synonymous with early retirement? As vociferously as many used to argue for the right to retire early, equal force is now frequently applied to arguments for working on and choosing the manner of, and the point at which one finally leaves the labour force.

However this position neglects the reality of older workers' experiences. There is no doubting the potential benefits for economies and older people from working later. Yet, it is easy to point to gaps in arguments concerning the value of blocking off early exit pathways and instead exposing older workers to the labour market via promoting re-entry and retention. As noted by Julie McMullin and colleagues in this volume, policy changes often appear to have been driven rather more by concern about the economic consequences of population ageing than by that for the well-being of all older people, despite arguments to the contrary. Frerich Frerichs and Gerd Naegele, also in this volume, put the criticism more strongly: 'that the true target of the anti-pre-retirement policy in Germany is lowering pension costs and not promoting employment opportunities for older workers'. It also appears that the current policy climate has skewed the nature of the research agenda to such an extent that there is scarcely a murmur of dissent regarding the current policy approach. But, if the evidence is picked through carefully, it is possible to mount a serious challenge to those who would make a case for 'active ageing' as it applies to the labour market. It is difficult to argue with the principle, after all, it appears to offer something to everyone, but for older workers serious risks are clearly present.

For it to work for them a number of factors need to be in place. Underpinning public policy is a prerequisite, but progress here has been described in this volume by Sol Encel as 'disjointed incrementalism' rather than demonstrating a strategic approach, even in so-called age strategy documents. A new, but somewhat hesitant and not particularly holistic policy approach is emerging in all of the case countries, which undermines efforts. The authors in this volume point to holes in retirement policy, in particular, which reduce the prospects for continuing to work. Mandatory retirement has not been eliminated from all of the case countries, with employer doubts about the performance and commitment of older people overriding the 'right to work'. For instance, Julie McMullin and colleagues note that, despite 'the current rhetoric around active ageing and extensions of working life, there are several policies in Canada, including provisions for mandatory retirement that discourage the labour force participation of older workers'. In the Netherlands, active ageing, in terms of stimulating people to remain active in some way after retirement, is not on the policy agenda. In Japan and the UK, working later is possible for those with skills in demand, but with questions about job quality and security. About the rest, even those wanting to work, policy makers have been rather more ambivalent. So here, active ageing has clear limits.

Active labour market policy, where it has emerged, it appears has made limited inroads so far, and arguably, may not be resourced to the levels required to make a real difference. Vulnerable groups, in particular, such as the older disabled and long-term unemployed have not fared well, and many remain unlikely to, considering the sheer volumes of benefit claimants and the complexity of the barriers they face. On the other hand, perhaps predictably, the creaming off the top of those with better job prospects and deadweight effects are common. Where jobs are found it seems that occupational downgrading is common. It could be countered that these jobs, such as they are, may at least act as a step towards better work later on, something that would be unachievable from unemployment or inactivity. Unfortunately, this does not actually appear to occur.

Deeper cultural change, for instance in the form of the stirrings of a shift towards lifelong learning, has been emerging in certain occupational groups, but as noted by Frerichs and Naegele in this volume, older workers still do not participate in learning and training in large numbers. Auer and Fortuny (2000) stress the importance of lifelong learning to meet the challenges of ageing populations. First, it can help the adjustment of workers' skills and competencies to labour market demand. Second, it can help improve the attachment of older workers to the labour market. Third, it can help to over-come productivity declines after a certain age. However research into individual-initiated vocational training among middle-aged workers indi-cates that it is primarily those with skills already who participate. Those with lower levels of education, who arguably have most to gain, are less likely to participate in learning activities (Elman and O'Rand, 2002; Jamieson *et al.*, 1998). It has already been noted that for older workers, flexible working may not be conducive to maintaining skills currency (Platman, 2003). Older workers often consider themselves unsuited to new learning and lack confidence in such situations. Given that the realization of lifelong learning is a major pillar of policy makers' strategies for tackling the economic pres-sures presented by population ageing (Auer and Fortuny, 2000: 29) these issues represent a substantial hurdle. While lifelong learning is a popular notion among policy makers, is it really achievable in the modern labour market, or will the skills gap eventually become just too great to be bridged?

Thus, while older workers may nowadays be somewhat closer to the labour market than they once were, their employability is often quite poor. Many unemployed workers will, in effect, be retired but lack the financial wherewithal to withdraw from the labour market, even though logic would dictate that this was the fairer course of action. Hard to accept in policy circles and perhaps even among some social gerontologists though such a suggestion might be, it should at least be acknowledged that 'active ageing' that is little more than unemployment is a denial of the modest dignity of early labour market withdrawal. Something that surely even its most ardent proponents must recognize is that 'activation' in terms of offering the 'right' of older people to work when there is no work to be had due to age discrimination, a lack of skills currency, or failing health may simply be condemning many to 'active' ageing in the form of labour force participation, but with little or no prospect of meaningful job opportunities.

Similarly, although policy makers would point to the individual benefits of working, if this is not good work then this may reduce the prospect of successful ageing. Research indicates that improvements in mental well-being on re-entering employment depend on the contractual arrangement. A return to permanent employment results in a larger increase in well-being than one to temporary employment or self-employment. Interestingly, exit to early retirement appears not to alter well-being (Strandh, 2000). It is apparent that much of what is available to older workers would not fall into the 'good' category. Flexible working has obvious appeal but as noted by Anne-Marie Guillemard and Annie Jolivet in this volume, difficult working conditions and meaningless jobs, which are monotonous, lack learning opportunities or do not provide recognition, are not conducive to longer working. In a similar vein, Sara Rix in her chapter points out that despite the shift to a knowledge-based economy, many workers are to be found in physically demanding jobs or unsafe or unpleasant work environments that do not lend themselves to prolonged working lives. A significant number also lack the skills and ability to make an easy transition to something new. While surveys show that large proportions of older workers would be inclined to remain in work under different conditions and 'flexible working' is promoted as a policy cure-all, in order for older workers to truly have 'flexibility' or a 'choice' about work or retirement, neither option should result in a serious risk of social exclusion or poverty. As noted be Kène Henkens and Joop Schippers in their chapter, while working may be better than retirement, those 'workers that fall out of employment despite restrictions to exit them may be less well off not only in terms of financial benefits, but also in terms of prospects to re-enter the labour force'.

The new policy rhetoric of working until the age of 70 or beyond must surely ring hollow to job-seekers aged in their 50s or those whose life expectancy, due to a combination of social and health risk factors is likely to fall short of this or exceed it by very little. This perspective is generally neglected in official statements and amid the recent deluge of media coverage on older workers. Though 'baby-boomers are once again reshaping their world' is a common refrain nowadays, it is a claim that does not stand close scrutiny. The reality for many older workers is that their choices are severely constrained. While they may be drawn to the idea of flexible retirement this is simply not an option for many, and as shown in this volume, even those with apparently valuable skill sets may struggle to maintain their employability. Added to this, while some economies have been growing steadily in recent years, it has been relatively easy to point to the business imperatives of employing older workers. How sustainable such a position would be in a recession is another matter. Indeed, one can speculate on whether fickle public policymakers would again resort to retirement under the threat of adverse economic conditions.

IS INCREASING DEMAND FOR OLDER WORKERS A MYTH?

That governments have been reluctant to open labour markets to all older workers has left plenty of room for organizations to dispose of them if they so wish, and even where protection has been applied, the cases of the UK and USA demonstrate that employers have the will and the capability to get around this. This seems to reflect the reality that, while new public policies are intent on increasing the supply of older workers, it is by no means certain that they will be welcomed by the market. As shown in this volume by Kène Henkens and Joop Schippers and elsewhere recently, where employer behaviour has been considered (Taylor, 2006), even in relatively buoyant economies, recruiting them may not be paramount in the minds of employers. The chapter by Henekens and Schippers should be a warning to those who would make claims about the changing attitudes and behaviour of firms. They show quite clearly that while active ageing is high on the agenda of policy makers, it is rarely so within organizations. Firms view the ageing of their workforces with great concern, but few are aiming to delay retirement and they are biased against recruiting older workers. Older people are generally viewed as employees of last resort.

Workplace age barriers are also manifested elsewhere. For instance, Masato Oka's chapter in this volume shows that companies will only entertain retaining older workers with certain skills, while Sara Rix notes that the policy makers' favourite, phased retirement, is not manifested in many formal programmes but instead, there are many ad hoc opportunities to ease into retirement, suggesting that employers want flexibility in deciding whom to keep. The company case examples mentioned in this volume notwithstanding, evidence of strong market demand for older labour is simply absent. Where older workers are targeted, certain conditions are attached. Sara Rix in this volume puts it well when she states that 'Employers, however, have considerable discretion over providing the flexible options that so many older workers say they want.'

It seems somewhat paradoxical that, despite remarkable unanimity among the social actors concerning the economic and social benefits of working later, much of industry does not appear to have been galvanized and older workers struggle to maintain a foothold in the labour market. Why might this be so? Understanding the context is important. Many years ago, Alan Walker and colleagues drew attention to the role early retirement played in some of the industrialized nations, acting as a release for some older workers and as a refuge for others (Walker, 1985; Westergaard *et al.*, 1989) as economies underwent massive restructuring. Among the, mostly older, redundant steel workers studied by Walker and his colleagues, there were two pathways into early retirement, depending primarily on socio-economic status. Some viewed early retirement positively, being relieved to give up work, but others withdrew reluctantly. They wanted to work but were 'discouraged' from doing so. Similarly, others have argued that much so-called 'early retirement' was really a kind of unemployment (Casey and Laczko, 1989). The causes are well understood. Older workers were over-represented in declining industries, underrepresented in those experiencing growth and were affected by reduced demand for unskilled workers (Kohli *et al.*, 1991; Trinder, 1989). Organizational delayering, downsizing of operations and process reengineering fragmented the traditional employment relationship and undermined the ability of older workers to sustain positions on age-stage career ladders (Tillsley and Taylor, 2001).

While the large scale devastation of certain kinds of manufacturing and production industry about which these authors were writing has ended, global forces continue to shape the employment landscape in ways that are not conducive to older workers' job prospects. Indeed, the recent actions of some employers, mentioned earlier, in facing the challenges associated with surviving in a global marketplace via programmes which involve the removal of workers over a certain age are highly reminiscent of the situation in the 1980s and early 1990s.

Twenty years later, Alan Walker (2005) stated that 'Future competitiveness in the private sector and efficiency in the public sector will rest increasingly on the performance and productivity of ageing workforces' (p. 691).

This scenario may eventuate, but employers are already thinking otherwise, and some taking steps that are at odds with it. If labour supply choices were, against a background of population ageing, really so constrained then those who point to a looming crisis facing industry would have a stronger case, but for some sectors at least, it may not be unrealistic to suppose that, in an era of increasing global connectedness, younger, cheaper and skilled labour forces will be sought out as opposed to what may be considered a more risky, home-grown and, of course, older solution. While European policy makers, in particular, describe a scenario consisting of dwindling numbers of young labour market entrants and continuing early exit, and conclude that this will inevitably constrain economic growth if drastic action is not taken, importantly, others have drawn attention to a doubling of global labour supply in the last decade and a half and argue that capital will find the lure of cheap labour impossible to resist (for example, Freeman, 2005; Roach, 2004). This raises questions about whether the expected labour drought brought on by demographic change really will exert such pressure on business that this will, in turn, result in a strong market pull on older workers, or indeed, whether instead, early exit, at least in some form, will be a continuing feature of labour markets if some employees are discarded in a drive to obtain supplies from elsewhere.

As Kohli *et al.* (1991) and others carefully mapped the changing contours of older workers' employment at the end of the twentieth century, there is surely a need for such a considered approach today. It would be easy to fashion a fascinating research agenda concerning the relationship between older workers and the globalizing economy, where labour flows more freely and both corporations and countries compete for the cheapest and the most skilled, and where there are clear limits on what nation states can do to protect their more vulnerable citizens. The easy assumption, or perhaps it is more appropriately viewed as a prescription, that 'age works', must be tested properly and if necessary challenged, if policy makers are to respond appropriately.

Other clues to understanding employer ambivalence towards older workers come from consideration of management theory. While policy makers would, currently, prefer business to view them as an investment, according to Lyon *et al.* (1998), this sits uneasily with new approaches to managing human resources, which stress the need to align strategic business planning and HR practices in order to achieve worker flexibility, organizational commitment and the retention of a 'core' workforce. While the importance of workforce investment over the long-term is also stressed, there is selectivity as to whom this investment should apply. Older workers' employment with the firm may pre-date, by some considerable time, the introduction of new practices. This may generate suspicion among managers who may view them as having ideologies and allegiances at odds with the new value system they are trying to establish. Such perspectives may provide the rationale for recruiting younger and inexperienced workers to new businesses and to the exclusion of older ones among established businesses seeking to emulate these conditions. According to Lyon and his colleagues, this perspective not only legitimizes existing attitudes, it also provides a seemingly more coherent and, above all, business-focused explanation for the apparent drawbacks in employing older workers. Older employees are not merely perceived as being less effective, they also represent a serious barrier to organizational change and flexible performance. According to the authors

> nothing better epitomises the contradiction between long-term employee investment and numerical flexibility than the treatment of older workers . . . [HRM's] philosophy can be seen to amplify older workers' problems by reinforcing ageism in management thinking through the provision of a commercially appropriate rationale which embellishes existing stereotypes and doubts about the commitment of older workers. (p. 57)

Such considerations are important if policy makers wish to promote a business case for employing older workers. A case for employing, training and developing older workers has been set out by Taylor and Walker (1995). This has five elements:

- return on investment;
- preventing skill shortages;
- maximizing recruitment potential;
- responding to demographic change; and
- promoting diversity.

However HRM theory provides managers with a convenient and powerful alternative rhetoric for legitimizing the exclusion of older workers. As a result, commonly used arguments for employing them may be largely ineffective. For example, what follows from HRM theory is that one of the so-called 'positive' attributes of older workers, corporate memory and experience, might be viewed as largely irrelevant or even disadvantageous by employers. As noted by Sennett (2006), investing in older workers may not be preferred by employers, instead sourcing already skilled and cheaper labour elsewhere, and as pointed out by Dickens (1999), the appeal of equality action may vary over time, leading to 'fair weather' policy making. In this regard, limited longitudinal research has challenged the notion that the emergence of workplace policy on older workers is a one-way street (Taylor, 2006), which should give policy makers and advocacy groups cause for concern. The 'lump of labour fallacy', which is a challenge to the notion that any increase in older workers' employment would come at the expense of younger ones (Funk, 2004), hardly fits with the day-to-day reality of workplaces, where difficult decisions concerning who to keep on are made. Here, employment levels really are finite. Even the commentator's 'sacred cow' of the inevitability of business responding to the imperatives flowing from demographic change has been challenged. Turning the argument on its head, in a recent article in *The Economist* (2005) it was argued that population decline might spur Japanese business towards greater efficiency in its use of labour, and as shown already, the overall global picture is one of increasing labour supply. In sum, the foundations of the business case may, in fact, be rather weak.

Moreover, some examples of employer good practice towards older workers that have been identified in recent years appear to resemble HRM's core and periphery workers, with them often appearing to have been relegated to the latter position. Masato Oka makes this clear in his chapter, where he states: 'the pay and working conditions of these [re-employment] schemes appears to be poor on the whole. In many cases, pay is halved, status reduced, while working hours and assignments are almost the same as the pre-*Teinen*'. Moreover, 'the quality of work of *Teinen* retirees also often appears poor. It seems likely that most post-*Teinen* schemes will not fulfil the needs of older workers, as their roles will be ambiguous and unimportant in many cases.' Thus, for policy makers the problem with promoting flexible employment for older workers is that it may push many towards certain roles or kinds of organizations, ones that may be associated with low status, skill, security and pay, and which carry additional occupational health and safety risks. Raising levels of employment may have adverse consequences that do not seem to have been much considered. Sara Rix in this volume points out that retail work, not traditionally considered high risk or dangerous to older workers, may in fact be so. It is more than a little ironic, therefore, that 'where older workers are positively favoured on commercial grounds, seem mostly confined to those widely-publicised policies of firms chiefly in the retail and catering sectors' (Duncan, 2001: 40).

The European Commission (2002: 27) has acknowledged the potential risks for older workers, when it notes that 'Transition rates into both unemployment and inactivity are considerably higher for older workers in jobs of low quality'. For the European Commission:

> The quality of jobs and the working environment will also make a significant contribution to keeping people at work, by reducing the risk of occupational accidents and improving workers' health, in particular the health of the oldest workers. (2005b: 8)

This issue has also been considered by Walker (2005) when he states:

> Unless the factors which limit work ability are mitigated, as well as combating the access barriers to employment, then it will not be possible for active ageing to be achieved widely and, therefore, nor will the age diverse workforce become a reality. To put it another way: if the health and work ability of workers is maintained then they will be more able and, in all probability, more willing to extend their working lives. (p. 692)

Here, it is important to consider the relationship between work and non-work activities. It is interesting to speculate on how working later might impede caring activities or reduce the amount of participation in civil society, that is activating in one sphere but deactivating in others. Frerich Frerichs and Gerd Naegele in this volume argue that welfare-to-work policies may increase poverty risks for those older people who cannot find a job or take refuge in early retirement measures. As a consequence, this group will also be lost to community involvement and volunteering, a sound income base being a prerequisite for this. An emphasis on work and the neglect of 'life' is a significant weakness in the older worker literature. The Finnish concept of 'workability' offers a holistic and coherent framework for the design of workplaces and jobs, management structures and behaviour, and to address individual factors associated with working which either limit or enhance a person's prospects of continued participation in the labour market (Ilmarinen, 2005). There is a growing literature on designing work for an ageing society (for example, Gay, 2005; Heather Hamlyn Research Centre, 2005). As well as focusing on new approaches to workplace design, research which explores the employment destinations of older workers would be of great value from an equity perspective. Evidence of continuing inequality in terms of types of employment opportunity would seriously undermine the case of those pointing to a simple measure of employment activity as indicative of changing labour market prospects.

However more optimistically, there is clearly some employer engagement with the issue. Putting to one side arguments concerning the possible ethereal nature of some actions, being wary of drawing conclusions concerning trends in the degree of employer engagement with the issue based on limited studies, and being cautious about applying the epithet 'good practice' when evidence concerning effects is often sketchy, an impressive array of organizations are focusing on adjusting workplaces with older workers in mind. It is clearly early days, with some ambiguity about outcomes for organizations and individuals. It is also the case that employer interest does not yet stretch far, with limited moves to recruit and retain individuals aged far into their 60s. Perhaps, as they get used to the idea of utilizing older workers, this attitude will soften.

The need to promote demand for older workers means that attention should be focused on employers. There has been a huge amount of employer case study research over the last two decades. Much of this might be considered more like propaganda than good science, but gradually a better understanding of the factors shaping employer behaviour and their response to issues of workforce ageing is emerging. More longitudinal research, in-depth case studies and action research would provide a richer picture. More broadly, taking study of the issue beyond the realm of gerontology, and particularly, much further towards that of management and business would benefit understanding enormously.

BETWEEN EARLY RETIREMENT AND ACTIVE AGEING

It is clear that, so far, 'age free' employment is more aspiration than reality. Indeed, as noted by Guillemard and Jolivet in this volume, trends such as towards greater work intensification potentially undermine older workers' prospects. While some observers point to a coming era of age-free employment, what might emerge instead is even greater age segmentation of labour markets as global industry demands a highly flexible, mobile and skilled workforce. While industrialized nations are ageing and some commentators draw an obvious link with ageing workforces, new labour reserves are increasingly being mined elsewhere. It cannot, therefore, yet be said with any certainty that a new era of employment opportunity is unfolding for older people. A plausible scenario is one of increasing labour market insecurity and personal hardship as workers can no longer fall back on early retirement when they begin to lose the struggle to maintain labour market competitiveness. The implications of employment instability for retirement transitions are understood (O'Rand, 1996). The prognosis for old age is often poor. Neglect of these particular avenues for research would be unfortunate.

The limits of demand for older workers must be identified if governments are to know where their responsibilities end. While they are quick to point to evidence of interest from industry, evidence of the continuing disadvantages facing older workers, as demonstrated in this volume, is all around. In fact, if individual well-being is the concern, then much of the current policy effort may be considered quite misguided. Broader consideration of the needs of older inactive people as they move towards older age would be of value. Further, there is a need to take a hard look at targets for older workers' employment. As noted in the case of the UK, the recent upturn in older workers' employment rates may be viewed partly as a cohort effect rather than representing a distinct turnaround in their fortunes, while there is uncertainty elsewhere that this apparent improvement will be sustained. At present, it often seems that wishful-thinking, as opposed to solid evidence, is guiding the policy response.

Public policymakers must, then, be wary of pushing older people into labour markets where their abilities are not valued. Based on this review, it might even be concluded that in some countries there is a 'lost generation' for whom the notion of working later has come too late. Unfortunately, but realistically, no programme of activation could now make very many of them work ready. This assessment might be criticized by advocacy groups as being defeatist, but appears to have been recognized by some public policy makers, tacitly at least, in the form of relatively weak activation measures. If commitment is measured in terms of resources allocated, then in Australia, Germany and the UK in particular, despite a great deal of rhetoric, it appears that older workers are not being prioritized for assistance. Initiatives so positioned to assist workers at critical points in their careers so they do not reach their 50s having accumulated a range of characteristics that put them at a disadvantage are likely to be more effective than remedial actions, though of course, this would require a significant ramping up of resources. In the meantime, while the good intentions of programmes specifically aimed at older workers should be commended, it is inevitable that they are always going to benefit a small minority.

While at odds with an activation ideology, it must surely also be recognized that the legacy of decades of early exit is a cohort who should be accorded the dignity of retirement, and not face what might be perceived as the threat of activation. Moreover, it is also my contention that targeted exit pathways will continue to play a crucial role in the volatile globalizing labour market of the early twenty-first century. Much of industry may simply feel unable to countenance ageing workforces, with the consequence that those who might hitherto have left the labour market for retirement would instead now be forced to remain economically active, but jobless or underemployed. The likelihood of significant social and individual costs resulting from 'activation' has been pointed to elsewhere in this volume. As a singular focus on early exit benefited some, but had unintended negative consequences, 'activation' has its own pros and cons. Rather than abandoning early exit entirely, new forms of social protection for older workers may be required, probably not on the same mass scale as the past, and not simply misusing other instruments such as disability benefits which has occurred (European Commission, 2002; OECD, 1998). Bridging the gap between work and retirement with something other than unemployment assistance would acknowledge the contribution older people have made and recognize their future prospects. The Social Protection Committee of the European Commission (2003) acknowledges the importance of maintaining a good social safety net for older workers, but to be implemented once integration methods have been tried. Once again, these are important, but neglected areas requiring full consideration.

Finally, there is a need to act at a basic level to change the way age and ageing is viewed. As argued in this volume by Anne-Marie Guillemard and Annie Jolivet in the case of France and Kène Henkens and Joop Schippers in the case of the Netherlands, modifying the institutional framework will not, by itself, undo the solidly anchored early exit mentality. Current efforts to ferment attitude change among employers and older workers are worthy but, in the words of Guillemard and Jolivet, by 'failing to focus on collective representations of age and on the cognitive basis of underlying actions, motivations, justifications and referents that shape behaviours', reforms will struggle to find traction. Put simply, the 'whole society is obsessed with age' (Young and Schuller, 1991: 14). This is a long-term project and the steps taken so far, small and faltering.

In the meantime, policy makers and commentators need to be brave enough to accept the current limits of active ageing and devise policy responses accordingly. Thus, while much work could still be done to adjust official provision for the older jobless and those seeking a career change, to protect people from discrimination on grounds of age, to promote the benefits of employing older workers to business and, more generally, to recast work for an ageing society, a pragmatic balance is required between, on the one hand, maximizing job chances, and on the other, an escape from diminishing prospects. It cannot be said with any certainty that labour markets will adjust easily or willingly to the ageing of industrialized society, and the ongoing reconfiguring of national economies on the back of global shifts brings with it the prospect of turbulent times ahead for at risk groups such as older workers. Recognizing this, 'active ageing' should then be a policy aspiration, but not an ideological straitjacket. Certainly, any policy armoury that did not contain adequate protection in the form of both activation and exit for its older citizens would not be properly equipping them to face the challenges of the modern labour market.

REFERENCES

Auer, Peter and Mariangels Fortuny (2000), *Ageing of the Labour Force in OECD Countries: Economic and Social Consequences*, Geneva: ILO.
Casey, B. and F. Laczko (1989), 'Early retired or long-term unemployed? The situation of non-working men Aged 55–64 from 1976 to 1986', *Work, Employment and Society*, **1** (4), 509–26.
Dickens, L. (1999), 'Beyond the business case: a three-pronged approach to equality action', *Human Resource Management Journal*, **9** (1), 9–19.

Duncan, Colin (2001), 'Ageism, early exit, and the rationality of age-based discrimination', in Ian Glover and Mohamed Branine (eds), *Ageism, Work and Employment*, Aldershot, UK: Ashgate, pp. 25–46.

Elman, C. and A.M. O'Rand (2002), 'Perceived job insecurity and entry into work-related training among adult workers', *Social Science Research*, **31**, 49–76.

European Commission (2002), 'Increasing labour force participation and promoting active ageing', COM(2002) 9 final, Brussels.

European Commission (2003), 'Modernising social protection for more and better jobs: a comprehensive approach contributing to making work pay', COM(2003) 842 final, Brussels.

European Commission (2005a), 'Integrated guidelines for growth and jobs (2005–2008)', COM(2005) 141 final, Brussels.

European Commission (2005b), 'Confronting demographic change: a new solidarity between the generations', COM(2005) 94 final, Brussels.

Freeman, R. (2005), *China, India and the Doubling of the Global Labor Force: Who Pays the Price of Globalization?*, 30 August, accessed 12 April, 2007 at www.zmag.org/content/showarticle.cfm?SectionID=15&ItemID=8617.

Funk, L. (2004), 'Employment opportunities for older workers: a comparison of selected OECD countries', *CESifo DICE Report*, **2**, 22–33.

Gay, Jeremy (2005), *Work Well. Inclusive Furniture for Older Office Workers*, London: Heather Hamlyn Research Centre.

Heather Hamlyn Research Centre (HHRC) (2005), *Capture It*, London: HHRC.

Ilmarinen, Juhani (2005), *Towards a Longer Worklife! Ageing and the Quality of Worklife in the European Union*, Helsinki: Finnish Institute of Occupational Health.

Jamieson, A., A. Miller and J. Stafford (1998), 'Education in a life course perspective: continuities and discontinuities', *Education and Ageing*, **13** (3), 213–28.

Kohli, Martin, Martin Rein, Anne-Marie Guillemard and Herman van Gunsteren (1991), *Time for Retirement: Comparative Studies of Early Exit from the Labour Force*, Cambridge: Cambridge University Press.

Lyon, P., J. Hallier and I. Glover (1998), 'Divestment or investment? The contradictions of HRM in relation to older employees', *Human Resource Management Journal*, **8** (1), 56–66.

Organisation for Economic Co-operation and Development (OECD) (1998), *Maintaining Prosperity in an Ageing Society*, Paris: OECD.

O'Rand, A.M. (1996), 'The precious and the precocious: understanding cumulative disadvantage and cumulative advantage over the life course', *The Gerontologist*, **36** (2), 230–38.

Platman, K. (2003), 'The self-designed career in later life: a study of older portfolio workers in the United Kingdom', *Ageing and Society*, **23** (3), 281–302.

Roach, S. (2004), *How Global Labour Arbitrage will Shape the World Economy*, accessed at www.globalagendamagazine.com/2004/stephenroach.asp.

Sennett, Richard (2006), *The Culture of the New Capitalism*, London: Yale University Press.

Strandh, M. (2000), 'Exit routes from unemployment and their impact on mental well-being: the role of the economic situation and the predictability of the life course', *Work, Employment and Society*, **14** (3), 459–79.

Taylor, P. and A. Walker (1995), 'Utilising older workers', *Employment Gazette*, April, 141–5.

Taylor, Philip (2006), *Employment Initiatives for an Ageing Workforce in the EU-15*, Luxembourg: Office for Official Publications of the European Communities.

Tillsley, Christine and Philip Taylor (2001), 'Developing strategies for managing third age workers', in Ian Glover and Mohamed Branine (eds), *Ageism, Work and Employment*, Aldershot, UK: Ashgate, pp. 311–26.

The Economist (2005), 'The sun also rises', 8 October.

The Social Protection Committee (2003), *Promoting Longer Working Lives Through Better Social Protection Systems*, Brussels: European Commission.

Trinder, Christopher (1989), 'Employment after 55', National Institute for Economic and Social Research, discussion paper no. 166, London.

Walker, A. (1985), 'Early retirement: release or refuge from the labour market?', *The Quarterly Journal of Social Affairs*, **1** (3), 211–29.

Walker, A. (2005), 'The emergence of age management in Europe', *International Journal of Organisational Behaviour*, **10** (1), 685–97.

Westergaard, John, Iain Noble and Alan Walker (1989), *After Redundancy*, Oxford: Polity Press.

Young, Michael and Tom Schuller (1991), *Life After Work*, London: HarperCollins.

Index